To Rob

CW00401144

ASK FORGIVENESS
NOT PERMISSION

Give me my Rolex back!

For
Mina, Olivia and Constance

ASK FORGIVENESS NOT PERMISSION

The true story of a discrete, post 9/11 operation in the 'badlands' of Pakistan.

HOWARD LEEDHAM MBE

Bene Factum Publishing

Ask Forgivenss

Not Permission

Published in 2012 by

Bene Factum Publishing Ltd

PO Box 58122

London

SW8 5WZ

inquiries@bene-factum.co.uk

www.bene-factum.co.uk

ISBN: 978-1-903071-67-0

Cover design: Ian Hughes, Mousemat Design

Typesetting: Carnegie Publishing

Printed and bound in Malta for Latitude Press

Contents

In Memory of

NK Muhammad Iqbal Butt, KIA, July 24, 2004

Mark Spring

Major General Sadaqat Ali Shah

The 'Pathan'

The Pathans, as they are known in Pakistan, (or Pashtun in Afghanistan), are characterised by their use of the Pashto language. Their 60 tribes inhabit the Hindu Kush down through the borders of Pakistan and across Afghanistan. The Pathan race numbers approximately 10 million in Pakistan and some 8 million in Afghanistan. The Pathans have earned the reputation as a 'Warrior Race'. They are noble brave, hard and tenacious but, on occasions, ruthless. They are noted as formidable fighters, and throughout history they have offered strong resistance to any and all whom they consider invaders of their territory.

Pakistan-Afghanistan border

Irregular war was far more intellectual than a bayonet charge, far more exhausting than service in the comfortable imitative obedience of an ordered army. Guerrillas must be allowed liberal workroom: in irregular war, of two men together, one was being wasted. Our ideal should be to make our battle a series of single combats, our ranks a happy alliance of agile commanders-in-chief.

T.E. Lawrence (Lawrence of Arabia)

Foreword by Frederick Forsyth

A phrase may be grossly over-used but still remain true and 'Fact is stranger than fiction' is one such. The hitherto unknown story that Howard Leedham has to tell could have come from the Northwest Frontier of Rudyard Kipling's time.

Before the story even starts he had had a career to satisfy most tastes for danger and adventure. Starting as a volunteer Navy entrant he became a Clearance Diver. (That's the dangerous stuff by the way.) Taking a commission he went on to become a Commando and helicopter pilot with qualification for fixed wing thrown in. Most of his career was spent inside the closed world of special forces and their equally special 'ops'.

By his mid-thirties he was out; married to an American girl, father of two small girls, emigrated to the USA and was working in the world of executive jets. And bored stiff. That was when the State Department Air Wing came over the horizon with an insane offer.

Personally I did not know that the State Department even had an Air Wing. Britain's equivalent, the Foreign Office, certainly does not. Washington's offer was to go to Pakistan and its border with Afghanistan and create with American Bell Huey helicopters, two private contractor pilots, half a dozen mechanics, Pakistani aircrew and twenty-five of the fiercest mountain tribesmen an anti-Taliban, anti-Al Qaeda night raiding force. Likely tasks: snatching high value terrorists and hostage recovery. Nothing to it.

The budget would be peanuts, the attitude of the US Embassy pretty unrelieved hostility, the cooperation of the

Pakistani bureaucracy almost suicide inducing and of their Army unrelieved obstructionism. As I said, nothing to it.

The following year, described in these pages, cost him his marriage and (several times) almost his life. The first months were spent multi-tasking. Wheedling out of the US Government enough helicopters to do the job; keeping the ultra-politically correct bureaucrats of the Embassy in Islamabad as sweet as possible by telling them almost nothing, cajoling an initially sceptical Pakistani general into trusting him, winning over the British, the American 'contracted' pilots and ground crew, purchasing weapons from dubious freelances round the back of the bazaar and gaining the loyalty of some of the most formidable killers those bleak mountains along the Durand Line have ever produced.

Kipling mentioned the Pathans with awe. They are pretty immune to fear or pain and regard taking prisoners as only for wimps. But starting with twenty-five he was later given fifty to train. And they had never been in a helicopter let alone in pitch darkness staring at the world through night-vision goggles.

Operating by day was impossible. Those trying it ran straight into Taliban ambushes. Traitors and spies were everywhere. Quetta, capital of Baluchistan, was and remains for a white unbeliever a grenade with the pin out. So that became his HQ.

Somehow it happened. Somehow, on a shoestring, the heli-copter-borne, night fighting intervention force began to frighten the black turbans out of the Taliban, Al Qaeda and opium barons who had with impunity denied those terrifying mountains to any forces of law and order, Pakistani included, since time immemorial.

But it was a one-year contract and when it ended it ended. The Pakistani military wanted to take over what Howard

Leedham had created. Since then reports have it that the wild country between Baluchistan and Afghanistan is as lawless as ever despite the spending of hundreds of millions of dollars.

And the Pathans? Those fifty dark featured, tough, lean, hard warriors, as dangerous as the land that made them; what happened to them? Who knows? But for a few months led by an infidel Britisher, they terrified those whose only language was terror. Kipling would have loved them.

Frederick Forsyth

Acronyms and Abbreviations

ANF	Anti Narcotics Force
Casevac	Casualty Evacuation
CO	Commanding Officer
C208	Cessna Caravan 208 Aircraft
DEA	Drug Enforcement Agency
DoD	Department of Defense (US)
DoJ	Department of Justice
DOP	Drop Off Point
FARC	Fuerzas Armadas Revolucionarias de Colombia (Revolutionary Armed Forces of Colombia)
FATA	Federally Administered Tribal Area
FC	Frontier Corps
FLIR	Forward Looking Infra-Red
FRV	Final Rendezvous
GOP	Government of Pakistan
HLZ	Helicopter Landing Zone
HNS	Host Nation Support
HQFC	Headquarters Frontier Corps
Huey	Bell UH-1N Huey Helicopter
ICITAP	International Criminal Investigation and Training Assistance Programme
IGFC	Inspector General Frontier Corps
INL	International Narcotics & Law Enforcement
ISB	Islamabad
ISI	Inter Services Intelligence

MOI	Ministry of the Interior (Pakistan)
MRE	Meal Ready to Eat
NAS	Narcotics Affairs Section
NSOP	Night Standing Observation Post
NVG	Night Vision Goggles
RIF	Rapid Interdiction Force
RPG	Rocket Propelled Grenade
HAF	Heliborne Assault Force
MOI	Ministry of the Interior (Pakistan)
NWFP	North West Frontier Province
OC	Officer Commanding
OpCon	Operational Control
OpSec	Operational Security
PUP	Pick Up Point
PSC	Personal Services Contractor
QA	Quality Assurance
RSO	Regional Security Officer
RV	Rendezvous
SF	Special Forces
Slammy	Islamabad (nickname)
SOCOM	Special Operations Command (US)
SSG	Special Services Group (Pakistan's Special Forces)
TLA	Three Letter Abbreviation
UAV	Unmanned Aerial Vehicle
USG	United States Government
VCP	Vehicle Check Point

List of Characters

Brigadier Shafiq	Director of Aviation, Ministry of the Interior
Brigadier T	Director Anti Narcotics Force
Caz	U.S. Huey Pilot and Instructor
Curtis	DynCorp Site Manager
Ed	Fixed Wing Mechanic
Frank	Quality Assurance (Aircraft)
Gerry	Huey Mechanic
Iqbal	The Punjabi in the RIF
Iqbal Butt	Huey Crewchief
Javed	Major Pakistan Army (Administration Officer HQFC Balochistan)
Jason	Aircraft Armourer (Guns)
Jay	Avionics Expert
Jerry	"The Cop". Country Head of ICITAP
Jim	DynCorp Security Manager
Keith	DEA
Ken	Head of Embassy Security
Kevin	Embassy Ops Coordinator
Mark	Huey Mechanic
Matt	Safety Equipment and FLIR "Volunteer Expert"
Nancy Powell	US Ambassador to Pakistan
Pervaiz	Captain Pakistan Army, Troop Commander 1 Platoon HAF
Robert	Diplomat, British Embassy Anti Narcotics

Saadi	Mr. 'Procurement' in Islamabad
Colonel Shaheed	50 Squadron CO MOI
Colonel Shaheed (2)	CO Ghazaband Scouts, FC.
General Sadaqat Ali Shah	IGFC Baluchistan
Smiler	RIF Sniper
General Stone	USMC, Head of DoD in Islamabad
Tanveer	Captain Pakistan Army, Troop Commander 2 Platoon HAF
Tom	Close Protection and Embassy Security
Pervaiz	Captain, No. 1 Platoon Commander, RIF.
Pete	U.S. Cessna Caravan Pilot
Colonel Wahid	Chief of Staff HQFC Balochistan
Wajid	Major Pakistan Army SSG, OC RIF

Preface

For several reasons, capitulating to the persuasion of others to put pen to paper about the *greatest* sustained adventure in my life has taken seven years of pondering. I suppose I have always been instinctively disinclined to impart my doings in public. However, this is now balanced out by the passing of time and circumstance that negates the currency of locations, techniques or sensitive information that might endanger past or present individuals. Also, so much has been said regarding the measure of the West's failure to contain the situation in Pakistan, that it now seems right to tell the story of how a few resolute souls from the State Department and some courageous Pakistanis utilised a discreet but publicly disclosed border security programme to forge a path against all odds. This combined 'under the radar', effort attempted to provide hope of stability by blending willing, allied indigenous capability with western assets in the land of the "Great Game".

While the world was distracted by what materialised to be a baseless war in Iraq, I became a lone advisor working and patrolling with a loyal and incredibly tough Pathan militia along the infamous Pakistan-Afghan border against an enemy who knew he could use this nakedly exposed flank to his own advantage to disrupt Pakistan, Afghanistan and the western world.

The main distinction between this and other efforts in the region was that the deference others permitted me to develop my own doctrine under the noses of the likes of Pakistan's Inter-Services Intelligence agency without them noticing until the job was done. Meanwhile, I worked alongside a few exceptionally brave individuals who, without permission, unofficially embraced the operational entrepreneurism that I came to represent. They grasped the concept that when on a forgotten flank, in order to make progress against subversive forces, it was necessary to do what needed to be done quickly and quietly until someone realised what we were doing and either gave us a pat on the back or ordered us to stop. Our team in Pakistan comprised one visionary General, one cunning Brigadier, fifty tenacious Pathan tribal militia fighters, some heroic Pakistani and U.S. pilots, magnificent DynCorp aircraft mechanics, and me, their 'Advisor'.

What you are about to read is as close to the truth as I can make it without jeopardising anyone's safety. I have merged and masked some of the events and identities to protect the "innocent" from harbingers of institutional retribution. I have purposely not disclosed my previous experiences in the UK's special forces nor compromised any classified organisations, individuals, or operational techniques.

Howard Leedham
London 2012

Introduction

With a little over two hours of darkness remaining, we moved up onto a small earthwork feature just short of a Balochi village in a godforsaken area of the Pakistan Afghan border dominated by the Taliban, Al Qaeda and opium traffickers. Inside the village was an individual who had been taken by one of these groups and I had led twenty-five heavily armed Pathan militiamen across a mountain range close to the border to try and rescue the poor bastard. This was the first time we had attempted anything like this and we were about to give some literal bang for buck to the American taxpayers' sixty-five million dollar contribution to a discreet State Department programme. Now we'd either have to kick some serious arse or potentially die trying.

Three hours earlier, the State Department's "gifted" Bell Hueys had dropped us off on a sandy plateau well up in the mountains to the east of Quetta, about ten kilometres from the village. It had been a perfect drop-off. The helicopters were only on the ground for about four seconds. The noise and commotion during the drop-off had pushed up everyone's adrenaline to near-toxic levels.

On the way down the mountain, I took "point" and came upon a small concrete irrigation aqueduct. I chose to follow this path down the mountain and the patrol changed formation to single file. To our left was a massive chasm. We needed to avoid treading on any loose gravel here because, if it gave

1

way, it would mean a fall of several hundred feet to certain death. The moonlight levels were very high that night and our Night Vision Goggles (NVGs) provided excellent clarity. As we approached the base of the mountains, the slope gradually surrendered its gradient and the landscape opened up to an undulating desert plain. We now had to turn northeast to the village, which was remarkably difficult to pick out through the NVGs against the bland background.

A Cessna Caravan, piloted by an American pilot, Pete, circled thousands of feet above us in the darkness with a Forward Looking Infra-Red (FLIR) camera mounted in its belly. Its operator, a Pakistani officer, had "eyes-on" the target village and reported that several dogs were in the area. There were also at least two armed sentries posted outside the village house where the hostage was reported to be held.

As we came close to the village, the shape of the single-storey buildings gradually took form though our NVGs. The light breeze to our back was doing us no favours and, as our scent drifted on the wind, the dogs began to bark. One of them picked up our scent and came dashing boldly out of the village, barking as he charged, with two less audacious pack members behind him. We must have been about 400 metres from the village when he came bounding up to see what smelled so interesting.

I dropped to one knee and the patrol did the same behind me. I reached down to my belt and slipped the retaining band from my dagger's handle and pulled the razor-sharp knife from its sheath. If the dog chose to attack, I would have no choice but to dispatch him. The dog was now thoroughly confused by the apparent lack of any fear or verbal aggression and thus waited for his two canine colleagues to catch up. He was now about ten metres away from me, standing his ground and wondering what he was up against. He reservedly barked

2

before taking a couple of steps forward. I stood up and did the same, *sans* the barking. I had my rifle in my left hand and dagger in my right. It was time to see who would blink first; I knew it couldn't be me.

No sooner had I stood up than the twenty-five Pathans behind me mistakenly took this as the signal to resume patrolling and were also on their feet. The dog instantly assessed that the odds of defeating this invading "rival pack" were decidedly not in his favour and turned tail, running back towards the village with his small gang giving an occasional bark of protest as he did so. The observer in the Cessna reported with some amusement that the dogs did not stop running when they reached the village but continued on, clearly not wanting anything to do with further events of the evening. I sheathed my knife and was quite relieved the dog had chosen not to escalate the situation.

As we closed on the target, the level of activity around the normally dormant village was much greater than expected. The initial phase of the build up to an assault was for our snipers to get "eyes on" the sentries. They were dispatched forward to find suitable firing positions. My best sniper was Sana Ulla, otherwise known as Smiler simply because he never did. He was an incredibly hard man and a brilliant shot. His stalking ability approached animal instinct and, at some time in his life, he had developed the skill of using terrain and cover to crawl silently into a position that enabled him to get within killing distance of any prey. He carried a 7.62mm. Draganov sniper rifle with ten sniper rounds in a short magazine. His spotter accompanied him to provide his rearguard.

We waited about twenty minutes before Sana and the other sniper whispered their respective codewords "Alpha 1" and "Alpha 2" over the radio to indicate they were in position, undetected, and had the sentries in their sights. The Pakistani officer operating the Caravan's FLIR was by now providing a streaming commentary to our earpieces on movement within the village.

One of the six man sections remained to the rear as reinforcement and rearguard. They would immediately mark the Helicopter Landing Zone (HLZ) as soon as the breach of the target occurred. The breaching team moved into the village, but the militia's Pakistani platoon commander, Pervaiz, became hesitant. I urged him forward and we were now within short reach of the target building. This was no time to go wobbly.

Crouching behind a low wall, we were still completely undetected by the sentries. I moved silently to the rear of the target building with the explosives trooper. We laid the two "homemade" distraction charges [detonators sealed in sand-filled washing-up bottles] on each of the high windowsills of the two rooms and withdrew behind the wall, trailing the wires as we did. Once we were back behind cover, the explosives trooper passed me the battery and I twisted the ends of the wires onto one of the terminals.

I looked along the wall and gave Pervaiz the thumbs up. I then saw him glance back along the wall at his Pathan assault group toting AK-47s, crouched close to each other and ready to go. These guys had killed before and they were ready to do it again. They hated the Taliban and for pay of seventy dollars a month were willing to risk life and limb to drive the jihadists out of their country.

I watched as Pervaiz reached for his Press-to-Transmit button on the lapel of his combat jacket. He whispered the codewords, "Bravo-Bravo." This told the entire force and the supporting aircraft that we were ready to make the assault. The Caravan responded, "Roger, that is a Bravo-Bravo." I knew that Caz, our American Huey pilot, and his four

Pakistani-crewed Hueys were in a holding pattern some sixteen kilometres away and would now be turning towards the HLZ.

One of them, a gunship that had been ably converted by Jason, a former U.S. Marine, would be over the village within minutes in order to provide suppressive fire should we need it. Now, there was no turning back. The clock was running and I knew the rearguard would move quickly to mark the landing zone after Pervaiz's next radio transmission.

He looked at me, I nodded, thinking that we were only metres from the sentries and, for now, completely undetected. Any second one of the sentries might realise they were not alone and if we lost the element of surprise that would cost us lives. We had to get it done and do it right now! He gathered himself for the sprint across open ground. By now, his team was a human force of pent-up energy and adrenaline waiting to be converted momentarily into shear unbridled aggression.

Pervaiz again pressed his transmit button. "Standby... Standby...Go!" I pushed the wire onto the battery terminal and instantly the detonators exploded, showering sand and causing stunned distraction. I saw two sniper lasers shine through the night, one from a small hole in a wall, the other from a shallow gulley. They had found their targets; I didn't see them fall but I knew the sentries were no longer a threat. Pervaiz and his Pathans were already across the eight or so metres of open ground, with the strongest, Ali, hitting the first door of the building with the full might of his body.

The door instantly gave way and the three soldiers who were right behind him were in the room as one, providing a crushing force against whoever might be with the hostage. In tandem, another trooper hit the second door of the alternate room. Both rooms were treated with equal priority until the hostage was located. There was shouting in Pashtu and several shots fired. The young male hostage was dragged from the first building and handed to two troopers who were specifically waiting for him at the door. They each grabbed an arm and ran him to meet the helicopters that were, by now, about two minutes away.

In an instant, the deafening noise of the Huey gunship was overhead. If there were any threat from outside of the village, its mini-guns would suppress it and permit the team to make its extraction. I moved forward to the building to tell Pervaiz to "Move it out." We were a small raiding force, with no reserves to help us if we became embroiled in a sustained firefight. We'd gotten what we came for and wanted no more. Ali and the "enemy" were in the room where the hostage had been held. Two men lay motionless and rendered harmless with their AK-47s' on the floor. Whether they were dead or alive would have to be left for the villagers to discover. We had no room for prisoners. The other room was confirmed as "clear". I knew we needed to get out of there "right now" to avoid being surrounded.

I bellowed at Ali above the noise of the gunship, "To the helicopters! Let's go! Let's go!" The Pathans knew we were probably only minutes from being heavily outnumbered so moved out at speed with each section covering the other in a rearward movement towards the HLZ. The Hueys were now on their final approach. I waited at the outskirts of the village and saw the snipers running at full speed towards them. We had allocated our only Punjabi, Iqbal, as "last man" and I recognised his gait amongst the Pathans.

"Last man?" I shouted as I touched his arm to ensure I got a response. "Last man!" he shouted back above the din of the Hueys. We turned and ran as a pair through the swirling sand toward the last helicopter that now nervously waited for us. I was running as fast as I could alongside Iqbal, who accelerated to a full sprint. I knew all the other section commanders would be confirming as their own last man on their aircraft. The ground was undulating and stony and Iqbal must have had about twenty years of youth on his side, so I was not going to be last man by choice but by vintage. I reached the Huey and rolled into it, screaming, "Last man, last man!"

The crewchief must have given the pilot the "Go, go, go," and we were almost instantly into the air in pursuit of the lead aircraft. As I tried to get my breath back from the sprint, I looked out of the open door and saw the shape of the gunship Huey closing to tactical formation distance. I spat some of the dust out of my mouth. We must have been on target for only about three minutes from the time of the assault. My militia had performed brilliantly.

Back at the airfield an ambulance was on hand but not needed. We made our way to the briefing room and went over the various points of the operation. Morale was high and the input from both pilots and troopers alike carried a tone of satisfied excitement. This level of operational efficiency was a new experience for them. Now they functioned as a unit, actively working to make things as slick for each other as possible. Amid the laughter of the men, I walked out of the completed debriefing and the daylight took me by surprise. I checked my cheap watch to discover, with some amazement, that it was 6am.

With sunrise came the stunning outline of the Sleeping Lady of Quetta, an uncanny but natural mountain formation that ironically flouts the curves of female form over the deeply austere and fundamentalist city of Quetta. Her welcome appearance brought by the daylight signified that our work was over for now. It was time for a shower and then to bed, but not without some reflection before sleep. This platoon of twenty-five willing Pathans had come a long way in a very short time. I even wondered if British or American soldiers could have adapted so quickly. These mountain men had proven themselves time and time again over the past few days. In the preceding hours, they had conducted one of the most difficult of manoeuvres with absolute professionalism and precision.

As my mind drifted and meandered towards a long-awaited sleep, my final thoughts hoped we didn't yet again fuck up the end game on the Pakistan/Afghanistan border. Of course, statistically, it was highly probable that the 'powers-that-be' would.

CHAPTER ONE

An Irregular Sailor

Unless you are a relative of one of the victims, it is not imperative that you can recall where you were at precisely 08.46 hours and 40 seconds (Eastern Standard Time) on the morning of September 11, 2001 when American Airlines Flight 11 smashed into the North Tower of New York City's World Trade Centre killing all on board and blotting out the innocent lives of 658 Cantor Fitzgerald employees. Because, like most, we assumed that it must have been a terrible mishap, a horrific accident, a catastrophic human error - but certainly nothing more.

At the time, I was Vice President of Operations and Chief Pilot for a business aviation company based in Hagerstown, Maryland. One of my junior pilots, Jay, rushed into the office and said, "Dude, a plane just hit the World Trade Center!" I so wished he wouldn't call me dude but asked, "What kind of plane? How can that be? It's an 8/8ths blue sky-day for Christ's sake. What's the weather doing in New York? How the hell could any pilot hit that?"

I had viewed those towers many times while piloting our Learjet 45 into New York's business aviation hub at Teterboro, New Jersey. How could a pilot hit the Twin Towers unless he was attempting some insane barnstorming manoeuvre, trying to fly between the towers and screwed it up? It simply made no sense. We went to the crew room and turned on one of the TV morning shows and were aghast to see smoke pouring furiously out of the North Tower. The woman on the news reported that a passenger airliner had hit the building. They had no other information at that moment. This just did not feel right. Something was very, very wrong and then, shortly, the world found out why.

At 09.03 hours and 11 seconds (EST) we watched in horror as United Flight 175 threw a steep left bank turn, in which the abinitio, jihad, kamikaze pilot almost misjudged the width of the turn caused by the speed of his hijacked Boeing 767. Unfortunately, he did not misjudge it enough and the aircraft slammed into the South Tower creating a flaming inferno. This was to be the defining moment that changed the direction of the modern world. I looked on and realised instantly what was going on.

"Jesus Christ!" I looked at Jay and blurted out, "We're under attack!"

Throughout the course of my life, I have learned our longest and most perilous journeys always begin with just a single step. Unbeknown to me on that sunny morning in September, my first step towards running a tribal militia unit on the Pakistan/Afghan border, the culmination of all the conventional and unconventional military skills that I had ever amassed had just been taken.

My next thought was whether my family was safe? I called my wife. She was already frantic and asking if she should pull our two little girls out of school. I told her to not upset them; we could let them believe, at least for the moment, that nothing was amiss in their perfect world. I was on my way home.

Along with every soul in the world that could view a television, I watched as the devastation and death of that day unfolded. While I was glued to the television screen, I received two significant phone calls. The first was from my friend, Paul, who was the number two executive in a state power company. He knew my background in counter terrorism and wanted to know my take on what was going on and, specifically, if there was anything he should particularly do. I responded by saying that the United States was under strategic attack and that he should initiate searches of all key-generating stations for improvised explosive devices.

The second call I received that day was from Steve, one of my Learjet pilots. Steve was a bright guy but in keeping with most corporate pilots was always paranoid about losing his job. He bizarrely asked whether the destruction of the Twin Towers would be good or bad for our business. I told him "this changes everything."

He asked "Which part?"

I responded. "No, Steve, you are not hearing me, this will change *everything*! And it will change it *forever*! Nothing will ever be the same again."

Suddenly Steve truly understood the magnitude of what had happened.

As I watched the chaos of the day's events multiply exponentially, I started to consider my own situation. I had lived in the United States since I had left the British Military in 1997, having married an American lady whom I had met in the early nineties when I was serving as the British Exchange Officer to the United States Marine Corps. The transition from the military had not gone smoothly. I went from being somebody who mattered in the eyes of the world to, frankly, somebody who didn't matter at all. But by 9/11, I had started the arduous climb back up the "matter ladder" in the world of

11

corporate aviation. At the end of the day, the only solace that any man really seeks is to know that his contribution truly does make a real difference and I was trying to get back on that path.

I had grown up in the countryside of Hampshire in England although my earliest memories are of Sierra Leone in Africa where my father was briefly tasked to form a national airline during that country's transition to independence.

My father was a World War Two veteran having flown Lancaster bombers, as he put it, for the purpose of making "car-parks in Germany". He subsequently saw action in the Korean War and then became an airline pilot.

My mother had served in the British Army's Pay Corps. She was a beautiful woman who was soft and gentle. She fell in love with this dashing RAF bomber pilot and that love never faded even though my father predeceased her by more than thirty years.

By the age of eighteen, I had spent two years at college studying mechanical engineering and, unfortunately, the only thing I took away from that experience was that I did not want to be a mechanical engineer.

Concurrently I had become aware that commercial divers in the North Sea were paid handsomely by oil companies and I wanted some of this. So I asked Dad if he would lend me £5,000 to attend the commercial divers course in Fort William, Scotland. He thought about this for a long moment and then asked, "How much do you think *my* Dad lent to me when I was a teenager?"

I glibly replied, "I don't know."

He then placed his hand on my shoulder and told me "Nothing. Not a penny - and that's the exact amount that I'm going to lend to you."

The refusal of funds from my father led me to seek support from a higher power. Not God, but, rather, Her Majesty the Queen. She would undoubtedly be happy to pay me for my service. So without informing my parents, I paid a visit to the Royal Navy Recruitment Office and boldly told the Chief Petty Officer that I wanted to be a Clearance Diver. He explained that the navy only accepted one in every twelve applicants and that there were 72,000 men in the Royal Navy but that just 200 (or two, one-thousandths of a percent) of them were divers.

"So what chance do you think you've got, Master Leedham?" he asked.

I looked him straight in the eye as a cocky eighteen-year-old who, in my own mind, was a Hampshire Rugby Colt 'superstar' and answered, "If I say I'm going to be a diver, I'll be a diver."

I'd like to say the rest is history, but that would belittle the freezing depths and soul searching endurance challenges that lay ahead. Anyway, in March of the following year I was badged as a Royal Navy Clearance Diver and, for the very first time in my life, I felt that I could look my father in his eye as an equal. During what turned out to be the last year of his life, we spent our most precious father and son moments as the best of friends.

I was hand picked from my divers course to serve on the Fleet Clearance Diving Team and spent several months clearing a Soviet mine field at the mouth of the Suez Canal. In reward, I was told I would get to choose the next location of posting (or draft as it is referred to in the Navy). I made no real preference of where I did want to go, but simply stated against the question "Places to avoid", "Scotland".

When I returned from Egypt, I learned that I had been assigned to the Faslane Submarine Base.... in Scotland. This was the busiest diving team in the Royal Navy and despite not wanting to go there, I quickly settled in. The diving team spent its days servicing submarines, recovering test torpedoes and conducting deep diving exercises just in case one of the submarines experienced a problem. Of course, as the so-called "elite" of the base, we also chased a lot of skirt in the shape of Women's Royal Navy Service and, in my case, especially a particular dental hygienist.

However, it was during a working road trip back from Scotland's Kyle of Lochalsh that our boss, Commander "Diesel" Davis (so named because he held a Masters degree in Science but had once fuelled a petrol mini-van with diesel fuel) suggested that I should apply to be an officer. I told him I wasn't interested because Diving Officers didn't dive enough. On my next long-weekend leave, while sipping a pint of beer with my Dad at the Kings Arms pub in Billingshurst in Sussex, I told him about Diesel's suggestion.

He went mildly berserk when I shared my response and sternly advised, "If you get the chance to gain a Queen's Commission, you need to grab it with both hands."

I repeated that I did not want to be a Diving Officer. My father then uttered what would be prophetic words. "There are other things in life besides diving, son."

I said "Like what?"

He replied "Like flying!"

I took his point.

I spent two years as a Commission Warrant candidate and served as a diver on the minehunter HMS *Nurton* for a year during which my father died. I was promoted to Leading Diver and completed my Leading Divers Course. I passed my Admiralty Interview Board that same year. I then joined the Britannia Royal Naval College as an Upper Yardsman (so called from the days of sail when the best sailors manned the

Upper Yards of the tall-masted sails) in February 1981 to commence officer training with a view to being a pilot. I passed out as a Divisional Sub-Lieutenant and, after a few weeks of junior officer's sea training, which is naval code for cleaning toilets, on HMS *Intrepid*, I volunteered for Commando training.

Whenever I ended up on an arduous course in the military, it was always winter and the All Arms Commando Course at the Commando Training Centre in Lympstone was no exception. The first three weeks of January were simply a build up to the "pass-in tests". The Commando course itself was a subsequent five-week slog through tactics and field-craft, endurance courses, load carries, and the dreaded final test, a thirty mile high speed trek across the boggy wastes of Dartmoor in the driving rain.

If I had to distinguish the main difference between the Clearance Divers Course and the Commando Course, it was that the cold on the diving course was intense but would end at the close of each long day. On the Commando course, however, the cold was less intense but could last for a week during the survival phase and final exercise. Other than that, whilst different in emphasis, the determination to complete the course and the necessity to be able to reach very deep into your own reserves of resolve was about equal. On a good day the rain or snow was vertical; on a bad day it blew horizontally. On completion of the Commando Course, I had an in-depth understanding of small arms and commando tactics and, most significantly, I was now entitled to wear the coveted Green Beret.

From Commando training I was inducted into the Number 12 Pilots Course, the next stepping-stone towards gaining my Royal Navy Wings and, for the first time in my military experience, I could not rely solely upon my physical prowess to get me through. I had to study long and assiduously to pass each flight test. Fortunately, I never found myself at the back of the pack and following the award of my Navy Wings after the basic flight-training phase, we were selected for our specialisation.

The routes were Harrier, Commando, Small Ship (Lynx), or Anti-Submarine. So when we learned that of the twelve pilots who had gained their wings only two slots would go to Commando, it was a bit tense to say the least. My interview with the Commanding Officer [CO], Commander Trevor Lockwood, was akin to one of today's television reality shows where the panel already knows the answer but chooses to play with the contestant. Given Lockwood's impish sense of humour he wanted to make me squirm a bit. He said, "You've worked very hard, Howard, but I'm very sorry we are going to have to send you..." He paused for a seemingly eternal second, "...Commando." Needless to say, I was elated.

The Wessex 5 aircraft was old in design but a fabulous helicopter to fly. We had no NVGs for night formation flying or night operations, no Global Positioning System (GPS), just a map, a compass and a pair of "Mark-1 eyeballs". It was a testing time to say the least but I had the satisfaction of leaving the training squadron having won the Double Diamond Flight Trophy, and I joined 845 Naval Air Commando Squadron.

Squadron life was everything I'd hoped for and, suffice it to say, we ripped the arse out of life from every perspective, pushing all limitations to the max be they related to aviation, booze or women. It wasn't until later in life that all the pilots would realise just how much fun they were having; but what *was* to prove most significant about this entire experience was that 845 Squadron did not have a Combat Survival Instructor, a billet it was absolutely required to have. The fact that I sported a Green Beret apparently made me an ideal candidate for such position because it required survival training by the Special Forces in order for me to be able to train fellow pilots how to evade capture and live off the land in the event they were ever shot down behind enemy lines. The Senior Pilot duly informed me that I should prepare myself for the training course - three weeks with the 22 Special Air Service Regiment (SAS) in Hereford. To say I went back into serious physical training was an understatement. I assumed that the SAS were the pinnacle of the Army Special Ops, so by the time I nervously reached Hereford, I was more than ready for what was about to transpire.

The well publicised, three-week course at Hereford concentrated on advanced survival techniques, escape and evasion, and tactics behind enemy lines and we were taught the full, unclassified gambit of ultimate survival in the wilds of the Welsh hills. I passed out with a grade of "B" which I later learned was exceptional for any officer who was not on Selection.

When I returned to the squadron, we were tasked to pilot an aircraft down to Dorset on a tactical exercise supporting marines who were attempting to become members of the Special Boat Service (SBS). This we duly did and then spent the night at their Headquarters in Poole. That evening in the bar I had a long conversation with their training officer, a mountain of a man who in later years became this elite unit's CO. We chatted about various things and, when he discovered that I was a commando, a pilot, a clearance diver, and a combat survival instructor, he looked at me and said, "Howard, you should be one of us. It's obvious you could pass. It's the diving that beats most guys and you've already got that cracked."

17

The next morning we flew the team on exercise out to the New Forest. I distinctly remember watching them exiting the aircraft, disappearing into the brush, and thinking how much I would like to be with them. On arrival back at the squadron in Yeovilton I went to the CO and asked if my next appointment could be SBS selection. I was soon to learn, however, that the Royal Navy had more elaborate plans for me.

Two weeks later, I was summoned to the offices of Flag Officer Naval Air Command where I was ushered to an office of a Lieutenant Commander whom I had never met before. He looked at some papers on his desk and then at me. He said that he understood I wished to join the SBS. He went on to commend my B grade from Hereford and declared it unsurpassed in the Royal Navy and, in view of all of the above, the Navy would like me to consider taking another route into special operations. He asked if I would consider "rubbing shoulders with the enemy?" Given the magnitude of the question and that I really did not have a clue as to what he was talking about or what such process might involve, with a shrug of my shoulders I heard myself say, "Okay Sir, I'll give it a go." And with that simple statement my life was never to be the same again.

I will not go into the six-month selection process that pushed every man to his limit, but of the 120 men who commenced the course only *four* were still standing on its completion. The prize was continuous operational deployment.

As I progressed up the ladder, I became the only naval officer to achieve two operational commands within the unit. I was promoted to Lieutenant Commander twelve months ahead of my peers and I became the first British Officer in history to take temporary command of a USMC Squadron (HMT 204) and married my American wife during that time.

The only return to normality during my entire career was a six-month stint as a Lieutenant Commander on the frigate HMS *Broadsword*, during which I earned my Ocean Navigation and Bridge Watch-keeping Certificates. These maritime qualifications were seen as essential by my peers to enable me to be a "career" officer in the Royal Navy and this evolution was carried out on active operations in the Adriatic Sea enforcing the Balkans blockade where we experienced the tragic loss of three of our crew by means of fire and accident on the high seas.

By this stage of my military career, I was considered to be a "grown up" and it was now time for Staff College.

The Navy decided that because I had spent so much of my time doing "Army things," I would be a perfect candidate to send to the Army Command and Staff College in Camberley. By the time I graduated I was capable of commanding an armoured brigade but, in truth, I wouldn't have recognised one if it ran over me! It was, however, during this time that I first recall reading about a man called Osama bin Laden.

However, in another twist of fate, following a specialist directorate's presentation at the Staff College, the Boss hosted a reception for 'selected' officers. He knew me well from previous work together and during a conversation at the bar, he asked me whether I would consider joining his team. This was an offer I couldn't refuse and during the next two years I was kept busy with various small team deployments.

On the domestic front, however, I was under increasing pressure from my American wife to leave the military and devote more time to my family life. It was then that I began to ponder the future, concluding that my service as a Naval officer, having been anything but "naval", had probably reached its end. The Royal Navy was unlikely to ever reward me with a promotion to one-star or above for I had not been on enough grey ships or even worn a blue uniform except to formal functions. That said, I owe the Navy a debt of thanks for permitting me to carry their mantel in a discreet, irregular and adventurous career path.

But it was now time to get out and see what civilian life could offer. In my last year in the military, I studied for my Civil Aviation Air Transport Pilot's License, spent my last four idyllic months back with 845 Squadron and drove away from Yeovilton Naval Air Station, no longer as a decorated officer but now nothing more than a plain "Mister".

A few days later, I emigrated to the United States to join my wife who was now pregnant with our second daughter. During the next two years, I tried my hand at being the General Manager of a fantastic Harley Davidson dealership in Wilmington, North Carolina before succumbing to my urge to fly and becoming a very poorly paid captain for U.S. Airways commuter service. The airline management had nothing but contempt for commercial pilots and a pilot's role had been diminished to that of a blue-collar worker merely disguised in a white collar. So when the opportunity came to join a small corporate aviation company, I took a leap of faith and *that* is how I came to be in Hagerstown, Maryland, on September 11, 2001.

On September 12th I woke up and concluded that if I was going to continue to live in the United States with my wife and daughters, all of who were American, then I should be prepared to do whatever it took to preserve the safety and freedom of the country that I now called home. I collected the forms from the U.S. Immigration Service and applied for a U.S. Passport. One year later, the passport was issued and, unbeknown to me, the door to go into Al-Qaeda's backyard as an "Advisor" had been opened.

CHAPTER 2

Recruitment

During the aftermath of 9/11, I watched on like the rest of the world as Osama bin Laden's name gained infamy. Unlike the general public, I had come familiar with his name and profile in 1995 during my last specialist tour in the military. In 1998, some three years after I had first been briefed on his nefarious intent and his growing destructive capabilities, the simultaneous bombing of the U.S. embassies in Nairobi and Dar Es Salaam momentarily captured the attention of the world and the citizens of the United States. However, even when just days after these bombings the FBI placed the name of Osama bin Laden on its Top Ten Most Wanted list, the American television viewing population was more interested in Monika Lewinski's blow-jobs than Osama's blow-up jobs.

By the time my U.S. passport had been issued, not only had bin Laden's name surpassed that of Lewinsky in the popular press but also a new and very different President was in power. In the weeks that followed 9/11, the U.S. Government had to be seen to be doing something and anything, and the initial foray by the SF and CIA into Afghanistan in October 2001 proved in the short-term to be incredibly successful. The U.S. and UK SF teams were permitted free rein to coordinate with the indigenous forces (Northern Alliance) under the brutally effective warlord, General Dostrum, in a joint effort to rout the Taliban and Al-Qaeda and they swept south from Uzbekistan to liberate Kabul.

The final assault against bin Laden was on Tora Bora Mountain by a joint task force incorporating U.S. precision weapons, American and British Forces, and Northern Alliance militia. To reduce allied casualties, it was decided that the Northern Alliance should go up the mountain to clear the remaining pockets of resistance, negotiate a truce and bring down the surviving Al-Qaeda members. A British commander on the ground later described how some *1,000* Northern Alliance troops went up the mountain. There then followed a twelve hour cease fire that had been initiated and brokered by the treacherous warlord, Haji Zaman, purely to buy Al-Qaeda time and some *3,000* 'Northern Alliance' members came down the mountain. Once off Tora Bora, the 2,000 newly aligned Northern Alliance troops instantly reverted back to their Taliban and Al-Qaeda patronage and faded away across the porous border into Pakistan; bin Laden was almost certainly amongst them.

Little could he have realised at that moment that he had unwittingly sealed the fate of Saddam Hussein who would now be the "bad Arab" that the Bush Administration *could* catch. This mission creep would move the focus from destroying Al-Qaeda in Pakistan to invading Iraq and serve to provide Al-Qaeda and the Taliban with enough time and space to lick their wounds, regroup, and ultimately reorganise.

By now I had finally settled into a "normal" family life, a luxury that neither the military nor the commercial airlines had ever afforded me. My new life actually permitted me the necessary time to devote to my children. I experienced the happiness of being the Under-Six soccer coach for my youngest daughter's team and sharing Saturday breakfasts with my eldest that often involved sneaking out the house in order to evade the desire of my youngest daughter to monopolise me. These were pleasures I had never experienced. My life running the business jet operation was a good one and, although the money could always be better, I had achieved a very satisfying level of personal contentment and professional success. The owner of the company, George Smith (or "Smitty" as he was known to all), although at times a bit cantankerous, was a thoroughly decent man with a big heart. And although all employees complain about their boss at one time or another, we could have done a lot worse than Smitty.

It was around this time in February 2003 that a Cessna Caravan aircraft flying over the southern jungles of Colombia got into difficulties and came down in the jungle in the very heart of Colombia's revolutionary guerrilla (FARC) territory. The pilot, Tommy Janis, clearly did a great job getting the aircraft on the ground in a relatively intact condition and none of the passengers, a Columbian sergeant and four U.S. 'defence contractors', were seriously hurt. However, a FARC reception committee was quickly on to them. The Colombian Sergeant, Luis Acedes, and Janis tried to escape and were summarily executed; the other three, Keith Stansell, Thomas Howes and Marc Gonlaves, were captured and joined the French aid worker Ingrid Betancourt in the makeshift gulag that was her prison deep in the Colombian jungle.

As plans were being made to recover them, a conversation occurred at the British Embassy in Washington DC between an old friend who was a special ops Royal Marines Officer serving in a liaison role and an American official who was involved in the search and rescue mission. During the casual conversation, the British officer mentioned to his counterpart that he knew a former colleague officer living in Pennsylvania who might have some knowledge of a successful hostage recovery in similar circumstance.

That afternoon I received a call from my friend warning me that a call might occur and an evening or two later it came from a man who introduced himself as Paul from the Department of State's Air Wing.

I would later learn that Air Wing was officially The Bureau of International Narcotics and Law Enforcement Affairs Office of Aviation (INL/A, also known as the INL Air Wing). The "Wing" oversees a combined fleet of more than 240 active airplanes and helicopters in some of the most challenging, remote, austere, and dangerous countries in the world in support of counternarcotics, counterterrorism, border security/law enforcement, and embassy transportation missions.

During the next few weeks, Paul called a couple of times; we exchanged some ideas and became somewhat acquainted. However, it seemed the hostages were lost to the dense and mountainous forests and it sadly transpired that the opportunity to launch a rescue operation was not to occur for another six years.

Concurrent to the periodic calls from Paul I was busy expanding Smitty's business. By this time we had two jet aircraft and two turbo-props under management and were about to add a third jet. Life was sweet.

As the war in Iraq went through its initial, euphoric stage the inept Iraqi army rapidly dissolved under the might of America's technical ability to fight a conventional war and Iraq descended into anarchy. I watched with bated breath, wondering how the hell the U.S. would ever get itself out of such mess.

It was sometime during April 2003 when I left the office in Martinsburg in West Virginia. I headed along Tabler Station

Road toward Junction 8 of Highway 81, making the forty-minute drive north to my home in the quiet village of Greencastle, Pennsylvania. My mobile phone was resting in the cup holder. I remember distinctly the moment it rang. I had just turned right onto the "on-ramp" of I-81 North. I picked up the phone and looked at the number; it was "Number Withheld" and I recall thinking, "Who the hell is this?" I pressed the receive button and gave my characteristic, "Hello, it's Howard" greeting. On the other end was Paul.

As we went through the usual "How's it going?" greetings, I assumed he was going to update me on the situation in Colombia. Instead he went on to other things.

"Look, H, we've got a programme running in Pakistan at the moment and we are having a few problems getting it to a point of efficiency..."

Having given about as minimal information as possible, he then went straight for the jugular. "...and we were wondering if you'd like to be our man in Pakistan?"

I'm not sure whether it was a question or a statement but I had an instant flashback to the Lieutenant Commander in Naval Air Command and his "rub shoulders" recruitment pitch. However, I was older and wiser now (or so I thought) and hopefully less impetuous.

"Well Paul, that's really very nice of you to think of me, but I'm married with two kids now so all that shit is over for me." Paul was undeterred and he adopted a more subtle approach.

"Well, that's OK, Howard, I fully understand but I'll tell you what."

He had moved from his preliminary approach to his alternative strategy – he had recruited men before and he knew this would take a bit more manoeuvring.

"Don't worry about necessarily coming on board, but given your experience, why don't you just come down to see us in

Florida and at least we can pick your brains on a few tactics? Help us develop a game plan."

I remember thinking I've told him I'm not interested in deploying so a visit could do no harm but, also, the visit would be bloody interesting; which was exactly what Paul wanted me to think. So I said, "Okay, as it happens, I have to come down to Florida next week on business."

"That sounds great! Let me know what day suits you and I'll line it all up. It'll be great to meet you in person and to talk about the problem at hand."

In the week that followed, I felt alive again. I once again mattered. Paul and I had multiple email exchanges honing the visit schedule. Meanwhile, my wife and I had some pretty deep discussions. From a personal perspective, I had been pressured to leave the military at her behest. At that time, our first daughter was an infant and Shellie had decided being a military wife was not for her. So she had laid down an ultimatum that is all too common for so many western military men; "Me or the Services. Choose!" One then is faced with the decision whether to lose one's family or one's standing in the military. At the time, my decision to leave the Royal Navy seemed like a no-brainer. In retrospect, however, I had regretted that decision for many years. So Shellie and I agreed I should check out the new opportunity. I combined the trip with another business opportunity in Florida but my focus and emphasis was my meeting with Paul, and the thought of once again getting my boots dirty; back into the game.

After flying down to Fisher Island in Florida, arguably the wealthiest Zip code in America, to persuade a hedge fund manager to buy and have us manage his new jet, I picked up a rental car and headed up the coast. Once in the area of the base where Paul was located, I conducted a drive-by so that there were no hiccups with my timing the following day ("time spent in reconnaissance is seldom wasted").

By 0950 the following day, I drove through the front gate of the secure installation and, following the issuance of a temporary security pass, drove to the hangar as directed. This was the home of the U.S. State Department's Air Wing. Paul, who looked much younger than his fifty years, greeted me and he was as affable in person as he had been on the phone. The offices, although not military, were in partition form with maps, photos adorning the walls. All the men to whom I was introduced were former United States military and those who wore flight suits sported their individual service wings on their State Department patches.

Paul offered coffee, which was just the same flavour as I used to drink when with the U.S. Marine Corps. I recall thinking, "If these guy are entrenched in Colombia operations, you'd think they'd get some decent coffee!" However, the cheap, stomach lining-destroying brand would have to do. We then walked along the centre walkway with partition offices on either side toward a large office at the end of the corridor. I was immediately struck by the memorabilia, which consisted of photos of well-known or very dodgy looking characters, maps and multiple wall mounted aircraft and gun parts. I knew I was about to be introduced to the boss, John. Interestingly, I had heard of this guy. He was a bit of a legend, to say the least. By now, he must have been well into his fifties, but still quite fit. Having put Air Wing together, I could tell there was little that could be said to impress this man. He had carved his own path up the mountain of special operations.

The most striking aspect about all the individuals I passed on the way to John's office was that they were clearly "operators". Not one was a door-kicking *"honey-monster"* (body builder) or a *glory boy*. If you had encountered any of them in a bar, you wouldn't have given a second look. This was a world I knew.

As I walked into his office, Paul could not even get the introduction out before John stood up and in a quiet voice said, "So you're going to be our man in Islamabad?"

I quickly replied, "Well, I don't know about that. I think we have a lot to talk about before that can be a true statement."

John and Paul took up their seats on a couch in a corner of the office. A map of Pakistan/Afghanistan was already conveniently laid out on the coffee table between them. As they commenced the brief and pawed over the map they went into surprising detail, undoubtedly knowing they were reeling me in.

John explained that he and an Assistant Secretary of State Bobby Charles had visited the Pakistan border on the first "site survey" to conduct an assessment and it was only then that they realised with compete shock that the entire Pakistan/Afghanistan border was wide open.

They returned to the U.S. and recommended the implementation of a full-blown border security programme beyond just an air component, which would permit Air Wing to concentrate interdiction of the flow of drugs, arms, and subversives between Afghanistan and Pakistan. However, Iraq was the mission of the moment and Air Wing was essentially told to get on with it and do what they could to strengthen border security.

Both John and Paul unashamedly exposed the operational shortfalls of the funded, equipped but unilateral operation in Pakistan and I soon realised they had some severe tactical and logistical problems.

Essentially the U.S. State Department had provided the Government of Pakistan with aircraft to enable them to tighten the non-existent border security. Furthermore, State had, via a DynCorp contract, provided two flying instructors to train Pakistan army pilots, along with maintenance personnel to train Pakistani ground crews.

All this sounded great in theory but no one had anticipated the cultural or tactical integration complications. The aircraft had been given to the Ministry of the Interior (MOI), which was neither military nor part of the Anti-Narcotics Force (ANF), so they were largely being used (and abused) as VIP transports for Pakistani generals. Such a perk was not surprising, given that the Pakistan Army ostensibly staffed the MOI.

So, in reality, not much kudos for the $65million of U.S. taxpayers' money that was supposed to help strengthen border security. Furthermore, rather than be located in Quetta, the main town in the border area, the aircraft were kept in Islamabad out of harm's way.

John and Paul explained that there were two Cessna 208 aircraft that could be used as Forward Looking Infra-Red (FLIR) surveillance platforms, with one more due for delivery and seven UH-1 Huey helicopters that could be employed for troop lift ops and logistic support. We then talked about limitations and armament for the aircraft and the operatives. I was shocked to learn that the diplomats in the U.S. Embassy in Islamabad were opposed to any operational personnel carrying weapons for self-protection. I couldn't believe my ears. Paul, however, assured me that there were legal ways around these totally naive policies. John cut in to explain that Air Wing was a highly operational unit but because it was a part of "State" had to whistle to the tune of diplomats.

He went on to make clear that his unit had taken more rounds in its aircraft than any other, including all U.S. military units, since Vietnam. These boys were used to getting shot at. In places like Colombia their role was the eradication

29

of narcotics at the growing stage, i.e. they sprayed poison on coca plants etc. while the bastards below try to shoot them down.

We finished our coffee and John calmly came in for the kill.

"The programme is at a standstill, we really do need someone like you to make it all happen. So what do you think?' he asked.

I responded that it looked like a heck of a challenge.

To which John said, "Look, we need a guy with your credentials to take this on. Otherwise, it's going to fail. It's that simple, Howard. Operators with your kind of skill sets are extremely hard to find."

I paused and asked, "How often will I get home?"

He answered, "We'll give you a month off at the end of your year."

I thought about that for a moment and I told him it wouldn't work - I would need ten days off every three months. Paul interrupted and said they couldn't do that because that wasn't how the programme worked. If they did it for me, they'd have to do it for everyone.

Standing up as if to leave, I said, "Well, I don't think that's so - but, if it is, then it's a deal breaker because I have two small girls and I need to see them. Sorry gentlemen but that's a show-stopper."

John, clearly surprised by my response, somewhat excitedly urged me to sit down and relax. I did.

He and Paul had a short quiet talk that lasted no more than twenty seconds.

"Okay," said John, "We'll make it happen. But you need to understand, it's very irregular."

"That works," I said, "and I need it in writing and talk about the money."

Paul then explained that I would have to negotiate my package with the State Department's contracts office, and added that whatever I was able to negotiate they would back me on it.

John went in for the kill a second time. "So are you in?"

I told him I would have to talk it through with my wife and a lot would depend on the package - but I was interested.

He was clearly elated and went on to say, "I just know you'll be perfect for this. We need someone with the Brit mentality to get it done. You Brits are great at what you do. The only problem is that I know when I unleash you, I just know I'm going to get a lot more than I ever bargained for."

And, he did.

Following lunch, Paul showed me around the facility and the various aircraft they had at the base. It was a very impressive operation and I could sense that this unit existed for one purpose and one purpose only - getting the job done. And they made no fuss about it.

By mid afternoon, I was driving to Tampa airport, starkly aware that my feeling of strategic uselessness had never left me since resigning from the military. I had never realised just how important being a cog in the gearbox that makes military/political strategies happen had been to me. But it was and the impact on my family since leaving the military had been pretty awful. Try as I might to sort out my priorities, I never seemed to do so to everyone's satisfaction. Shellie did her best to bring me round with anger and occasional threats of leaving. Olivia and Constance would simply wind their Dad around their little fingers to get their way. Gradually, and a bit too late, perhaps, I learned that those years were both valuable and irreplaceable, that the love between a father and his children would shape their lives and, significantly. I had pulled my head out of my arse and showered them with as much love as possible. Sometimes that love would be returned, sometimes not. It didn't matter. The realisation of the absolute beauty of my family was with me, but so was the realisation that I needed a role!

With all of that spinning around my head, I dumped the car at the rentals and caught AirTran back to Washington. Now the real dilemma of "what to do" would have to be thrashed out. During the drive home from the terminal, Shellie and I spoke about the guys I had met. I described the personality of the unit and how it was just what I had been used to in the past.

I reflected that I was the only guy *I* knew who could do the job and that if I could get in, get the job done, and then get out, it would be a lot less than the time I had spent on previous, difficult operations.

The following day I arrived at the office in Martinsburg pretending the meeting with John and Paul had never happened; it was time to live a lie again, even if for all the right reasons. I debriefed Smitty on my business meetings in Florida. I hated to conceal the fact that I might be leaving but at least I would be leaving the company in great shape and I vowed to myself to work diligently until my last day with his company.

During the day, Paul called and told me that a woman from contracts, Linda, would be calling me. He described her as a very tough lady and that I should be prepared for a potentially abrasive conversation.

When Linda finally called, I recognised the Washington DC area code and answered. Her inflection was immediately dour and monotone. She explained that I would be a Personal Services Contractor (PSC). This is essentially the government's way of employing someone, but not employing them. In other words, deniable if you screw it up or get killed on the job. A PSC is not afforded such perks as language course, or for that matter, any in-depth preparation for the task he/she is about to undertake - a fabulous penny-wise, dollar-foolish shortfall dreamed up by some idiot who has never been thrown into a high-threat environment.

Linda ran through the basic package. Frankly, if the President ever needs someone to guard the government U.S. Treasury and protect the taxpayers' money, he needs only to haul Linda into the Oval Office.

This lady was a fiscal control monster and her offering was surprisingly meagre. In fact, I was a bit insulted. I was considering restructuring my life and risking my neck to run a $65-million covert programme and yet the price of my service, from the very start, was being grossly undervalued. Did this woman truly believe that just *anyone* could undertake this complex and dangerous assignment for a base pay of $80K a year? I told her the compensation package would not work for me at its current level. She then advised me to go back to Paul to see if they were willing to upgrade the position.

Terminating the call, I immediately contacted Paul and let him know that the package was too low for me to consider leaving my family for an entire year to risk my life for Uncle Sam. Expecting my likely refusal after Linda's first offer, he told me that there was a grade or two on top of the current offer and that he and John could nudge things along to bump me up to those levels. The next day I received an email from Linda offering the higher amount.

Once I had decided that I would likely accept that offer, I contacted my insurance company to determine if I could buy coverage in Pakistan. Not surprisingly, the answer was a universal "No." From their viewpoint, a "whitey" living in Pakistan was tantamount to suicide. And had they known what I was going to be doing there, they probably would not have even taken my call. After contacting several other insurance agencies, it became obvious that I was going to have to figure out some kind of self-insurance plan.

The State Department's offer actually took into account that I might be on my way to an early death. In the event that I was killed, they would pay my wife over $100K per annum until the children were eighteen. Thereafter, it would be reduced to $75K for life unless she got remarried. If she remained unmarried until age sixty-two, she would remain on that amount for life. I did my sums and sent a polite email to Linda presenting my financial requirement to do the job.

It was two days later when I was on the ramp in Martinsburg viewing our fleet of corporate aircraft when Paul called. He informed me that Linda had received my requirements and had basically gone berserk, demanding, "How can this man justify this outrageous amount?"

"She clearly has no concept of what it's like to be shot at, mortared or bombed," I said.

Paul went on to emphasise that they had explained that my skill sets were quite unique and that they considered me to be an absolutely vital addition to the operation. He then told her to do whatever might be necessary to meet my requirements and that the operation had little chance of success without my involvement. With that, he wished me luck and I awaited Linda's dreaded call.

As it happened, I didn't have to wait long. Linda called almost immediately and she had clearly prepared her opening salvo. She said she had looked at the numbers and having a big problem figuring out how I had arrived at those figures. It was now time to get firm, so I played my Ace.

"You need to put yourself in my position Linda," I told her, no longer jovial. "I am standing on an aircraft ramp looking at three very decent jet and turbo-prop aircraft. I manage them all and run a team of pilots. I write the flight programme, manage all the programmes, and am away whenever I want to be and home whenever I don't. The total value of the planes is about $26million and all are owned by high net worth clients. I'm number two in the company and I earn a good wage. Furthermore, I've had my run of adventure and excitement. So I don't need a job and I certainly don't need to do *this* job."

It's up to you. You know where I stand on the amount and I'm not budging."

There was a long pause.

"Okay," she said, "but in order for us to meet your numbers we would have to move you into the highest civil service pay bracket, basically ambassador level."

She further explained, "If we were to try to do that then it would have to raise a memorandum and go through all sorts of approvals in all sorts of departments and that will likely take months."

I let her continue. "What we can do is put you on the very highest dollar level in the current bracket which would actually come out to about a $2K shortfall per annum. If I can do it, would that suffice?" she asked.

I told her we had a deal and with that she hung up.

Within minutes my phone rang again. It was Paul. He was laughing.

"What the hell did you say to her?" he asked.

I replied, "Why? What did she say to you?"

"She asked, where the hell did you find this guy? He's not the usual kind of guy I deal with. He really seems to know his stuff and I don't think we're paying him enough!"

"Shit," I replied, "I left money on the table?"

"No," said Paul. "You took her to a dollar amount she has never paid a Personal Services Contractor before. Not ever! And you know what? She doesn't mind. Well done, buddy!"

He concluded by saying Linda that would send through the contract immediately.

I wandered back towards the office from the aircraft ramp, it was a beautifully sunny day and the Smokey Mountains of West Virginia were green and lush. The excitement coursing through my veins made me feel alive again, I reflected that the last time I'd felt this way was probably my passage into the besieged Sarajevo during the height of that godforsaken war. But along with all this excitement came the inevitable conflicts and questions: Was I letting my family down? How would I cope with the separation from my precious daughters? Would Smitty think I had betrayed him? And, most significantly, what would become my relationship with Shellie?

What ultimately led to Shellie's acceptance of my decision, grudging though it was, is that she realised that I would be forever restless (as I had been in those years since leaving the military) until I got this out of my system.

Perhaps naively, I truly believed our relationship was strong and could withstand the stress of a prolonged separation. We loved each other and that was all that really mattered. I even recall commenting to Shellie, "If this will cost me my marriage, I won't go." But she agreed it would not. She understood that I was acting for the benefit of the family and our future.

Two days later I arrived home to find a Federal Express package from Linda. Inside were two Personal Services Contracts with the title of "Senior Aviation Advisor (Pakistan)." Linda had also been thoughtful enough to enclose a prepaid self-addressed FedEx envelope. As I read the contract in my study, I realised that perhaps I had left a bit too much on the table. I then went to the kitchen to discuss this with Shellie and asked whether I should sign. She sat down and watched me ratify each section. My two little girls were in the family room watching television, blissfully unaware that their Daddy had just signed a contract that would change all of our lives forever.

The clock was now ticking and I had only eight weeks before I would need to abandon my quiet, predictable life and leave for an uncertain future in a primitive war-torn region of the Pakistan-Afghan border. I commenced physical training, running at least four to six miles a day and concentrated on weight training that wouldn't add bulk. I rewrote my will and rehearsed what I would say to Smitty. I hoped that I wasn't letting him down - but I knew that he was, in his heart, fiercely patriotic and, with the utter mess regarding the fallout from the initial invasion into Iraq and George W Bush's premature "Mission Accomplished" declaration, I trusted that he would understand. As it happened, he was more gracious than I could have ever imagined and although he was profoundly disappointed that I was leaving him, Smitty also understood the concept of "sense of duty". We parted as good friends and remain so to this day.

Smitty and I came to an agreement on a departure date from the company and I booked a ten-day holiday in St Thomas for Shellie and the girls. It was an absolutely idyllic time. But, sadly, unknown to any of us, it would be the last vacation, the last bit of genuine, prolonged quality time we would ever share as a family.

CHAPTER 3

Induction And Training

On my return from our family vacation in St. Thomas, I felt refreshed but, at the same time, I harboured a sense of dread that it was the calm before the storm. My family had never felt so together and my marriage was as strong as it had ever been. Shellie and I had long, heartfelt talks about what was about to unfold. I promised her I would not take any undue risks and that I would return in one piece. I felt that the many years I had spent leading specialist operations had prepared me for this mission and that my diverse and extensive training, and personal security awareness was second to none.

In cynical terms, the best way to survive a bear attack is either not to be noticed by the bear or, if you are, to simply run faster than the person you're with. It was this personal doctrine that I always metaphorically applied and followed.

The following Sunday, it was time to commence my training at a facility in Wichita, Kansas, where I would be trained to fly a Cessna C-208 "Caravan" in a simulator. The C-208 is a single engine turbo prop so it was considerably slower and less complicated than the Learjet 45 or Hawker 800XP in which I had been booming around. It almost equated to climbing out of a Ferrari into a FedEx delivery van.

Even the check ride was a breeze, with the instructor recognizing the aircraft wasn't stretching me in the least. A great start, I thought, and at that stage, I must have been the best-paid abinitio C-208 pilot in the world.

A week later I arrived at a hotel convenient to the Air Wing's Florida base and reported first thing on Monday morning. I received the usual welcome from the team and sat in on the daily Ops briefing, which gave me an insight of the global operations. Of all the current Air Wing actions it seemed, somewhat incredibly, that less was happening in Pakistan than anywhere else. I recall thinking, "I'll have to change that."

The first couple of days were spent obtaining various passes and being briefed on each department and how they interacted with each other. DynCorp were contracted to provide all the aircraft maintenance support and these guys outnumbered the Air Wing staff, but the cooperation and cohesion appeared to be there. It also became blatantly obvious that everything was run on a tight budget.

I was issued equipment, flight suits and other required gear. The first thing that struck me that almost all of this was green. Was I not destined for a mountainous desert region? To my knowledge, there was virtually no *green* in Balochistan or anyplace else in that region. When I requested desert cammies, I was told they didn't have any. These guys were geared up for Colombia and they clearly had never considered or even realised the colour of Balochistan's terrain. Like any soldier, I took all equipment on offer in the knowledge that I would only use about ten percent of it once I was out of training.

Within a couple of days, I was on the flight schedule with Kevin as my instructor and we worked through the C-208 flight syllabus in a real aircraft. There was only one shaky moment during manoeuvres when a light aircraft came through our airspace and almost hit us; another hundred feet higher and it would have all ended right there. Kevin and I spent the week running through every emergency and conceivable adverse situation before progressing to Night Vision Goggle training. This was real "back in the saddle" stuff for me. I hadn't flown on NVGs since leaving the military in 1997, so I had to work on relearning those skills, which are akin to flying an aircraft while looking through a pair of toilet rolls with green light filters on them. It took just over a week and a half to complete the C-208 training module.

I then commenced my Bell UH-1 Huey helicopter training under the guidance of John, Air Wing's instructor who, I reflected, probably spent more time in a helicopter than he had spent in bed with his wife.

I quickly became aware of the aircraft's simplicity and its forgiving nature. No wonder it had saved so many lives. I tried not to think about the fact it had effectively also delivered so many men to their deaths. The aircraft had just one engine and pretty much two of everything else - blades, doors, skids, and instruments. For some reason, when these helicopters were designed in the mid-fifties, their limited fuel tank and power-plant pretty much meant they could go nowhere with a lot of people or a long way with no people. Over the years, technological advances in engine, gearbox and blade engineering meant that the aircraft could now carry full fuel, an auxiliary fuel tank in the cabin, and its troop load. So it had 'legs', even if it was a bit slow with a cruising speed of around ninety knots.

The other marvellous aspect of the Huey was that it was relatively simple to maintain and therefore about as perfect as it could get for Pakistani mechanics in austere conditions to keep it flying. It had also undergone a considerable upgrade in armour and Kevlar that now protected many of its vital components from small arms fire, including the pilots' seats and the cabin floor. This added measure gave its occupants some testicular reassurance compared to the grunts in *Apocalypse Now* who sat on their helmets preferring to take a shot to the head than to their balls.

My previous helicopter experience had been in the Gazelle (3 blades, single engine), Wessex 5 HU-1 (4 blades, twin engine), the CH-46E Sea Knight (6 blades, twin engine) and the Sea King Mk4 (5 blades, twin engine). So to be in a twin bladed, single engine helicopter was something new and it took a couple of flights to become familiar with its handling.

Thankfully, it didn't take long before I felt comfortable piloting this aircraft. The only manoeuvre I found challenging was when John, my instructor, repeatedly failed the engine and I had to put the aircraft into autorotation to keep the blades spinning and then glide it down to a selected landing spot.

During the week we cracked the full mandate of the syllabus and also had the opportunity to fly some gun-ship profiles, where we would practise providing fire support to an OV-10 Bronco, which was practising its crop-spray profiles for Colombian coca eradication ops.

The culmination of the Huey training was the walk-round and check flight with Dave. He was a former Chief Warrant Officer and came over as one tough bastard with an outwardly intimidating aura of "Get it right or I'll chop your arse." I suppose if some examiners can put you at ease, there are others who don't and all the indications from Dave were that I was not going to get an easy ride.

He put me through my paces, and corrected me without hesitation if I was not doing anything the way he wanted it. His standards were high and rightly so, for this was not a game we were about to play. By the time we finished the check-ride we had both relaxed and it actually turned out to be a very enjoyable flight. As we wandered back into the line to sign in the aircraft, I reflected the next time I would fly a helicopter would be in Pakistan itself.

In the three weeks I spent completing my flight training, there was a lot of what the military call 'concurrent activity'. Most of my time, when not flying, was spent with Paul going over the various intricacies of the Pakistan operation.

The picture that he painted was one that, to say the least, was quite bizarre. He described the hierarchy within the U.S. Embassy in Islamabad and those to whom I would have to answer. My superior in Islamabad was to be a young lady named Dorothy. She was not a career State Department employee and it was widely rumoured that she had been some sort of junior staffer during Clinton's second term.

When State had no takers for the Narcotics Affairs Section in Islamabad, this bright young lady, who had a degree in law, volunteered for a job for which she had no experience but as the *only* volunteer, she got the position. She now had a driver, a car, a massive house, servants, and so on, a far cry from the one bedroom, staffers' apartment she had come from in Washington's Dupont Circle. From Paul's description, I knew Dorothy and I were going to be poles apart on doctrine.

She was known to have issues regarding her department being armed when deployed on the border. I found this mindset absolutely naive and frankly, preposterous. There was no way I was going to operate without a gun in a veritable hotbed of jihadist extremists. Paul could not explain or understand her illogic but simply said it was something we would have to overcome. To that end it was decided that I should be put on State's weapons handling course in the Berretta 92SB pistol and the M16/M4 rifle. He also expedited the approval process to have a number of weapons shipped out to Pakistan in support of my task.

The weapons course was pretty basic and, having had the benefit of firing thousands of rounds in my 'previous life', I completed the class with quiet confidence.

Every evening I would take a run along Coco Beach and understandably enjoy the "in-your-face" microscopic bikinis on display. The percentage of beach fit women in Florida was amazing and I figured I might as well soak up the scenery because there would certainly be nothing to compare where I was going.

The operational discussions and sessions with Paul intensified with him providing profiles on all the personalities involved both stateside and in Pakistan.

Unbeknown to me our Boss, John, had reached his own crisis point seeking "top cover" for his teams and at some juncture, he had become so frustrated that he had written an unclassified memo that fell into the hands of the media. It stated within that, *"Dodging trees and ground fire over jungle terrain at 200 mph is not diplomacy and diplomats cannot be expected to fully comprehend the complexity of the task and the level of support required."*

Even though the statement had its merits it triggered a knee-jerk reaction and the "diplomats" immediately turned it round with spin to say, "We don't understand why he is attacking his own programme".

Everyone in Air Wing acknowledged it was brilliant misdirection from the ivory tower and just incredibly ballsy to essentially ignore the memo and attack him instead. The real lesson was, though, that John had publicly crossed "city hall" and those who approved his position and paycheck.

Someone would have to go.

John voluntarily retired from the Unit that he had built from inception. It was a great pity, but at least John went out as he had commanded; coolly, calmly and with an operator's honour. Now this epitome of a quiet hero would have time to ride his BMW motorcycle at characteristic breakneck speeds during his well earned, albeit somewhat forced, retirement.

As the new guy on the block, I didn't know quite what to make of all of this. Paul suggested that I take a week off while waiting for my deployment clearance. By now, I was understandably more worried about the internal politics of State than any pathological Taliban carrying an AK-47.

I spent the week at home cramming fitness and quality time. I took the opportunity re-read the Holy Quran and work my way through Afghan Guerrilla Warfare by Ali Jajali and Lester Grau. The books were entirely at odds with each other, with the first preaching a good way to lead your life and the second detailing Mujahedeen tactics as described by the fighters themselves. I also read anything else I could on travel in Pakistan.

I re-wrote my Will, finished as many of the family DIY duties as I could and went to a dental clinic Hagerstown where the gold cap on one of my molars was replaced with enamel. It was just one more temptation removed for any would be cutthroat whose need for the gold was greater than mine. Then on to a specialist in Chambersburg who administered a combination of needles into my buttocks to protect me from the delights of cholera, yellow fever, hepatitis A & B, typhoid, meningococcal meningitis and a variety of forms of encephalitis, not forgetting the obligatory boosters for polio and tetanus.

I put together a med-pack for myself. In times past, I had learned the value of preventative medicine. Having strong medications in your kit was potentially life-saving. For example, a few doses of Cipro at the first sign of the shits can eradicate an infection before it becomes disabling.

I called my old friend, Dr Bob in North Carolina, who used to be my girls' physician. Bob is a truly great doctor with whom I had struck a friendship and we have remained close friends ever since.

Bob's raspy New York voice came on the phone. "Howard, you big sissy, what are you up to?"

I explained my upcoming journey to Pakistan. After a prolonged silence followed by multiple expletives describing my insanity he got serious.

"Here's what I'm going to do," he said. "I'll package up some samples and preventative medical supplies and get them to you with precise written instructions. And for Christ's sake, Howard, be careful out there. There's some really nasty shit to be caught, bugs you only read about."

The very next day a FedEx box arrived filled with medical supplies and a handwritten note enclosed:

Howard, you big fairy, here is what you will hopefully not need.

If you have any doubts, call me. I don't give a shit what time it is, just call. Okay? You're in my prayers, ya crazy limey wanker! Your friend Bob.

By now, I was mentally and physically prepared to deploy and it was time to AirTran it back to Florida to meet John Mac's replacement. I must admit I was a bit taken aback to discover that it was woman with no operational aviation experience whatsoever. What the hell was going on?

I arrived at the base and was briefed by Paul that the new boss, Sharon, was pretty cool. The first thing I noticed was that she was a tall woman with a pleasant smile who appeared to be in her forties, it was clear that she was the polar opposite of John, but she was sensible enough not to try to replace him at his own game. She asked many questions, listening intently to my responses, and told me she considered Pakistan to be the Air Wing's biggest challenge and, as the only operational unit in State, we were going to have to "cut the path." She explained that she intended to use her experience in funding and procurement to get the Pakistan operation everything it needed.

I left Sharon's office feeling mightily encouraged. She seemed like a lady who could kick arse and who I could trust to back me and, as it happened, she more than lived up to that first impression. Sharon was to develop great pride for "her boys" and that respect became a two-way street. It didn't hurt that she also enjoyed a beer or two and the camaraderie of her team.

My deployment clearance finally came through so there was no time to lose. Shellie and I had a farewell dinner at Roccoco's in Hagerstown. It was very personal and about as romantic as anything I can remember. We discussed the strength of our marriage and how we would get through this coming year. The next morning, feeling a little shabby from a bit too much Pinot Noir, we went as a family to Trinity Lutheran Church on the outskirts of the Village. I prayed that I would come back in one piece and see my girls again. I remember holding Constance's hand during the entire service while she was completely unaware of the intense, heart-wrenching emotion her Dad was experiencing.

It was time to be on my way. I gave my Rolex watch to my daughter Olivia for safekeeping and caught the Saab 340 commuter jet to Pittsburgh.

As the aircraft lifted from the runway, I looked down on all the landmarks that were so familiar, having piloted so many aircraft in and out of that airport. I realised that I was now truly alone. As we climbed noisily through 10,000 feet, the pilot turned off the seat belt sign and I reach down to pull out the New King James Holy Bible that Shellie had given me.

On the inside cover she had written, *"To My Darling Howard, I want you to read this whenever you are feeling unsure of life's little challenges. Don't be afraid but know that God is right there with you and if you can't quite find the answers, put your challenges in his hands. I love you, Honey, with all my heart. Please take special care and come home soon. Forever yours, Shellie."* She completed the passage with *"xxx"* (three kisses,), which I assumed were one from each of my family.

Many hours and four flights later on the approach into Islamabad, I strained to see the terrain and city. Islamabad was created as a new capital in the Sixties to replace Karachi as its political centre. The international airport actually sits within the teeming sprawl of the old city of Rawalpindi. As the aircraft banked, I could see the mass of buildings that were built on top of each other in what was a veritable maze of ancient and modern structures.

My mind was now racing with questions: "What the hell was I doing here? Would this be my last hoorah? What if I never got back to my daughters?" The only upside of the moment was that, with every metre the aircraft descended, it was one closer to me getting out of that stale-sweat stinking pressurised cylinder in which I was temporarily imprisoned.

The runway at Islamabad is something to behold. It is one of the most uneven of any international airport and aircraft have to use the full length in order to turn around and back taxi to the terminal. Out of the window, beyond Mr. Smelly next to me, I could see greenery and the odd soldier on sentry duty. We taxied past the military C-130s and the presidential Boeing 737 on the military ramp and towards a row of Pakistan International Airlines (PIA) aircraft.

Our Emirates Airbus came to a halt and the scramble to get towards the door started. Despite my yearning to get away from the offensive odours, I thought, "What the hell, there is no point in pushing and shoving with this lot." As I approached the door, I got my first whiff of Pakistan on a beautifully sunny morning and thought of the memorable quote by Rudyard Kipling, "The first condition of understanding a foreign country is to smell it."

So the first whiff was to forever recognise Pakistan - and, although hardly aromatic, I had certainly smelled worse. However, as I walked down the aircraft steps one question rang in my ear, "How the fuck did I end up here?"

At the base of the aircraft steps all of Emirates Airlines meticulous attention to detail and quality ended abruptly as we clambered on to a shitty airport bus.

At the 1950s style terminal I learned a few seconds too late that there is no such thing as queuing in Pakistani culture so I became the third to last passenger to pass through immigration and smiled as I presented my Diplomatic Passport to the FIA officer. The scanner on the way out of the airport, as in any Islamic Republic, checked my luggage for booze.

As I walked out of the airport, I was confronted with a throng of people who had all come to meet their friends and relatives. The chaos and the noise were overwhelming to the senses. Out of the mass, I noticed a white face and it was focused on me. We smiled at each other and I asked, "Curtis?"

A thick Georgian drawl came in reply, "Welcome to Pakistan!"

Curtis was the senior DynCorp 'Site Manager' in the country and ran the aircraft maintenance team. He also filled the Senior Aviation Advisor's slot while it was gapped or non-existent. He helped me with my bags and we made our way to his white Toyota 4x4.

I must admit, I wasn't sure if Curtis would be pleased to see me or not. He had clearly been ruling the programme's roost for a while but, as we began to chat, he seemed genuinely pleased, if not relieved, that I was there. He couldn't wait to tell me that relations between the American Embassy and the Government of Pakistan (GOP) were "fucked up." Our helicopters had basically been kidnapped by the Pakistani military and were impounded in a hangar at a nearby military airbase. That had occurred six weeks before. He explained that there has been a major "shit-fit" between the Embassy and the Pakistan Ministry of the Interior (MOI) over operational control. The Paks wanted it and the Embassy didn't want to give it to them. It was that simple.

Apparently the row had reached Presidential level and, as a middle-finger snub to the Ambassador, the Pakistani leadership had decided that, if they couldn't have complete operational control, then the helicopters would be impounded until the Americans changed their minds. It was a complete mess by any measure - but as Curtis drove along the highway towards Islamabad breaking all the speed limits, I recall thinking, "At least the only way is up."

The roads at 7:30 in the morning were busy with everything from jingly-jangly trucks to bicycles and donkeys. As we entered the city, we passed a number of signs each declaring "Islamabad the Beautiful" and a large memorial which, in reality, was basically a rock representing the mountain where Pakistan had conducted its first nuclear test. Looking around at the squalor and dishevelment, it was almost inconceivable that this struggling country could actually be a nuclear power. However, thanks to the arguably misguided genius of Abdul Qadeer Khan, Pakistan had developed the ultimate doomsday defence against its mortal enemy, India.

The first impressions of Islamabad are that of an extremely well planned city. In keeping with most things in Pakistan, however, much of what has been achieved in terms of infrastructure or construction either looks unfinished or unkempt by Western standards; although compared to other cities such as Lahore, Karachi and Quetta where the main thoroughfares are surrounded by narrow streets and cramped housing, Islamabad is well organised in a grid format. The beauty of this system is that a stranger can get to know the city quickly since finding locations by the grid address is the epitome of simplicity.

We passed through a junction known as Zero Point, which was where the city started in earnest and Curtis turned northeast along a road that paralleled Jinna Avenue past the United Nations building. He then swung left into a picturesque road with trees and greenery on the right side and walled villas on the other.

Outside every villa was a small security hut manned by either uniformed or non-uniformed men. Curtis explained that most of those in uniform belonged to the SMS security company who were contracted by the various embassies. However, their presence essentially was a double-edged sword because it indicated to the bad guys that a foreign diplomat or embassy worker was within. I was slightly alarmed that not a single guard was armed.

We stopped outside a solid iron gate and the SMS guard duly opened it. Curtis pulled into the courtyard. A pleasant villa with no round edges dominated the property. As we entered through the front door into the large, austere marble hallway the saying, "A thousand men can make an encampment, but it takes a woman to make a home" sprung to mind. It was readily apparent that no woman's touch had graced this domicile for many a year. There were boxes containing equipment just about everywhere and a large supply of beer in the kitchen. The only marks of real comfort were the vast counterfeit DVD collection by the widescreen television and the well-worn couch where Curtis obviously chose to view many hours of movies in a horizontal fashion.

Curtis began to give me the low down on Dorothy and her deputy Suzanne. His description of Dorothy was pretty much as briefed back in the U.S. but perhaps a little harsher. Reading between the lines, he had obviously been kicked around, or at least prodded, by her and a tone of resentment was apparent. Curtis clearly knew his job and didn't like being told how to do it by someone who had next to no experience. He also thought Dorothy had overplayed hardball with the Pakistani generals, which had resulted in the impounding of the aircraft. He explained that the Ambassador, Nancy Powell, was a woman with an inclination towards rugged fashion sense and comfortable shoes, and she and Dorothy were noticeably good friends. This resulted in Dorothy achieving leverage for position, power and influence way beyond her age or experience.

By now, I was thinking that my biggest obstacle to making this work was not the enemy but the apparently "dove-inclined" bureaucrats who were supposed to be in charge. I wondered how I would handle Dorothy. I'd decided long before that I would take a friendly and cooperative approach and see which way she wanted to play it. After all, wasn't I the advisor they had gone so far out of their way to recruit? Surely she would recognise that my success would be her success too? The only thing for sure was that I wouldn't have to wait long to find out. I had an appointment to meet her at 10.30. So it was time to shave and clean up.

Although Curtis had advised me that I could wear slacks and a polo shirt, I opted for a collar and tie. It was important that her first impression of me was of someone who was serious, who meant business - and I did not want to appear casual in anyway. I had often joked in business that "the smarter I dress, the more I want," and today I was going to want plenty.

As we headed northeast, we passed the Marriot Hotel, which, unbeknown to me, would be a place I'd come close to death on a later date. We swung a hard right onto Constitutional Avenue and headed down hill with all the official governmental buildings on our left. As we did, Curtis informed me of the purpose of each: Ministry of Interior, Parliament, Presidential buildings, National Library, Supreme Court and so on. We came to a red light outside the Supreme Court and all of my previous situation awareness training came to a peak. We were unarmed "whiteys" in a large white sports utility vehicle on what must be the main route to the cluster of Western embassies. It was not a comfortable feeling but Curtis was either blissfully unaware of the threat or, after a couple of years in country, no longer gave a shit about the chances of being assassinated.

He swung the Toyota left at the roundabout and we headed toward a chicane checkpoint where the armed security guard casually waved us through.

The red brick and concrete and high walls and lookout towers of the U.S. Embassy compound came into sight. We turned left to another chicane and drove to the main gate. A guard checked Curtis's pass and I was asked for my diplomatic credentials.

We had arrived early, so Curtis suggested we grab another coffee. We walked to the theatre/cinema where there was a tea-stall. Sitting outside was a lady grinning from ear to ear at Curtis. She turned out be Suzanne (nicknamed "Spray-chick"), she was Dorothy's deputy. Suzanne immediately struck me as having the potential to be a "bit of a lad" after a couple of beers. She was clearly good fun and, once we had bought the teas/coffees, we joined her outside. It was a beautiful morning now that Islamabad, at some 450 metres above sea level, was moving out of its summer. We quickly moved past the small talk phase with Suzanne and she commented that I must be "fucking crazy" to volunteer for such a job. I explained that I had not exactly volunteered; she then surprised me by saying that I shouldn't rush to unpack. With the aircraft impounded, she was not entirely sure there would be anything for me to do.

Once inside the Embassy, we entered an office that was divided into three sections. Suzanne was front and centre, already at her desk, having breezed though security. On the left was a large room where, behind the gap between the hinges and the doorframe, I could see a blonde woman sitting behind a large desk. On the right, there was another small office known as the "cop's office". In reality, it was the Department of Justice staff that were attached to the International Narcotics and Law Enforcement arm of State. Sitting behind a cramped desk was a gentleman who was introduced to me as Jerry, or "Jerry the Cop". He must have been a good-looking guy at some stage in his life and he still looked fit, but the rigors of police work, foreign deployment, and wild parties had clearly taken their toll. Standing up, he looked me in the eye as he shook my hand and, with a wry smile, mumbled in a deep voice, "Welcome to Slammy." I warmed to the man immediately. He was clearly the proverbial "man's man" and appeared to be the type of guy who said more by what he *didn't* say than what he did say.

Suzanne then craned her head around the door and said, "Dorothy is ready for Howard."

Curtis almost ventriloquisted, "I'll be in the next office along when you're finished."

He clearly had no intent of becoming involved with this one. "Here we go!" I thought.

My first impression of Dorothy was that she was a young woman trying to be an older woman. Her dress style was bordering on matronly and it didn't really suit her. I guessed that such incongruous attire was purposeful. She had strikingly well conditioned blonde hair of which she was clearly proud. Her complexion was blush but pale. I guessed that her lineage was Nordic. There was a couch and chair by a coffee table, which I presumed she used for "greeting" meetings. However, she stayed behind her desk and I sat in the armchair.

No sooner had I sat down than she picked up a piece of paper from her desk and said that I should be aware of its contents. It was a memorandum from Dorothy to the Ambassador and others recommending that the aviation programme be terminated. As I read it, I was staggered. "What the fuck is this? Why did she even bring me out here?" I thought.

I knew that neither Paul nor Sharon could be aware of this memo and this was clearly the reason why Suzanne had advised me not to rush to unpack. She went on to say that the whole programme was more trouble than it was worth and that the argument regarding operational control had brought considerable embarrassment to both her and the Ambassador. She said that there was no way that the aircraft could be handed over for the Pakistanis to use as they wished and that they were not in the country to conduct operations for the Pakistani Army.

I explained that I could understand the political issue from both the U.S. and Pak perspectives but that both parties should stay focused on the long-range objectives of the programme and not be deterred by these temporary difficulties. She said that nothing could happen until the aircraft were released and, by then, it would likely be too late to meet those objectives. I told her that I would meet with the Generals and, hopefully, that I would speak their military language in regard to rectifying the problem of operational control. I then told Dorothy that there were a number of other matters I needed to discuss with her.

Almost snapping at me, she said, "Weapons, right? You want to carry guns!"

That actually had not been the first matter on my list - but I let her continue.

"Look, I don't know why everyone is so keen on carrying guns. These people don't want to hurt us and, anyway, we can't even find Al-Qaeda. So how are they going to find you?"

I was utterly staggered by naïve logic but fought my rising emotions to stay calm and explained that State back in the U.S. had already approved the issue of defensive weapons for those personnel trained to use them, especially in high threat areas like Quetta. I added with a bit of humour that if Dorothy didn't want me to carry a weapon, that would be fine but she would then have to accompany me everywhere and protect me. If she planned to place me in danger, then she had to also be prepared to accept that same personal risk. Not surprisingly, she said that she was a diplomat *not* a soldier. To which I responded, "My point exactly."

I must admit I walked out of that meeting feeling totally disillusioned. I would have to tread very carefully with this young lady who had somehow concluded the jihadist sympathisers out in the border regions did not wish to hurt us.

The next few days were spent on induction; creating a survival plan and figuring out what the hell I could do to make an operation out of this pig's ear. I was given the keys to my house, which was a nice little villa by the Margalla Hills but it was far larger than I really needed. Also, it was almost next door to one of the most radical Madrassa's (Islamic school) in Islamabad and I had all its bearded teenage pupils passing by my "unbeliever's" house twice a day. These young men could be a threat either directly or even indirectly if they percieved me as an infidel, living in their neighbourhood.

The next stage was to get a vehicle. I was taken to the Narcotic Affairs Section Annex, which was in town and separate from the Embassy. Host Nation Support (HNS) personnel staffed these offices which, in layman's terms, means that they were Pakistanis. All were very cooperative and pleasant from the start of my tour to the very end, a truly great bunch of men and women for whom I was to develop the utmost respect.

At the back of the compound there were a number of cars, all 4x4s, and all jumbo size. The Pakistani in charge of the car pool told me I could have my pick, so I asked if there was anything smaller. He pointed to a two-door Rav 4 covered in dust and bird-shit in the corner of the compound. I told him to clean it up and I'd take it. He was clearly surprised that I hadn't taken the biggest, newest and best available. Of course, he could not have realised that my plan to survive in Islamabad and, more imperatively, escape the undue attention of the Madrassa under-graduates, was to look unimportant compared to others that were being metaphorically "chased by the attacking bear".

That afternoon, he called me on my newly issued mobile phone to let me know the vehicle was ready. He had done a great job cleaning it up. It was then I noticed that had green Pakistan government license plates. He explained that it would appear to all to be a Pakistani government vehicle and not a U.S.-sponsored vehicle (many, like Dorothy's car, sported diplomatic plates). I told him okay but to also get me a set of black and white plates with the same number. He did not question my motivation and simply responded, "I'll have them by tomorrow."

I drove to the Embassy and was now thinking that I had to get myself armed. I simply could not wait for the weapons to arrive from the States; it could take weeks and this could mean life or death in consequence. If I couldn't rely on either the Embassy or the Pakistani authorities to provide me with adequate protection I would have to organise my own protection and, if it all went pear-shaped, I would rather be judged in a room by twelve men (a jury) than carried out of room by six men (in a coffin).

A resource that will remain unidentified had given me an unofficial contact specifically for the purpose of self-protection and I made the call. We arranged to meet the next day.

Once back at the Embassy, I picked up all my passes and made my way to my new office, a narrow corner room next to Dorothy's. Curtis was there and all smiles. He said, "They just informed us they are going to release the helicopters!" This was great news but, after six weeks of sitting in a Pakistani hangar, one could only wonder in what state of disrepair we would find them. Curtis went on to explain that he had arranged for some of his mechanics to go to Qasim Airfield in Rawalpindi to undertake an inspection. He added that our meeting with Brigadier Shafiq-Ur-Rehman Awan, who was in command of the MOI Air Wing, was scheduled for tomorrow at 10am.

Three unarmed SMS security corporation men working in shifts guarded my house. Two seemed pleasant. The third guard had an orange henna-dyed beard and was clearly radical in his religion; I could tell he just despised unbelievers. The only reassurance was that none of these guys actually offered any real protection except a few seconds delay because in all likelihood they would willingly, and understandably,

57

step aside if threatened. I made sure they knew that I wanted the gates closed at all times and, that if anyone called, they should keep them outside the gate and ring the doorbell themselves. I asked them if they needed extra supplies and they requested chai (tea). I told them it was no problem and I would buy some. I also had asked Curtis if he tipped his guards. He said that it was the normal course of business was to tip them about 1,000 rupees per month. Applying the "bear attack" theory I gave mine 2,000 rupees on the premise that even a radical would value cash-in-hand in this life rather than everlasting life in the next. They would be presumably less keen to see me dead if they were getting paid more by me than my replacement in the event of my untimely death.

The house itself was quite secure, however, anything but cosy. All the windows had bars and, because I only used the kitchen, the living room and one bedroom, I drew all the curtains and locked the internal doors to delay anyone coming at me through those routes. The bedroom itself was a "safe room". It had a metal door and double locks. The ensuite bathroom had an escape window arrangement that would drop away the bars if I needed to get out quickly. From that window, if the shit hit the fan, I could reach the opposite wall in a downward leap. From there I'd identified a drainage ditch along which I had cover from view to reach the Deputy Head of Mission's house (who did have an armed guard) about 800 metres away. I was also provided with a VHF radio that provided a direct communications link to the USMC security post at the American Embassy some twenty-five minutes away over which I could call "Help!"

So if the shit went down I knew this would be about as effective as a fart in the thunderstorm. The only person who could save me if the bad guys came would be myself and I would have to prepare for that accordingly.

The following day I went to rendezvous with Curtis and, like a rabbit coming out of its warren, I exited my house cautiously. Before leaving, I had checked the activity on the road from my upstairs perch and made certain I had everything I needed was by the front door. No sooner had I left the house than I was out of the gate and away. Once out of the drive, I could turn either left or right. In those early days, without a gun, I felt extremely uncomfortable and vulnerable - but I employed "bear attack" avoidance in every aspect and ensured that I didn't raise any undue attention. The combination of a small car, looking unimportant, varying times and routes, knowing my immediate area, looking after my guards, and, not least of all, years of protecting my arse in all manner of covert scenarios would likely keep me way in front of that godforsaken bear.

After picking up Curtis, we headed for the Ministry of the Interior. At the entrance a seething mass of locals were going in and out. I noticed my first green and black turbans since coming to Pakistan. This traditional, tribal headgear tends to be worn by the more radical Muslims and, at least in Islamabad, it symbolises that the wearer is at the extreme end of the Sharia enforcement scale. Most locals in the metropolitan areas simply don't wear headdress. In fact from what I could gather most inhabitants of Islamabad simply want to live a peaceful life, however everyone is aware that the penalty for blasphemy in Pakistan is death.

On the way into the MOI, the car was searched externally but to my surprise, not internally. I noted this for a later date when I would be carrying a weapon. Curtis then directed me to the very last building where we parked up. At the crowded entrance, we were expected to exchange our IDs for a pass, which I wasn't happy about and would have to figure out how to avoid. We were also made to walk through a metal detector so, in the future; I realised that I would have to take great care. We then got into a crowded and stinking elevator that actually had its own operator.

Curtis and I exited at the 8th floor and walked almost to the end of the corridor. We entered a cramped room with about eight men dressed in Pakistan's cultural attire, the Sawal Kameez. All simultaneously jumped to their feet as we walked in. We exchanged "Aslam-Aleekhams'" and "Wa Aleekham Salams'" and one of them went through the side door to inform the Brigadier that we had arrived. I had worn my business suit, not least because I wanted plenty that morning.

Brigadier Shafiq came to door and greeted us like old friends. This man was an absolute gentleman from his demeanour and his style, conveying an air of modesty and understatement. I later found out as I got to know him that he was a deeply religious man in the very best of ways. His father had been a mullah and he had learned the good and bad that his religion could bring out in a man. We were welcomed into his office where a giant of a colonel sat; he stood to shake our hands. His personality was larger than life and he clearly wanted to impress us that he had a good command of the English language. As we sat down, chai and water was served and I could not help but wonder how relations could have broken down to the extent that these refined officers were forced to impound the aircraft.

The Brigadier opened by saying, "You have your helicopters back, so you are off to a good start." I joked that it was just as well; otherwise Dorothy was going to send me back to the airport.

The Brigadier then got straight down to business. "We have agreed to release the aircraft, but we must now have operational control."

60

I needed to employ a delaying tactic if I was going to get this operation off the ground without denting anyone's pride.

"Brigadier," I said, wanting to emphasise my recognition of his rank, "I really believe that we are having a conversation about OpCon too early."

I wanted also to employ the appropriate vernacular so he would hopefully view me as a military counterpart. I continued. "The argument that has caused so much acrimony when viewed from a tactical or operational point of view has been absolutely pointless."

I needed to be firm but fair because I knew this officer could torpedo the entire operation if I overstepped the mark, "But, potentially, it could have enormous strategic and political impact if the U.S. should pull the plug."

I continued, "We are, after all, talking about a very limited operational capability as it stands today. What is being discussed is almost tantamount to arguing over OpCon of seven Land Rovers rather than seven helicopters!"

Now I really had his attention. "We, and I mean *we*, need to develop an integrated capability, then look towards handing over OpCon to you because then, and only then, will it be *truly* worth having."

The Brigadier was now leaning forward on his desk and the Colonel was also listening intently.

"Also, we need to ensure that your maintenance capability is in line with Curtis' guys." Now I also had Curtis' undivided attention. This was going well, I was on a roll.

"And get Quality Control (QC), maintenance and operational capability to a place where everyone is comfortable."

It was time to pitch the deal. "I think, given what has been achieved so far, and the point from which we are currently working, that we set a goal of OpCon handover when Level-2 Maintenance has been achieved.."

I stopped talking and waited. I was aware that I had promised nothing but had given tangible points that we would all have to meet to make it happen.

The Brigadier looked at me and smiled, it broke the ice of the pause. He said, "I can already tell you are going to be a very difficult man to argue with because what you say makes sense."

He paused. "But you have to realise both my Minister and my President have been very insulted over this matter and we feel Ambassador Powell and Dorothy have not been at all reasonable; in fact quite the opposite. After all, why would U.S. diplomats want OpCon?"

He was using my term, which was great. "What do they know about helicopter operations?"

He was irritated. "I am the most experienced Huey pilot in Pakistan."

Now he was on a roll. "What can they tell me about when or when not to use a ruddy helicopter?"

He made a really good point and I sensed "ruddy" was at the top end of his profanity scale; so I had to jump on his side without going over to it.

I responded. "Brigadier, I'm not a diplomat, I'm an operator. I know from an operator's point of view what I have told you makes sense."

Now it was time for brothers in arms. "Our job as soldiers is to clean up a mess when diplomats screw it up. You have gone to war for such mistakes and so have I. Your President was Special Services Group (SSG), so he's an operator; he knows that when diplomats fail, it comes down to a soldier with a bayonet to sort it out. I'm not saying that I can work miracles but I am saying that I will work alongside you to try to make it happen for both of us. The only snag is that when we are done and successful, you can be sure it will be the diplomats who step in and grab the glory. We do what we do and they do what they do - so never the two shall meet."

The Brigadier beamed. "I couldn't have said it better myself."

He continued, "I will convey to the Minister this new wind of change and hope that you can convince Dorothy that we are back on track."

I replied, "Brigadier, we will deal in deeds not words, this is our job as soldiers."

He stood up and reached across his desk to shake my hand, saying, "I am so very happy you are here."

"And so am I, Brigadier. And so am I".

As we left the office, I said to Curtis, "How do you think that went?"

In his rich Georgia accent he replied, "It was fucking unbelievable! You should have seen how these guys have behaved over the past few weeks. They even refused to meet with us!"

I told Curtis that if I were the Brigadier and a lady in her late twenties who was totally unqualified tried to tell me how to operate helicopters, I would be pretty pissed off as well.

Curtis then asked, "What are we gonna tell Dorothy?"

I said, "We'll tell her the truth. The OpCon issue has gone away pending an increased maintenance and operational capability."

I added that I would talk to Brigadier Shafiq on the phone during the next week to discuss serviceability and, hopefully, we would agree that he and I would keep in close touch regarding deployment of assets.

I dropped Curtis off at his place and told him I would have to run an errand before coming into the embassy.

Now I had to see a man about a gun.

I made sure I was early in the Koshar market and sat in my car for a few minutes scoping out the activity. It all looked

63

quite normal but the escape routes were crap because there was one way in and one way out. There was a mosque at the far end and I noticed a lady with two small girls selling flowers by the exit just across the road. She had perfect surveillance of the market. I parked my car parallel for an easy getaway and walked across to the lady with all my senses working overtime. Her children were delightful. They had obviously picked up English lines and used them to enchant any Westerner out of a few extra Rupees. I picked out some flowers and she gave me her price. I handed over a note and told her to keep it. Realising I had given her over double the price, she tried to give me another bunch of flowers, but I refused. This flower-lady had just become part of my personal protection plan. She just didn't know it. I had figured if I always bought flowers from her before I entered the market *and* gave her twice the asking price then it would give me time to scope out the area and she might just warn me of anything unusual if there was a threat to her high paying customer.

I walked back to my car, dumped the flowers and then moved across the parking area to the French Patisserie, where I sat at the back of the room with a clear view of all in it and entering. I ordered a coffee. Shortly after the allotted time, I saw a local man with a sports jacket over his Kameez get out of a car and walk slowly towards the bakery. As he did, his eyes were busy as he scanned the area and he dialled a preset number on his mobile and put the phone to his ear. I answered my vibrating phone and said his name. He walked into the front of the Patisserie. I smiled. He hung up his phone and came to shake my hand.

This man exuded the aura of a thug by any measure. I suspected he would cut a throat for less than a dollar. He smiled, sat down and ordered coffee. He asked me how I was settling in and how I knew our mutual friend. I lied and told him I was enjoying Islamabad so far and then fed him some benign fiction of how I knew our mutual acquaintance.

He asked what I was looking for and I told him 'a self-protection device', carefully not using the word 'Gun' in case I was being set up.

I elaborated. "Once that is achieved perhaps we could move onto something more ambitious."

He was stoic in expression and said he could put his hands on a pistol overnight but that it wouldn't be anything fancy.

He then asked, "Would you accept a Makarov PM with 9mm short rounds?"

I replied that would be fine provided it worked and that he should please make certain that the ammunition was good. I knew that if the shit hit the fan, no one would care about the guns or the calibre that were used - just who lived and who died. I added that I would need three magazines and fifty rounds. He smiled as he sipped his coffee and told me it wouldn't be a problem.

I then asked him how much he needed.

He smiled again and said, "I do not take money from friends such as we have in common."

He paused and I knew what was coming next. "But I do have a need for refreshment and I believe you can get me a bottle or two of that."

Now he was being purposely vague because he probably knew our mutual friend had already briefed me on his passion for Johnnie Walker Black Label.

I told him, "No problem. Just give me a call tomorrow and we can sort it all out."

He nodded and with the transaction completed, I knew I needed to get the fuck out of there so I explained that I had to dash for a meeting but looked forward to seeing him the next day when I would have more time. We shook hands and I walked across to my car, scanning for any surveillance whilst taking a long look view at the vehicle to determine whether a booby trap had been put underneath it. As I pulled away, the flower lady and her daughters gave me a big wave. It was time to get back to the Embassy for Happy Hour.

CHAPTER 4

Quetta. A New Beginning

My first soiree to the American Club Happy Hour to meet the DynCorp aircraft support team was a necessary but an inconvenient event during which I knew I'd be under the spotlight.

As we entered the building the noise coming from upstairs was considerable. I thought, "These guys must like to get started early" - and from the DynCorp team's perspective I was right. As Curtis and I walked into the bar the team was already sitting around a group of tables that they had commandeered and the beer was in full flow. I reflected the entire operation was rudderless in a hazardous environment so it was hardly surprising that these hardened veterans had somewhat turned to booze.

As Curtis made the introductions I reminded myself that the eastern flank of American interests depended largely on the effectiveness of these individuals:

Caz	The Huey pilot
Pete	The Cessna Caravan pilot
Jay	Avionics
Gerry	"The Spanner"
Jim	Security

Mark	Maintenance
Frank	Quality Assurance
Ed	Fixed wing maintenance
Jason	The Air-Gunner
Matt	Safety Equipment

Their personalities were as about as diverse as you could find anywhere. The most engaging were Caz and Jay. Caz the Huey instructor and rotary-wing pilot was from Hawaii and actually had somewhat of a local appearance. As a former U.S. Army OH-58 Kiowa pilot and more recently an airline pilot with Commair his flying profile was not unlike my own. He was clearly an intelligent guy with stacks of ideas that he was eager to impart.

Jay was strikingly enigmatic and had a sense of humour that was just dying to get out there. If a general observation is that in order to be amusing you have to be intelligent then Jay had that more than covered.

Pete was tall and sharp featured; he was the Cessna 208 pilot and a former U.S. Army Apache Helicopter pilot. He was instinctively quiet, but clearly committed to his work and very engaging.

Mark and Gerry "the spanner" were more restrained. The former was noticeably haggard and had clearly seen it all be it in Pakistan or Colombia.

Gerry was younger and a former Marine. I immediately got the impression he had developed a dislike for officers at some stage in his life and still didn't like them now. Matt, another former Marine, gave the initial impression that he was a follower. And then there was Jim, a former Army Ranger who had been commissioned in the U.S. Special Forces. Along with his short, powerful build Jim came across as amicable but quite capable of kicking some serious arse if he deemed it appropriate.

Jason was the guns specialist and in country to ensure the Hueys could be fitted with the Gatling style mini guns. He was physically fit but had decided he wanted to look like anything *except* a former Marine. His van Dyke style beard was an outward expression of his interest in music and art.

Ed was the fixed wing mechanic; he was the quintessential caricature of how you wish your grandfather could look. He was a Vietnam veteran and, from what I could gather, had served his country for most of his life, he was a placid man who moved at a leisurely pace, but he was also a man who knew his job and harboured a great deal of practical wisdom.

Finally, there was Frank, another Vietnam veteran who had been a U.S. Army helicopter crewchief during that conflict. Frank had literally "seen it all" and took charge of Quality Assurance, and although he was getting up there in years and had the complexion of a rhinoceros, he would prove wisdom to match his age. It was a practical quality of judgment that became invaluable to me and which only comes from arduous life experiences.

After the first beer the conversation flowed in equal and copious amounts and free bar snacks were placed on the table. Dorothy and Suzanne turned up so I went across to talk to them and we chatted about the first week and the elation that the helicopters were no longer impounded.

The conversation with the ladies moved to chat about life in Slammy, with both telling me about their favourite restaurants and places to go. From a security perspective none of the U.S. personnel were permitted to leave the city of Islamabad without the Embassy's Regional Security Office (RSO) providing its prior approval.

Almost on cue, a tall fellow with a greying beard came over. Dorothy immediately stopped talking about carpet shops and introduced him as Ken – the Regional Security Officer of the Embassy. At first impressions he didn't seem like a security type, but he did seem really straightforward. I liked him immediately. He clearly had a lively personality and explained he wanted me to meet his Deputy RSO over at the bar. I followed him to the bar where a guy who was built like a brick shit house was sitting opposite an extraordinarily beautiful woman. Jerry the cop was there as well. Ken's Deputy was clearly a player; he was fit and confident, he'd certainly pulled himself the best looking woman in the place. Ken put his hand on his shoulder and simply said, "Tom meet Howard."

Tom spun on his stool and gave me a handshake that suited his demeanour. He said. "Great to meet you! Jerry has just been telling us all about you. By the way this is my wife, Marie."

His wife? Wow. It turned out she also worked for State and I wondered if he was the only guy with a striking woman on tap in Slammy. The male to female ratio in the bar must have been at least 10:1.

Tom leaned over and smiled, "How you getting on with Dorothy?"

The sarcasm was apparent for all. I told him everything seemed fine and all three guys burst out laughing.

"Oh man," laughed Tom, "Jerry is so pleased to see you because now Dorothy has a new whipping boy!"

Raucous laughter again; clearly these men had a bond that I hoped I would later share. Tom told me that he'd been part of State's close protection detail for many years and he and another 'bodyguard', Brian, would help me in any way they could.

He went on, "We are here to do a job so let's try to get 'er done! And by the way, welcome to the team."

He raised his glass.

The other key introduction of the evening was Keith who was from the DEA. It was obvious this guy had borne weapons for his country many times and, more significantly, was a renegade. What we didn't realise at the time was that the combination of Tom, Jerry, Keith, myself and two men from other departments would lead to the development of a mutual trust that, ultimately, would pull the stars into alignment and achieve a unique resource pool, creating a synergy that had likely never previously existed between the various allied sections and departments in Pakistan.

This capability would be developed not by any memorandum or policy issuance but rather, by half a dozen dedicated men who, although their prior battles had been fought separately on the streets of Bosnia, Iraq, Kuwait, Colombia, Panama, Miami, Northern Ireland and Phoenix, were to become brothers-in-arms

The following day was my first day off, so I optimistically unpacked my suitcases, which had remained on the floor since my arrival. The TV in the living room was almost permanently tuned to CNN World News where their weather reporter, Jenny Harrison, was about to become the sexiest thing in my world until I next got home. It was late morning when my phone rang and the local voice on the other end asked if I was at home.

As I made arrangements for his reception, I bumped into a tiny old man at the gate who introduced himself as Rafiq, the dhobi wallah, and asked if he could do my laundry. He gleefully declared "I do everything sir! I used to dhobi for British Army in India." We agreed on eight U.S. dollars for all my washing and ironing just as the "Lord of War's" car pulled into the driveway. I went to the door so he didn't have to linger and he came straight in. I offered him tea and he accepted, watching me with some amusement as I emptied water from my still into the kettle. He could doubtless drink the infested tap water that would have put me flat on my back within days. While the kettle boiled, he placed the newspaper-wrapped package from his carrier bag on the counter-top, revealing a brand new, heavily greased, Makarov PM.

He handed it to me so I immediately pulled back the slide and pushed up the slide catch, locking the slide to the rear to ensure it wasn't loaded. I then checked its general condition, which looked good to my trained eye. I then let the slide go forward. I could see the man watching me carefully and he was recognising that handling weapons was something I was used to. I pulled down the trigger guard and cocked it to one side so it was lodged open and pulled back the slide and lifted it off the gun, feeling the strength of the main spring trying to pull it out of my hand. The spring felt in good shape so I pulled it off the sticky barrel.

The kettle's whistle started to sound so I laid all the parts on the counter and made the tea, commenting that the weapon was in good condition. He said the gun was new and I agreed, thinking that it was either new or it was recondi-tioned. I doubted, however, that the original manufacturer had made it. The illicit arms manufacture in Pakistan is not simply good at replicating appearance, it is exceptional. In the legendary town of Dara in NWFP there is a flourishing national, cottage industry that manufacturers identical weapons to the originals in all respects. This Makarov was undoubtedly from this bandit's haven.

I poured the tea and placed the milk and sugar next to the mugs on the counter. I moved my attention back to the pistol and rotated the safety catch, which permitted it to detach, and then tipped the firing pin onto my hand. I needed to make absolutely certain that this was intact. If it had been tampered with or shortened, the weapon wouldn't fire making it worthless. Once content, I put the pin back in, replaced the safety catch, and rotated it to the fire position. I picked up the spring and eased it in a twisting motion back onto the barrel of the pistol; it was a tight fit, which was exactly the way it was meant to be. I then replaced the slide and let it move forward and let the trigger guard snap back up into the gun.

I looked at the provider who was now sipping his tea and stated, "So it will work."

"Of course, only the best for my *friends*." He responded, which, in all candour, made me bloody uncomfortable. He reached into the bag and placed three magazines and a box of ammunition on the table. I looked at the springs of the magazines; they looked in good condition and then took a look at the ammo. I recall thinking, "I just hope to Christ this is good stuff." It would be sometime before I could test fire the pistol.

I said, "Thank you, I really appreciate it," and bent down to the cupboard where two bottles of whisky had been prepositioned for him. Perhaps he would notice that I'd removed all the bar codes and reference numbers on the labels - or perhaps not.

I smiled and said, "Now don't go drinking this all at once."

He laughed and said, "Oh no, I won't. This is for special triple-X night with my friends and some ladies."

After he departed, I loaded the magazines and pushed one of them into the pistol grip. I pulled back the slide and let it go, snapping it forward as it picked up a round from the magazine and pushing it firmly into the barrel. I then removed the magazine, pushed another round into it and pushed the mag back into the pistol.

I loaded the other magazines and looked contentedly at my small but lethal insurance policy on the counter top. I knew for sure I would be in deep shit if anyone found out I was carrying, but reassured myself that covert carriage of weapons had previously been my world and, in any case, my only self defence option was "judged by twelve men or carried by six", it was a no-brainer. My personal security matrix was complete and I would do what needed to be done if my life was threatened.

That afternoon I went to meet Jerry the cop. It transpired that he lived in a veritable mansion. He went to the fridge, pulled out a couple of beers and during the next four hours we got to know each other.

Jerry had started out life as a bull-rider but when he got hung up on a bull as a young man, the animal had nearly ripped off his arm and put an end to his career in the rodeo. Recovering from this accident he joined the Phoenix, Arizona Police Department where not only did he get shot, but was the only white police officer to win the Martin Luther King Award for Community Policing. At some juncture he was recruited to the Department of Justice and had ended up in Pakistan in order to restructure and train their police force and implement immigration's electronic monitoring.

Jerry was a practical academic and thoroughly knowledge-able on his subject matter and the situation in Pakistan. He was deeply concerned over the disconnect between the local diplomats in the Department of State and his task as an oper-ative of the Department of Justice. He clearly hated to have to answer to those who had neither any real understanding of his job nor the amount of on-the-job training he had received to get to a place where he could effectively change the direction of a nation's entire police force. I left his house fairly late and drove back to my place. I went to bed with my insurance policy under my pillow. For the first night since entering Pakistan I slept soundly.

During the week that followed the seven helicopters were relocated closer to Islamabad and the DynCorp team worked around the clock to get three of the aircraft serviceable. When it became apparent we would be able to get the aircraft down to Quetta the following week I informed Dorothy and she took delight in telling me that I would need permission from the RSO to leave the confines of Islamabad. I dropped into the RSO office to have a chat with Tom who assured me "No problem".

I also needed to complete the pain in the arse, "light reading" produced by the various governmental agencies, these included: The letter of agreement between USG and GOP, The Contract, Statement of Works for DynCorp, The Border Security Project Augmentation Plan, produced by the Narcotics Affairs Section, The Air Wing Directive and my personal favourite, The Embassy Rules and Procedures.

The read was more powerful than Valium in terms of sleep inducement and it took the best part of two days of my life to complete it, but I had already learned from business that "life is a contract" so it was essential to be aware of which particular rules or policies I would be breaking at any given moment during the year to come!

I kept coming back to one question, asking myself, "Given all the restraints, policies and rules how the fuck was I *ever* going to get this done?"

In Islamabad it was far too unsafe to jog in the streets, so the only place I could run was inside perimeter of the Embassy, which boasts the largest US Embassy compound in the world. On the way round the circuit, I passed two memorials, one was dedicated to the Ambassador Arnold Lewis Raphel who was on the doomed aircraft carrying Pakistani President Zia ul-Haq that exploded in mid-air on August 17th, 1988 killing all on board, the other was dedicated to Barbara Green and her young daughter Kristen Wormsley who were both gunned down when attending a church service at the Protestant International Church on March 17th, 2002. I stood in front of this simple memorial and tried to imagine the last horrific and ironic moments of little Kristen's short and innocent life. She had been murdered in cold blood, in God's house, by men justifying their murderous actions in the name of God.

There was a third memorial in the Embassy grounds, the U.S. Marine's Bar named after Corporal Steve Crowley USMC, who was shot dead by a sniper when a mob tried to storm the U.S. Embassy on November 20, 1979. I reflected on the turmoil that this small patch of earth had seen since the messy partition between India and Pakistan and resolved that no tree, no garden, bar nor piece of stone would *ever* bear my name.

By the time the early hours of Monday morning came around, I was itching to get out of Islamabad and into the combative zone. The big city had already started to represent "admin city" for me and, although I knew my work in Islamabad was going to be a crucial enabler for the programme, it was incredibly frustrating. I couldn't wait to get down to Quetta and the sharp-end of the operation.

I had packed my kit the previous evening and, when the driver rang my doorbell at 5am, I already had the insurance policy down my belt and secreted underneath my shirt; I was ready in all respects to head out to the Qasim Army Airfield in Rawalpindi where Pete and his Cessna-208 awaited to fly me down to Quetta.

By the time we reached Qasim the sun was just coming up and Pete was already with the aircraft in the hangar. Somewhat ironically this was the very same hangar that had imprisoned the helicopters. Our equipment and supplies were crammed into the underbelly pod of the aircraft and any remaining bags were strapped down inside. I reflected that, for a single engine aircraft, the lift capacity of the Cessna Caravan is considerable.

Pete taxied the aircraft out to the runway and we climbed leisurely over the urban clutter and chaos of Rawalpindi. Punjab's landscape quickly gave way to the greenery of the Potohar Plateau. Pete would now hold an average course of 237 degrees for the next 435 miles and the next three hours. It was a route I would get to know only too well for the best part of the next year, which I rarely found boring or uncomfortable.

The three-hour flight passed and the infamous city of Quetta became visible to the forward and right of the aircraft. The first thing that struck me was the sheer size of the place. The visibility was reasonable but I still could not make out the far side of the city, so it must have stretched on for some miles. I then recalled that it had a population of about 600,000 people, so I don't know why I was so surprised.

Quetta is also the closest city to Kandahar in Afghanistan and the deep blue beauty of the gin-clear skies beguiled the reality that we were now truly in "The Great Game" territory, the Graveyard of Empires and the home of Mullah Omar, the leader of the Taliban, and his declared "Government in Exile".

As Pete continued the descent, on the right of the aircraft I could see a short and narrow runway with some former Soviet helicopters parked close-by. In our final approach Pete eased the aircraft over a set of wires that seemed ludicrously close to the runway and got the aircraft into a flare. The Caravan would have floated in the ground cushion had he not eased back on the power to the point where the variable propeller flattened out, which effectively acted as an air brake and lift-dump.

The enlarged "tundra" tires bit the runway and, because of their size, the aircraft tried to make sideways movement as they flexed. Pete now had the aircraft in full reverse thrust; we were on the ground in Quetta.

I looked out across the stony desert with scrub bushes and with the exception of numerous mosque minarets, the view of the city was almost non-existent because there are no high-rise buildings beyond the first rows of houses, which obviously were outskirt properties, so there was not much to see.

Across the other side of the airfield I could see a local village with no apparent barrier between it and the airfield. Behind the village were significant mountains, which must have rose to 12,000 feet above sea level. The scenery against the deep blue sky was stunning, however, the terrain close up was anything but.

As we taxied into the flight line I could see Jay and Jim who had pulled two trucks close to our position. Caz and Gerry had stayed behind with the helicopters, by now, they were hopefully with the Pakistani Pilots of 50 Squadron and would be making the long helicopter flight down through Pakistan. With luck and good weather they would arrive in the evening.

We got out of the plane into the clean air of Quetta. Jay quipped, "Welcome to Hell," and I laughed, commenting that it wasn't warm enough to be Hell.

"Oh yeah?" he answered, "Just wait until summer!"

After loading all the kit and equipment into the trucks, Jim told me to hop in with him and we drove along a dirt track towards a walled compound. As we approached, I could see a soldier with a dark grey salwar kameez operating a barrier.

Jim explained that the soldier was a trooper of the Frontier Corps and they were responsible for guarding us. Did my security in Quetta *actually* depend on this guy? I needed to make sure it didn't.

The Frontier Corps (FC) in Pakistan is classified as "paramilitary". Their volunteers are not afforded the same status as the military and therefore they do not enjoy the same kudos. The British founded the FC in 1907 to guard the border areas in North West Frontier Province, Waziristan and Balochistan. The men are recruited locally, commanded by Pakistani Army officers but politically controlled and paid for by the Ministry of the Interior. If there is a pecking order in Pakistan's order of battle, then the FC does not feature any place close to the top. These men are generally poorly paid and poorly equipped when compared to their regular military counterparts. The force, therefore, although numbering 80,000 men, represented to the border what a cheap lock is to a door; they would only keep *honest* people out.

The State Department had recognised this critical flaw and its upside for Al-Qaeda. They had therefore pushed funds to the Narcotics Affairs Section [NAS] to provide equipment (aircraft) and logistic development (roads) towards the MOI's border security efforts. The reason NAS had the mandate was so State could keep the initiative "in-house". State was up against the radicals of the Taliban and Al-Qaeda who used opium production in Afghanistan as their main source of income.

These narco-terrorists were now supplying at least eighty percent of all illicit opium based drugs that were on the market in Europe. It was a huge problem that had also been permitted to worsen significantly thanks to the diversion of military resources to Iraq.

Our helicopters and aircraft provided by the State Department supported by the International Narcotics and Law Enforcement's Air Wing for Pakistan's 50th Aviation Squadron represented the organisational chain of the anti-narco-terror response. Here at the MOI stage of that link, the connection between the Frontier Corps and the aircraft was made.

At the large metal gates of the compound, Jim exchanged a greeting with the guard as we pulled into the compound and stopped outside a large building marked "Simulator". We unloaded my kit from the back of the truck and Jim led me through two sets of doors into a stale smelling, large tatty room with six beds placed around the outside wall. He pointed at two of the beds, "That one and that one are taken. So just pick any one you want."

I picked the bed in the corner to the hard-left of the main entrance door. I knew that if anyone burst in firing it would be those in the first thirty degree arc of view who would be shot first. Once again I was applying the "bear attack" theory. If, God forbid, it happened, my "out of the arc" position would buy me seconds and provide the best chance of surviving. I threw my kit on the bed to claim my patch and Jim walked me through to the communal washroom and toilets, which after three hours in the Caravan was a welcome sight from my bladder's point of view!

Jim and I walked down the length of compound, which comprised four simple buildings - my makeshift barrack room, a lecture theatre/store-room/makeshift gym, the cook-house, and the stores.

In each building there were small unused store rooms that some of the men had commandeered as their makeshift bedrooms. Even though they had no running water and it was an outside walk to the toilets, they nevertheless had the most important element - privacy.

From a security standpoint, this was also good news. Any enemy infiltration into the compound would not take all the team out in a one-room hit. This ad hoc arrangement would buy us time and space.

I asked Jim if any of the men carried weapons and he told me they had asked for them but they had been denied by Dorothy. I could hardly believe that these Americans were in Pakistan's "Taliban Central" helping the effort against the drug and insurgency problem and they were unarmed. The only saving grace is that the enemy would never have believed it if they were told.

I explained to Jim I had received appropriate approvals from the U.S. and the weapons were to be shipped by diplomatic pouch, but it would take a few weeks. We might have to look at a contingency plan, (meaning I had already started one). The back gate of the compound opened up onto the airfield, so if the shit ever hit the fan, this would have to be our escape route.

Jim explained that there were layers of security toward the town formed by the military base and housing, referred to as the "Cantonment" that had an outer and inner cordon. Of course these cordons were only as good as the men manning them and we would be vulnerable to a rogue guard attack by any of the military or FC who were turned. But, whilst far from safe, we would hopefully have warning that an attack was imminent and be able to react.

As I sat with Jim and drank my first cup of tea in Quetta, Pete and Curtis walked into the cookhouse to join us. I asked if there had been any contingency for a bug-out and Pete told me they had gone over it. I told him it was vital that at least one aircraft was fuelled at all times and that we should insist that this aircraft is always parked nose out so we didn't have to waste time turning the thing around. If it was only Quetta that had gone pear-shaped then we could head to Islamabad. If, however, it was Pakistan's government that had fallen, we would have to head for Muscat, Oman and sort out the paper work thereafter.

Additionally, I explained to Jim, all the guys should have a run bag with water, passport, some cash, credit cards and a change of clothes and they should know any valuables that they would throw in it if the shit hit the fan. I wanted this implemented post haste.

The first night in Quetta would turn out to be much the same as any that were spent in the compound. The evening meal typically consisted of curried lamb, goat or chicken and, on one occasion, camel. Everything, and I mean everything, that was cooked was curried and served with rice and a simple salad. The choice of drink was water or cola. After dinner, tea was made and we would either watch communal television or retire to our respective bed-spaces for conversation or private time with a book or an IPod.

On the first evening there was much to go through. Each man had his hit-list of shortages within his work-scope; each was a barrier to taking the battle to the enemy. We were short on spare tyres and aircraft jacks for the Cessnas. We had UHF radio problems and the crews had no high-powered binoculars for identifying opium poppy fields from a distance. We also needed adhesive cover for the U.S. registration N-numbers. These needed to be more discreet. The aircraft had no FM radios for communication with ground forces and no Oxygen recharging connectors. As it stood, if O2 were ever needed in flight, the flight crew and passengers would die of hypoxia, (lack of Oxygen to the brain).

There were problems with fuelling the aircraft. The tanker truck that had been bought and paid for by the United States Government turned out to be a water tanker rather than a fuel tanker so, although brand new, it was totally useless, a small example of the U.S. taxpayer being ripped off. There was also no fuel-flow available directly from the fuel farm because the pipes were broken and we therefore had to rely on the Pakistani military who put us at the bottom of the rung in delivery. The level of cooperation was inversely proportional to the resentment the Pak Military had towards our presence in Quetta.

We had two Forward Looking Infra Red (FLIR) equipped Caravans but no operators and we didn't know when we would get one. The runway had no lights so only NVG equipped aircraft could land after nightfall. The 50 Squadron Maintenance Officer was not achieving efficiency in his team; we would have to help him if Maintenance Level-2 was ever going to be achieved.

The team had been told that, in order to travel within Quetta, they had to use an armoured vehicle, yet the closest available vehicles were in Karachi, 370 miles away. There was a shortage of tangle-foot wire around the compound that was used to channel potential intruders. We required empty surveillance camera covers to at least give the impression security cameras were in operation. We had a shortage of parts both for the helicopters and the mini-guns for their conversion to gunships. The men used shipping containers as their workshops out on the flight line and we were two sets short of safety equipment. We required covers for the FLIR sets in the aircraft in order to disguise the equipment to the casual observer. We needed the Squadron to provide gunners for M-60 and mini-guns on gunship operations and we needed portable fuel pumps so that the helicopters could refuel from barrels if necessary. This was just the first shopping list, so there was shit loads to sort out.

I would have to lean on Paul to pull some strings with the team in America for a lot of this and I'd have to move into the "beg, steal or borrow" mode for the rest. What was for sure was that I would have to delegate duties. Following the meeting, Curtis and I decided who could lead on which particular aspect.

I lay on my bed that first night in Quetta and reflected on the day. There was so much to do, so much to fix and, even if we achieved it, would anything come of it? The system seemed to be stunningly resistant to progress but, thankfully, most of the men within it were not. I realised that if we sought permission for everything we wanted to do then it simply wouldn't happen. We would just have to find another way.

With my insurance policy under my pillow, I thought of home, my daughters and my wife and how I missed them. The first few hours in Quetta had seemed like a long first day. I lay on my front placed my right hand on my pistol and slept like a baby.

The following day, Curtis accompanied me to meet the CO of 50 Squadron who turned out to be a man who set his own standards and met them to his own satisfaction. I had long thought that in the military there are two categories of officers, those who are better in training jobs and those who are better in operational jobs. I could tell almost straight away that this guy fell into the training category. He was a very short, stocky officer who was immaculately dressed.

I explained to the colonel that my mission was to turn the programme into an integrated operational unit but emphasised as a matter of courtesy that what had already been achieved was impressive, (and it was), but we must now look to putting the NVG skills that had been amassed to good use.

It was not enough for 50 Squadron to be a casualty evacuation and VIP transport unit. (Curtis had previously told me that the colonel would offer up the aircraft to his superiors in order to impress them and that this really pissed off the entire team.) I added that the concentration by the ground team must be to bring the maintenance level up to "Level 2" standard so that this matter of OpCon could be put behind us and concluded. I told him that, if we failed, it was both he and I who would be held accountable. I could see this comment unnerved him enough to make him agree. We also needed to push forward on the Cessna training. The pilots needed to be NVG-qualified and we would need to train FLIR operators.

The meeting had gone well, but I knew I was only scraping the tip of the iceberg with this guy. He would have to be dragged kicking and squealing out of his conventional mindset and I would have use the momentum of the programme to sweep him along with the operational current. The big question in my mind was: How the fuck could I do it? We had the aircraft and the potential to make them work, but we had no ground forces. The FC troopers that manned the border posts and wore traditional dress, they had no clue about helicopters or how to use them and I needed a dedicated ground force.

That afternoon, Major Javed, the Admin Officer from the Headquarters Frontier Corps, arrived at the compound. He was as friendly as his belly was big and his promises of everything and anything were a bit hard to swallow. He told me that IGFC, General Sadaqat Ali Shah, was aware of my arrival and that perhaps, next time, I would be able to meet him.

Javed was in charge of ensuring the compound was in good shape so I suggested we take a walk and it was no accident I took him to the ablutions. I pointed out that the start of a good relationship would be to make sure that more than one shower out of six worked. He noted it down and told me it would happen. I then asked for the tangle-foot wire and security camera cases, he thought he could get the former but was not sure about the latter. We drank tea in the cookhouse and he departed. No sooner had he gone than a staff car pulled into the compound. It was a different Colonel Shaheed who commanded the Ghazaband Scouts, the local FC regiment from which our guard force was comprised. This colonel was quietly spoken and very sincere, he explained over tea that his base was on the other side of Quetta but his responsibility was for the greater Quetta area and involved many complexities. He said everyone was aware that Quetta was the Taliban's capital city in Pakistan and that the insurgents would cross the border at will to raise havoc in Afghanistan then return to Quetta.

It struck me that he was frustrated to be with FC but was doing the best job he could. He added that he knew General Sadaqat Ali Shah, very well and that the General was a good man and a tactician. I told him I was keen to meet the General and hoped that this could be achieved during my next stay in Quetta.

The remainder of the week and a half was spent gaining an understanding of the various elements, meeting the individuals involved and the barriers they had to overcome to get their job done. Caz and the helicopters had arrived two days late after having had one of the Hueys develop problems on the fuel stop in Multan on the way down.

I was now three weeks in country and we had at last got the air team together in one place and started to address the shortfalls. However, the most significant event of the week would emerge from a casual conversation with Jim when I raised the subject of ground forces. I told him that it was all well and fine to develop an integrated fixed and rotary wing capability but it would be useless without a ground force trained to use it. Thus far, I hadn't seen any indication that the FC would have the slightest capability or intent to do so.

Jim then unwittingly dropped a bombshell. He said, "I don't know, but I heard that General Sadaqat has set up a specially trained force within the FC." He went on to say that he'd heard they had been recruited in Peshawar at the other end of the country and brought down to Quetta for training by the Special Services Group (SSG); who are Pakistan's Special Forces. I asked how many and where they were. He didn't know.

I called Major Javed who immediately asked how I was enjoying my new showers. He wanted to make quite sure I recognised his efficiency in getting them fixed. I told him they were great and joked that we all smelled much better thanks to him. I went on to ask about the special FC unit, giving him the impression that I already knew more than I did. He spilled the beans.

"You mean the RIF?" he asked. I thought he had said RAF (which was Royal Air Force in my book of three letter acronyms) and corrected him "No, it's a ground force." He told me that RIF stood for "Rapid Interdiction Force". He then endorsed what I had learned from Jim.

Javed explained that they were "Corps troops" which was to say they came under the direct command of General Sadaqat who had created and funded them. I asked how many there were and he told me one company, but they intended to go to three companies (which would have formed a Battalion). I asked where they were based and he told me they were co-located with the Ghazaband Scouts (Colonel Shaheed's base). I asked if they were operational and he said they were, and that they were training more men. Interrupting, I asked if the SSG were training them? He told me they were. I hung up the phone knowing these were my guys, but how? I would need to conjure up a hook to get close to these troops. Realistically, the only way would be through the General. That said, we probably needed to get our own aviation unit in order before I could approach him.

I met with Pete, Caz and Curtis and told them what I was thinking. Caz was truly enthusiastic and acknowledged this was why he'd come to Pakistan. I told them it was a long way to go in a short time and that we needed to concentrate on NVG capability in both fixed wing and rotary wing and get FLIR up and operational.

A couple of days later Curtis and I climbed in the Caravan for the flight back to Slammy. It was a beautiful blue day and as the Pakistani crew climbed the aircraft away from Quetta avoiding the peaks to our right I couldn't help but crave the relative civilisation of Islamabad. The life in Quetta was austere for the locals and for us, but at least our presence was somewhat by choice and, thankfully, temporary.

My days spent in Islamabad sometimes felt very similar to that of the movie, "Groundhog Day," in so much as the repetitiveness and the monotony felt identical. The Embassy frustratingly ground to a complete halt on the weekends, so I quickly figured out that by returning from Quetta on a Friday I could scoop a few beers at the Happy Hour in the evening then unwind and catch up on paperwork for the next two days.

On my arrival in the embassy compound, I put my insurance policy under a rag in the side pocket of the door and made my way to Dorothy's office, knocked and went in. She listened intently and seemed content with the Quetta hit list. She made a caveat, however, that it would have to be assessed if the requirements would qualify under the current budget and I would need to work with the staff at the NAS Annex on this aspect, I told her "No problem." As the meeting drew to a close I mentioned the ground force. I explained I thought these troops would be ideal for the programme but thought I'd need U.S. military assistance in order to achieve training. Dorothy told me that she didn't really know the military people in the Embassy, so it would be better if I approached them directly.

I excused myself and paid a visit to Jerry in his office next door. We walked up to the Embassy theatre for a discreet cup of tea. I described the situation and Jerry said he would get me in for a discussion with General Stone, the Embassy's' senior military officer who was described as an energetic extrovert.

The meeting happened the same day and Brigadier General Doug Stone turned out to be a USMC Reserve officer, who also ran a software company in the U.S. He was a businessman overcome by his passion for the military. We hit it off straight away, especially when I told him I had served with the Marines in the Gulf and had been the first British Officer to take temporary Command of a USMC Squadron. I dropped some names of brother officers namely, General Fred McCorkle, Colonel Mike Butler and Colonel Bill Hammerle. These were three of the finest USMC officers I had ever met and I was delighted that he knew two of the three.

I briefed the General and his staff that I needed a small U.S. SF training team. I assessed that two trainers would suffice to train this indigenous force; they had after all received some level of proficiency by SSG standards. I explained that I thought the hook of U.S. SF training would pull the Pakistani Commanding General, Sadaqat, into the loop.

General Stone and his team gave the impression that they would do their best but I had to accept that they hamstringed because Iraq had priority over everything. It was agreed that the request for support would be submitted to the Special Operations Command (SOCOM) in Florida.

As I left the General suggested a beer later in the week and told me to bring my "bull-riding cop". "Bull-riding or bull-shitting?" I joked.

General Doug laughed and boomed, "Both, but let's make it happen!" I left hoping he meant the training *and* the beer.

Over at the NAS Annex I had tracked down the individual called Saadi as "Mr. Procurement". He was an incredibly well versed Pakistani who spoke English with an accent as refined as most British aristocracy. I went through my list of requirements. He figured that most of the equipment could be attained within the budget and assessed whether he would have go back to the U.S. to source it, or if he could achieve it locally. I told him this was just the start and that, as we increased our capability, there would be more requests from where this came from. Saadi decided he could pretty much cover everything except the ammunition and the maps, explaining that I would have to source those through Brigadier Shafiq.

Before making an office call on the Brigadier I called Major Javed in Quetta. I had to be sure that General Sadaqat was going to be in town during my next stay in Quetta and I asked him if he could arrange a meeting. Javed confirmed the General's presence in Quetta the following week and told me he would talk to Colonel GS (General Staff) to see if a meeting would be possible. I asked whether I should call the Colonel direct to which Javed stated that he would "fix it." For some reason I did not feel too assured.

I survived another ride in the MOI building elevator and having learned how to wave myself through the building's security checkpoint arrived at the Brigadier Shafiq's office. He seemed very content with my progress, so I pitched him on the rounds for the mini-gun and the allocation of manpower for gunners, he scribbled down notes as I spoke. He could smell the momentum that was building, he told me to leave what he had to do with him.

I returned to the Embassy and asked Jerry about satellite imagery and where could I find it. He directed me to the "satellite spooks upstairs," so off I went. I explained to a polite but defensive young lady that I required *unclassified* imagery of the airfield at Quetta and out to the border area. I told her my reasons and my clearances. She wasn't sure whether she could have what I needed in twenty-four hours, but she would do her best. And as it happened, that was good enough. The roll of giant images was sitting on my desk on Friday ready for my departure to Quetta on Monday.

During the week I had been deluging Paul in the U.S. with emails, to which he always responded. The support from Air Wing was unwavering during these early days and it was to remain so for the duration of my tour.

By the time we were getting to week's close it had been a highly successful beg, steal and borrow week and my little Rav 4 certainly had the cobwebs shaken out of it running the various errands through the back-streets of Islamabad and Rawalpindi.

One of the main obstacles to getting things done in Pakistan at that time was not just that the Iraq War had been given overwhelming priority of resources or that there was almost no coordination between the Allied Troops on the Afghan side of the border with the Pakistani military. It was having to wade through or avoid the dysfunctional bureaucratic departmental quagmire within the Embassy itself.

Many of the staffers in the Embassy were working in their own vertical columns where knowledge was considered power and, therefore, never not to be shared with another agency, just in case they derived some recognition or, God forbid, success by having such information. This might sound jaded but, in my experience, the most effective crossover between agencies took place at unofficial level and was purely based the personal friendships between certain men and women within those agencies who were willing to go out on a limb for the sake of the cause.

These unofficial links within the Departments of Justice and Defense, the Drug Enforcement Agency and the FBI, the Defense Intelligence Agency, the Department of State, and members from a couple of other organisations. "wheeled and dealed" to figure out how we could help each other and, in most cases, such liaison had to be purposely concealed from leadership elements that would have felt threatened by such cooperation.

During a Friday evening in the Embassy bar, the Ambassador, Nancy Powell, appeared in the bar with Dorothy and an entourage of women that I didn't recognise. Dorothy came over and commented that it looked like I was getting to know everyone and would I like to be introduced to the Ambassador? I said I would. The conversation was short and sweet and Ms. Powell seemed like a nice lady. She wore her hair short cropped, no make-up, a rugged expression, a stocky build, a pantsuit and her 'signature' comfortable shoes. In her fairly deep voice she commented on getting the helicopters back and that Dorothy had done a great job in making that happen. I was confused, but it would not have been appropriate to ask how or why, because I truly didn't have a clue why they had been returned and I strongly suspected, neither did Dorothy.

The Ambassador and her ladies-in-waiting stayed for one drink before departing for their own party in the Ambassador's residence. Apparently one of the women on the

Ambassador's staff was leaving, which was the reason for the social visit. With Ms. Powell's exit, the rowdiness started again.

Later in the evening my phone rang and I dashed outside to take the call. The local voice had a refined English accent and introduced himself as Amir. I had heard a lot about him from Brigadier Shafiq and I suspect it was all part of the introduction process. He was a commercial defence representative. He explained that he was hosting a dinner the following evening and invited me to attend. He told me he had also invited others from the Department of Defense.

The following evening I made my way to the home of Amir where a servant greeted me. Immediately behind him was a distinguished looking gentleman sporting a pipe. He addressed me as "Commander" and guided me into the living area where several men and women were already sitting and partaking in the various forms of alcohol that were available. I had put my 'insurance policy' in my bag so, after taking out the wine, I placed the ostensibly empty bag in the corner of the room where nobody would bother it. The company was extremely pleasant and well educated with a wide cultural mixture that included women who were Pathan, Afghan, Hungarian and men who were British, American, and Pakistani.

During the Dinner the lady from Afghanistan was complaining about the U.S. aerial bombings in her country. She asked me, "Why does everyone want my country?"

I replied, "They don't. They just don't want anyone else to have it."

There was resounding agreement around the table.

The following day I headed to Quetta in what would become my own effort to deny others the right to the territory. It was time to find my militia.

CHAPTER 5

Finding the Militia

It was still dark in the early hours of Monday morning when I heard the iron driveway gates of my villa open just and the glow of headlights shone in through the frosted glass and surrounding iron bars of the front door. My equipment was ready to go and one of the drivers, Hussein Shah, was at my door by the time I opened it. I'd not really seen much of Hussein Shah, but he had always appeared friendly and Jerry had recommended him as one of the most trusted drivers.

Hussein Shah was a Pathan from Peshawar; during the drive to the airfield in Rawalpindi he explained to me that, in his view, Pathans were very different from other Pakistanis. They had their own language (Pashtu) and their own code of conduct. Although his English didn't stretch to the word indigenous this was the point he clearly wanted to make. He described his as a warrior race and one that didn't flee from anything - clearly a veiled criticism of the Punjabi and Sindh Muslims who had fled from the Hindu hordes when India and Pakistan disastrously partitioned.

By the time we arrived at the airfield he'd left me with the impression that Pathans are a proud people who have under-gone much pillage and intrusion of their lands. Hussein Shah described the current scourge on the border as people who were "not proud". He said the Taliban were bullies and Al-Qaeda were invading foreigners. He considered neither beneficial for the secure future of his family. He invited me to Peshawar to stay with his family and I told him, "That would be nice." I reflected silently that, on occasion, even I had developed a diplomats tongue.

Even though this was only my second visit to Quetta, I rapidly settled into the routine. There was no wireless and the cable Internet connection, like everything in Pakistan, was predictably unreliable. There were not enough sheets for the beds, so I'd brought my warm-climate sleeping bag rather than use the massive, communally used blankets I'd had to use during my first stay. Also, because the locally prepared cooked food was generally abysmal I'd brought some favourite snacks like tins of fish, tomato soup, Alpen, McVities chocolate home-wheat biscuits, and Marmite. These few edible luxuries would at least give my palette something to look forward to each day.

On Monday afternoon, I called Major Javed to try to get an appointment with General Sadaqat and he said he would check with Colonel GS (General Staff) and get back to me. He provided hope by saying, "*Inshallah*, maybe tomorrow." Which literally meant, "God willing, *maybe* tomorrow." I didn't feel reassured.

I spent the rest of the day out on the flight line observing the work on the aircraft on and getting feedback from the DynCorp team. It was vital the aircraft were operationally prepared. The conditions were atrocious for man and machine, with the slightest breeze leaving a layer of fine sand in every crevice whether mechanical or physiological. Not unexpectedly the mechanics constantly complained about everything. However, as a general rule, I knew that when men are holed up in such shitty conditions, if they aren't bitching and complaining about something then this was symptomatic of really serious issues.

Of all the guys who were there, it was Jay who surprised me the most. He was the avionics expert and was destined to excel given the challenges of equipment and environmentals. He was also an avid photographer and reader so he possessed the depth and the skills to promote endless conversation, which I sensed he used on ladies to good effect.

On the second morning in Quetta I stepped outside to be greeted by a cool breeze under absolutely beautiful blue skies. Jay asked if I'd seen the Sleeping Lady of Quetta. I hadn't got a clue what he was talking about. Jay then pointed to the mountain range to the south-south east and said, "Look over there and see if you can see her." As I looked at the outline of the mountain ridges and the craggy shadows I saw the incredibly formed the shape of an amply breasted woman laying on her back; her face chin, lips nose and closed eyes and breasts were as clear as if a skilled sculptor had somehow been able to chisel away the correct pieces of rock. This, however, was no Mount Rushmore, carved by men for the amusement of men. This was a natural and fabulous freak result of the elements wearing away the rock over millions of years to form a stunning optical illusion over one of the most fundamentally austere cities in the world. I couldn't believe it. "Holy shit," I said. "That is mind-blowing." It really was - and from that morning I would gaze at the Sleeping Lady everyday and look forward to the day I would see her for the very last time as my choice and not that of anyone else.

I purposely delayed my call to Major Javed until 10am. He told me that the Colonel GS insisted on knowing the subject matter and would I call him? The Colonel picked up almost immediately. I made my introduction and explained that I had come to Quetta especially to meet the General. I plunged in and asked if I could get an audience that week. (I knew I only had four days to get this done.) The Colonel told me the General was *very* busy and he wasn't sure if he would have time to meet with me.

Half bluffing, I told him that, if necessary, I would stay into next week because it was vital that I speak to the General on a matter of extreme sensitivity. I desperately did not want to stay any longer than absolutely required because if I achieved my mission in Quetta I had plenty of organising to do back in Slammy, but I was also acutely aware that I was getting the run-around. The colonel asked me about the subject matter and I explained that it was something that only the General could solve; however, I did explain that it concerned the re-employment of some Frontier Corps troops. I put the phone down knowing that I had got as far as I could in one call and knowing this could turn out to be a frustratingly long stay.

Brinkmanship is almost a regional pastime in all dealings in south Asia and Arabia. So with this screwed up, mind-game process in play, I had to give the colonel the impression of unlimited investment of my time to get the meeting. I knew I had to get these troops as my ground force; otherwise, to use a technical term, I'd be fucked. I was in a high stakes game and an all or nothing gamble.

To my surprise, my phone rang that afternoon and it was Colonel GS. He actually sounded like a reasonable man but I knew he was lying when he explained that the General's schedule was truly jammed that week and that he would be travelling during the following week. Shit! I'd have to revert to persistence. I was destined to waste at least another day of my life in Quetta.

The following day I waited until 10am to pester again.

The colonel explained that the General's schedule remained completely full and he couldn't identify any gaps. He went on to say the General was due to be in Karachi on Sunday for a week so he didn't see how the meeting could happen during the next two weeks. The odds had just been raised. We were down to shit or bust, so I went "all-in" and asked the Colonel, "What time does General go to the bathroom?"

"I beg your pardon?" the Colonel sounded off-balance.

"What time does he go to the toilet? Take a shit?"

"I don't know what you mean." The Colonel was now indignant.

I cut in to explain, "By the time you reach our age Colonel, we pretty much have habitual bowel movements at a given time of day, every day. Therefore, if you can tell me what time the General takes his constitutional, then I'll make sure I'm at HQ at that time and, once the General is in his closet, he can take a shit while I stand on the other side of the door and explain my concept *and* why I need his decision."

I continued quickly before the Colonel had time to interrupt, "That way the General will have his bowel movement, which he would have to have taken in any case, and I will be afforded the opportunity to explain the matter upon which I urgently need his decision. Whatever the outcome of his decision, there will have been *no* time wasted on his part and the *only* inconvenience he will have to suffer is me talking to him from the other side of a door while he's doing what he has to do whether I'm there or not." I added, "Which is a lot less than the odorous inconvenience I will have to suffer."

"You *are* joking." the Colonel asked somewhat incredulously. I honestly didn't know whether it was a question or a statement, so I replied, "I've never been so serious about anything in my life Colonel. This matter is very important to me and I believe it will be to the General, too." I paused. "Please convey my offer to the General." The final sentence was truly a plea but I sounded firm.

The Colonel paused and exclaimed that, in his entire career, he'd never before heard a request like this but he would convey the urgency of my plea to his superior.

It must have been an hour later when my phone rang and it was Colonel GS's number. The Colonel simply said, "The General will meet you at 1030 tomorrow morning." I asked, "In the toilet or in his office?"

It was a genuine question to which the Colonel jovially replied, "In his office!"

I was elated, but now I had to deliver, I would only get one shot at this and first impressions would win the day. I would practice my lines for the meeting in my bed space that evening. In the meantime, I wandered across to the little hut where Sergeant Moussa and three other FC troopers lived. As soon as they saw me they leapt to their feet. These men lived in conditions just above squalor but never complained.

I exchanged greetings and asked Moussa if I could have a quiet word.

Moussa was a man of small stature but big personality. He sported a thick beard in step with his religion but was invariably jovial and friendly, he was always polite and willing to help with just about anything. We stepped outside and I told him I would need to go into Quetta in the morning but I didn't know where or when just yet. It was a lie because I knew he'd have to be ready to go so I had to tell him of the requirement, but if I didn't give him the time, this way he couldn't pass on precise information. I added that he should use one of the little vehicles. He responded, "Yes Sir" before, during and after each sentence, even though I was trying to make him very relaxed.

After the instructions, he asked if I'd like to join them for chai. So I sat in their cramped hut drinking hot, sweet chai with milk, which is effectively cooked tea. As I drank, I knew that this would be made from tap water but tried to look nonetheless relaxed and grateful for their hospitality, even though it had every likelihood of containing pathogenic bacteria that would soon turn my innards to liquid.

By 0930 the following morning, I was ready to go. I wore non-descript, khaki trousers, a ventilated button up shirt and a brown casual over jacket. I needed to look smart and casual but with a blend of military civilian order for the General.

Whilst in the car I'd look inconspicuous and, with the addition of a local, Pakol hat, I should be able to avoid any undue attention. "Mr. Makarov" was held by my belt firmly against my stomach with my shirt carefully puffed out at the waist so that it wouldn't be noticed. I pushed two magazines into my left pocket with the base up and the rounds facing forward to enable the most efficient mag-change method and one that I had practiced countless times during previous deployments.

By the time I emerged from the cookhouse Moussa was in the car with one other FC trooper who had put on civilian clothing but still carried an AK-47. He moved to sit in the front but I told him I'd like to sit there. There was no way he would be able to react quickly enough with that weapon if we were stopped or attacked by the jihadists, whereas I'd be able to get at least a couple of rounds off through the windshield or side window if the situation warranted it. All three of us wore Pakols but only mine drew a laugh from the two men in my car as we set off into Quetta toward HQFC.

The strict Islamic code was enforced very stringently in this city and local rules did not permit women to walk out unaccompanied. As we progressed through this hostile town

Moussa pointed out the various landmarks. Meanwhile I was taking note of who was taking notice of me, and, at least for the moment, nobody was. We were three guys in a shitty little car surrounded by other shitty cars. However, the abundance of black headdresses that were the mark of the Taliban on the streets of Quetta was significant. The atmospherics left no illusion that I was in the middle of an urban bandit country.

Moussa was sensible enough to realise he shouldn't drop me at the main entrance of the headquarters so he pulled around the back of the main building. The side door of the building was a working entrance and there was the hustle and bustle of soldiers trying to look busy while walking around with pages of papers in their hands. Moussa said he would wait around the back of the building. I guessed I'd be about an hour but I didn't tell him.

As I walked in the double doors, Major Javed appeared from his office, which was the first on the right. You'd have thought I was his prodigal son by the way he greeted me whilst insisting that I come into his office. He was in conversation with two NCOs about something in Urdu and clearly wanted to impress me with his authority.

Major Javed then turned to me. He was completely out of condition with his belly pushing out over his uniform belt; he was almost the archetypal supply/administration officer. He offered tea but I refused and explained that I was due in with the General in ten minutes so I'd wait. He then said we should go to see Colonel GS.

We walked along the corridor to where a soldier stood wearing ceremonial headdress. As he saw me approaching, he knocked on the open door nearest to him. I drew level with the door to see a dashing Raj cavalry colonel with a broad smile. He came out from behind his desk to shake my hand and offered me a chair before returning behind his desk. A batman appeared with a glass of water and the Colonel offered tea. I told him that he was very kind but I would wait until I saw the General; I was clearly assuming the meeting would be "with tea" and instinctively hoped it would be.

The Colonel asked me how I was enjoying Quetta and I smiled saying, "I haven't had a chance to see much of it yet Colonel, we're a little confined to say the least." He went on to say that safety was paramount for us but that he would show me around the town one day and I told him I would like that very much. With that, one of his many phones rang and he put it down saying the General was ready to see me. We walked out of his office and across a large entrance hall, which was the main, ceremonial entrance of the front of the building. Standing next to the double doors opposite me was another soldier in ceremonial headdress.

I noticed the Deputy Commander's office on the left, which was directly opposite from that of the General. The colonel knocked the General's door and indicated I should walk in. The General was behind his desk but already standing and coming across his sizeable office with his hand outstretched. He was a man with a similar build to my own but perhaps slighter. He was wearing the dark grey salwar kameez uniform of the FC with a Major General's insignia on his shoulder. I noted they had retained the British design of rank but substituted a crescented star for the royal crown.

The General's light skin betrayed him as a Pathan, his traditional uniform was immaculate and he sported a thin beard as a token gesture towards Islamic tradition. His accent was immaculate English and he indicated for me to sit down on one of the three sofas. He sat down at the far end of the sofa on my left, which was at a right angle to me. A batman appeared and put a glass of water in front of me, the General smiled and said, "It's okay, it's bottled." I thanked the batman and looked at the General while taking a sip from the glass, "Rank rightly has its privileges, General." I smiled. He offered tea and I accepted. He then lent forward and picked up his cigarettes. He offered me one, which I refused, and he said he wished he didn't smoke but it was too late now.

The tea arrived with cakes and sandwiches while we made some small talk and he then asked what he could do for me. I knew that the entire future of the Department of State's programme in Pakistan had just reached a defining moment.

I began my pitch with the term, "As you know, *General...,*" I wanted him to believe that I assumed he was all informed, even if he wasn't.

I described the USG programme for the MOI and said that it had naturally commenced as an equipment reinforcement programme in order to increase border security (these were specific and precisely chosen words) and that the night flying capability of 50 Squadron was now nearing what was probably the best of its kind in Pakistan. Concurrently, the induction of the Caravan Cessna 208 and of FLIR would, for the first time, provided the FC's ground operations with real time, over the horizon (I actually meant over a mountain ridge) capability at night. Such capability, *if* integrated, and I emphasised "*if*", could afford for the General a manoeuvre capability that could respond to real time events and, in doing so, his forces could respond to reliable intelligence reports and events on the ground as a proactive rather than simply as a reactive force.

I had his full attention as he finished his first cigarette, sipped his tea, and slouched back on his sofa. I continued, not giving him a chance to cut in, by explaining that my task over the next few months would be to integrate the fixed wing and rotary wing capability whilst concurrently introducing a ground force that was specifically trained to use the equipment to maximum effect, essentially providing a helicopter assault force that could be utilised for both 'hard' or 'soft' operations. I wasn't entirely sure that he would understand the meaning of that last term but I assumed he would play along even if he didn't.

With the stage now set, I turned to what I *really* wanted. I told him that I'd heard he had put a special force together within the FC and that they had been trained by the SSG. I explained that when I had heard of this force, I was deeply enthused because the development of such a force was the right move at the right time, not just from an operational aspect but also from a strategic point of view. I was now purposely complimenting his visionary initiative without making it sound like brown-nosing.

I explained that the UK had learned its counter-insurgency operations from Malaysia and Northern Ireland, so we of all people understood the value of using specialist forces to "unhinge the enemy". Likewise, we learned that it was often more important to undermine the leadership of an insurgency than to rid them by other means. I added that it was always better to have the other side destroy their own for reasons of mistrust or incompetence than have our own side risk all to achieve the same.

I came back to his force and lied that I had choices of which ground force to use, (I hoped he would think I was talking about the rival Anti-Narcotics Force). I then explained that, from what I had heard, his force would be the ideal fit within a joint task force and I would like to provide him with force capability that would allow him increased reach and permit him to use his team as a surgeon's knife rather than as a sledge hammer to undermine and confuse the enemy. I closed by saying that, since Lawrence of Arabia fought in the desert eighty years ago, the desert has not changed as an environment, but now we can use helicopters instead of camels and night vision in order to take on the enemy when he doesn't want to fight all on our own terms.

I expressed my belief that, with an allocation of just fifty of his special troops, I could provide him with a capability that neither his fellow Generals nor the enemy would ever think possible. I chose not to mention the possibility of U.S. SpecOps trainers because by now he was leaning forward with full attention. I stopped talking.

The General reached over to his cigarettes on the coffee table again and lit up. I took the opportunity to take a drink of chai and grab one of the pastries that might otherwise go to waste or be eaten by the batmen after the meeting. The General slouched back on his couch; he was clearly relaxed with me, which I took as a good sign. It was his turn to talk.

"Howard, I appreciate what you say, but this U.S. Helicopter programme is a failure and an embarrassment, everybody knows it is."

He took a drag from his cigarette and put the ashtray on the arm of the sofa.

"You've got Nancy Powell and Dorothy trying to command the bloody things, so why would I subject my troops to something that might be here today and gone tomorrow? That's no good to me." Another puff and flick. "I put the Rapid Interdiction Force together myself," he explained. "When I sought approval it just never came, so I found the funding myself from my own budget. I looked for Pathan volunteers from NWFP and Waziristan because, if I used local men, they would be corrupted, intimidated or strung up by their balls by the Taliban who would inevitably find a way to threaten their families. These are the toughest Pathans we have. They go through a selection managed by SSG and only about half of them pass. They are given combat uniforms, they are given preference of equipment, they live in separate accommodation from the other soldiers, *and* they are given extra pay. We now have about ninety men and I intend to increase these to 300, so why would I want to take a force that is capable and motivated and put them under the command of two women who have no idea of my troop's capability or, more importantly, the enemy's capability?" He closed, "They would be better to concentrate on building proper schools instead of giving money to ghost ones!"

This last sentence was a direct reference to the fact that millions of U.S. tax payers dollars had been funnelled into schools programmes only for it to be discovered that many of the "schools" that received funding simply didn't exist.

I admitted straight away that the programme had experienced obvious problems, but this was the very reason that USG had sought me out. I told him that I didn't come looking for this job but that there must be less than a handful of operatives in the world who had the combination of Special Ops, Commando and Pilot qualifications.

I explained that, on day of my arrival, Dorothy had shown me in writing that she intended to shut the programme down. Despite that the aircraft were going through intense flying, maintenance levels have been renewed, equipment requirements have been approved and an agreement with MOI has been achieved regarding OpCon with a very definable point at which time it will be transferred.

I went on to explain that Maintenance Level-2 was likely to be achieved by February (3 months). So, if I were allocated a number of his specialist troops then the completion of the training of the first raiding platoon would coincide with the transfer of OpCon. I could personally guarantee that, not only would his troops never be commanded by the Ambassador or Dorothy (which clearly neither lady actually wanted), but also that I would provide for him and the Rapid Interdiction Force a capability that neither he nor anyone else would ever have thought possible. I would prove wrong the same kind of doubters who had not believed in him when he initially sought to establish his RIF. This close was to show I was simply trying to overcome resistance, which must have been similar to that which he must have experienced.

He sighed and paused. "You know what Howard, I've heard it all before," he said in a resigned tone. "The Americans make many promises then either fail to live up to them or change the terms leaving people like me to pick up the pieces."

Now I was on the back foot and fighting for the very existence of the programme, I needed to go all-in.

"General," I knew he'd warmed to me using his title. "I absolutely realise that you have heard it all before," I paused, "But there is a very big difference between then and now."

I stopped talking; I needed him to ask.

"And what is that?"

"The difference is that whatever you heard before, you didn't hear it from me."

I was now locked on to his eyes and he harboured no doubt that I was deeply serious. I continued, "I'm here because I know I have the skills and the experience to make this programme work and, together, we can do this. If you provide me with the opportunity to integrate your men with the air assets, to form a skilled ground force, you will never be disappointed with the result. You also have my word that your command will never be undermined by anything this programme does nor will I expose your men to any of the issues that may or may not be generated from Islamabad."

I was careful not to use the word "Embassy" and I maintained my eye contact as I finished.

"You have my word, Sir." He must have noted this was the first time I had used the word Sir.

He paused for several seconds that seemed like an age but I knew whomever spoke next would have lost, so it couldn't be me.

He leapt to his feet, which took me aback a little. As he did so, he said loudly, "Okay, I'll tell you what. You go out and visit the unit. I want to you do an assessment of their capability and then report back to me with your findings."

I wanted to leap up and hold both fists in the air but I didn't. He continued. "When can you visit them?"

"Tomorrow morning, General." I was back to his title.

"Okay", he said and walked over to his desk, pressed a button and, within seconds, his ADC appeared through the door for his instructions. "Howard will visit the RIF tomorrow," the General told his man. "Get hold of Major Wajid and tell him to lay on a full demonstration of their capability and get back to Howard. Confirm a 9am grouping at Belili."

The only answer possible was, "Yes Sir."

The General looked at me and held out his hand, "It's been a pleasure, Howard. You are a breath of fresh air but I hope you can make this work."

I replied simply, "General, the pleasure is entirely mutual. I thank you for your opportunity and trust; I will not let you down."

As I walked to the door, the General asked, "Oh by the way, when can I have that report?"

I told him that I knew he would be in Karachi next week so I could be back a week from Monday to brief him and provide a full assessment. He instructed his ADC to put it in his diary. I thanked the General and headed to the back of the building to find Moussa.

When we arrived back at the compound, I found Caz on the flight line where they had been ground running one of the Hueys. I explained to him that I would need to be out at Belili tomorrow morning, timing to be confirmed, and I required a Huey to take me there.

It would only be a ten-minute flight to the base, which was at the northern edge of Quetta beyond the international airport, so we agreed I would be out on the flight line by 0840.

The following morning, I donned my kit knowing that I would be under inspection as much as the RIF. Thus, I was careful with my choices. I had the civilian equivalent of combat trousers but with no camouflage pattern. I wore my trusty brown leather belt for its robust capability to hold a pistol covertly against my stomach. It was also way too long for my waist, just in case I ever needed to use it as a tourniquet or tie a flashlight on the end of it as a rotating signal device. I threaded the sheath of my six-inch dagger on my right hip. I donned my British military desert camouflage jacket, which already contained the basic equipment located in the same pockets I had always used. In the case of "vitals" such as compass and penknife, these were 'lanyarded' to the buttonholes so they could never be lost.

I took the conscious decision never to wear sunglasses when in Quetta or with the Pathans. I needed to meet them eye-to-eye and I never wanted to be an anonymous figure to whomever I spoke to. I took the view that by making them always look me in the eye it would make it just a little harder for them to think about direct betrayal.

As I walked out of the accommodation, I slung on my faded CAO cigar hat, which was to accompany me on every patrol, and as Jim drove me out to the flight line, my mind wandered back to the day at the Preakness Stakes in Maryland when a beautiful young lady selling CAO cigars had not only sold me half a dozen on the back end of a big win but also had given me my now "lucky hat."

When we reached the flight line, Caz was ready to go. I greeted the Pakistani crewchief and co-pilot. I knew it was going to take a while to learn all of their names, so I concentrated on trying to call them by their name as often as I could.

We skirted the city and, as we climbed. The main airport became visible, beyond that point the urban sprawl fell off. A small set of mountains forced the main road to skirt the low ground to their west before it could continue north and split in two. The traveller by road had a "devil and deep blue sea" choice of a north-east route to Zhob in Pakistan, which lies just to the south of the Federally Administered Tribal Areas (FATA), or a northwest route to the closest city of Kandahar in Afghanistan.

As we drew closer to Belili, the parade ground was the dominating feature with military-style administration and accommodation buildings emanating from its perimeter on three sides. The eastern perimeter, to which we were the closest, paralleled the public road. Here was the main entrance, the guardhouse, the ceremonial flagpole area, and the large white "H" indicating it was a helipad. To our right, we could see sentry points on the hills overlooking the camp and I wondered if they were manned. They also had a commanding view of the camp and the road into Quetta.

There were three officers to greet me at the Helipad. I immediately recognised Colonel Shaheed of the Ghazaband Scouts. With him were a major and a captain who were both dressed in U.S. style combat clothing. I exited the aircraft, gave the thumbs up to Caz. Within seconds, the wind and the noise caused by the departing Huey was fading to the south. The Colonel welcomed me to Belili and introduced Major Wajid who I immediately noticed was sporting a set of SSG wings with a maroon backing above his right breast pocket. The junior officer wore a set of parachute jump wings in a similar place but had a badge that appeared to be a silver falcon with outspread wings above his left breast pocket. He was introduced as Captain Pervaiz.

The Colonel explained that Major Wajid was the Commanding Officer of the RIF and Captain Pervaiz was the Number One Platoon Commander. The colonel, being ever gracious, invited me for tea in his office, but I could see about thirty uniformed men sitting over by the small grandstand on the southern side of the parade ground. I politely acknowledged the Colonel's kindness but told him that I only had a couple of hours because I needed to catch a flight that afternoon.

As, we approached the thirty men, they stood up and were called to attention with the Senior NCO saluting the colonel.

The platoon relaxed again and I complimented the Major on his SSG wings and noted that they had a maroon backing indicating he had conducted at least fifty parachute jumps. He explained that he had been seconded from the SSG to train and command the RIF and that they had used three SSG personnel to put the RIF through their initial three-month training. He made clear that the course was very physical but had progressed into SSG tactics and that all the men were volunteers with all but one of them being Pathans from FATA and NWFP.

The men I was about to see were the first batch and had been with the RIF for about six months in total. He went onto say there were another ninety men in training. I then brought Captain Pervaiz into the conversation. He explained that he was the first and only officer to pass the training and that the platoon I was about to see was under his command.

I asked him if they had conducted any operations and he described a substitution operation where intelligence had been received that a border outpost was going to be attacked. They then substituted RIF dressed as normal Frontier Corps soldiers in the hope that the attackers would walk into an ambush but the attack didn't happen, doubtless because someone had told the enemy that a substitution had been made. As he spoke, it became all too apparent that these soldiers knew that the Frontier Corps was infiltrated by enemies and informants. The sad reality was that this was hardly surprising given their extreme poverty and low pay. Operational Security (Opsec) in such a setting would be of constant concern.

The Major asked if there was any demonstration I would particularly like to see but I courteously suggested he show me what he wished me to see. With that, Pervaiz went forward to direct his men, who initially formed a three square, to demonstrate their weapons handling. The SNCO barked orders in Pashtu and the men conducted snapped and precise movements with their AK-47s. I noted that all the men were between twenty-five and thirty-five and all were clearly in robust physical shape. Some of them sported fundamentalist type beards and I wondered what these tribesmen would think of me. Having grown up in FATA and NWFP, it was likely that, as boys, all of these men would have owned an AK-47 in lieu of a train-set and this was reflected in natural way in which they now handled their weapons. I just hoped they could shoot them as well as they could perform their drills.

On completion of the drill, they retired to my right and then demonstrated their fire and manoeuvre exercises across the parade ground. It wasn't an ideal setting but at least they demonstrated that each section understood how it needed to be positioned and the requirement for suppressive cover during movement under fire. The only alarming aspect is that the men did not "hard target" (zig-zag) when moving but, so far, so good.

They then set out a square with six white bricks and placed a chair within the square. Two of the bricks were placed in proximity to each other on the side of the square closest to the observers. It was explained that these represented a doorway into a room where a hostage was being held. A chair was placed within this "room" where one of the RIF's number, dressed in a salwar kameez, duly sat. Two other men, ostensibly the Taliban, donned black turban headdress and the main RIF team retired about half way across the parade ground.

It was explained to me that the RIF had received a local report regarding their location and an order had been given to "recover the hostage". While the "actor" postured and slung insults at the hostage, the team started its "covert" approach across the parade ground, presumably assuming that the two enemy jihadists had no line of sight, given the assumption that there were no windows in the "building". The assault team grouped well and moved swiftly and quietly to the rear of the structure. One of the enemy was outside walking back and forth, the other was inside with the hostage.

Despite there being no real walls, they did quite well with "make-believe conditions" and, when the section leader was confident the sentry's back was turned, he moved forward quickly and dispatched him. As this happened, the team behind him moved to breach the door and quickly overpowered the remaining enemy.

It was all a bit 'Mickey Mouse' and I wished they'd thought to use a real building, but at least they showed they had been taught some of the basics.

I then asked Major Wahid if three men with full kit could step forward and that I merely wanted to see what equipment they would typically carry. Of course, it was a little deeper than that. I needed to ascertain if they had any standardisation of their equipment. They did not. The backpacks had a broad variation of equipment that ranged from a blanket to rope, there was even food wrapped in a handkerchief. It seemed the SSG instructors had concentrated on fitness and the "glamour ops" but had not bothered with the basics.

As I worked my way through their kit, I was gracious and made the odd joke or contorted face that they would all understand when I found something untoward. The entire platoon watched me carefully and I could tell they were trying to size me up and understand what I was doing. I especially wanted them to see that I knew what I was talking about, so I asked the last man for his rifle. He obediently offered it to me and I instructed him to take the magazine off and prove it was clear. He slipped off the magazine, pushed the safety lever down, and pulled the working parts to the rear. I checked the breach and tapped his arm, indicating it was indeed clear.

I knew I was now the one being assessed for my knowledge of how to strip an AK, so I concentrated on the task far more than I appeared to be.

Having broken the weapon down, I took a look at the cleanliness. The weapon was well kept but had obviously been around the block a few times.

I turned to the Major and said I was very happy with what I had seen and would report back to the General. I asked him to thank the men for their impressive demos and then dismiss them. Caz brought the Huey back for my pick up. It was then a quick turn at the compound before heading up to Islamabad the following day. I had found my ground force. Now I had to turn them into a cohesive unit with the aircraft. I had no other resource, no other choice.

That evening, I received a bizarre phone call from Dorothy. She explained that Deputy Assistant Secretary of State Steve Schrage was visiting the Embassy and, to her apparent irritation, he had insisted on an unaccompanied visit to Quetta. She added that he was a George Bush appointee and asked if I could I arrange for an aircraft to bring him to Quetta and deliver him back to Islamabad the next day. I told her it wouldn't be a problem and that I would simply delay my return flight to the afternoon.

I was bewildered by this impromptu visit and placed a call to Paul in the United States. Paul explained that Schrage was a "get it done" individual and had influence over the distribution of funds. He added that Steve had a reputation for wanting to get to grass roots rather than rely on diplomat's hearsay. Because the programme had recently come under a lot of scrutiny, Mr. Schrage's visit could tilt the balance between progress or closure.

All I knew that was this man's decision to come alone to Quetta was pretty ballsy and it would give me an opportunity to sell the programme, warts and all.

The following day, Steve Schrage arrived wearing a suit which somewhat served to conceal a small paunch, I guessed he was in his early forties. I welcomed him and joked that he must be the only person within 150 miles wearing a business suit and tie.

Curtis and I showed him round the basic facilities we utilised in Quetta. We started on the flight line and Caz showed him around one of the Hueys. We then went to the metal shipping containers that formed our workshops, stores and flight line offices. I had arranged a truck to drive him around the facilities, but he wanted to walk everywhere and take it all in. It helped that it was a beautiful, blue-sky day and that he was an energetic and affable man.

In the compound, he asked to see the living conditions and was clearly taken aback by the austerity of it all. In the wash-room, I explained, such was the difficulty of obtaining non-programme equipment, that Jay had actually bought a quality second-hand washing machine in the United States and had it shipped to Quetta so that our clothes could be washed properly.

In the cookhouse, Cha-Cha, the local and alleged cook, managed to rustle up a curried lunch on his bacteria encrusted stove while I updated Steve on what had happened over the last few days with Sadaqat and how I thought I had located a suitable ground force for the programme.

As we wandered out to the flight line to board the Caravan, Steve paused and looked back at Quetta. After some thought, he said, "This is unbelievable! You guys are out here pulling together an eastern flank of American interests on a shoe-string." I had to agree. He went on, "If you can continue to get this programme back on track, Howard, I'll give you all the support I can." This man from Capitol Hill was my modern day Charlie Wilson. I told him I would do my damnedest to keep my side of the bargain and, as it would transpire, Steve did more than his part to honour his end.

On the flight back to Islamabad, we took a detour to show Steve the porous and ill-defined border between Pakistan and Afghanistan. He now clearly realised the immensity of the problem we faced but that we were building something special; we had won the day.

CHAPTER 6

Final Preparation

As ever, I was relieved to be back in Slammy and a cold glass of beer always seemed to taste just that much better when I'd had to go without for a week or two.

We dropped Steve at the Serena Hotel, he was headed back to the U.S. via Dubai that evening, but we agreed to clean up and rendezvous at the Embassy. I needed to get to Dorothy before the close of business, but it was going to be tight.

Friday was always a weird day in terms of atmospherics in the city. This Sabbath day in Islam is always marked by Friday Prayers and there was always an air of tension for an aware unbeliever about town. On occasions parts of the city would, in an instant, turn into violent protest against anything western.

In Islamabad, the fervent sermons of the sibling mullahs, Maulana Aziz and Maulana Ghazi, at the Red Mosque had a reputation for generally being the source of the most violent post-prayer protests. It was thus prudent for an unbeliever to avoid that blessed but potentially deadly area on a Friday afternoon at all costs.

I headed straight to Dorothy's office and asked if I could have a quick word. She immediately wanted to know what had been said to Steve. She did, after all, have the programme closure proposal to annul. I told her it was a "vanilla" visit. He saw everything he needed to see regarding the actuality of life in Quetta and I thought that his visit was entirely positive given he had seen the realities of what we were up against.

Even though I was purposely using the word "we" I could sense her discomfort at not having personal control of the flow of information to Steve so I didn't dwell on the matter but switched the subject to the militia.

I segwayed into the meeting with General Sadaqat and that I had gained his permission to review the capability of his specialist troops. I added I would push a proposal for the use of his troops with our helicopter team the next time I met him, which I hoped would be in about ten days. I didn't mention that he'd asked for a written assessment because she might have asked to see it and edit it from her myopic civil servant's perspective. I also decided not to mention his reluctance to get his troops involved due to fear of political interference. Given Steve's visit Dorothy's concern regarding her lack of control over his visit was likely running rampant anyway so I'd let that sleeping dog lie unless she awoke it.

My doctrine within the bounds of the Embassy had rapidly become the less said the better. I was confident Sadaqat and I could make it happen and that could speak for itself.

Dorothy listened carefully and I could only imagine what was going through her head. On top of the Steve Schrage visit, I wondered if she also resented me meeting Sadaqat. I really wasn't sure, but I got a clue when she asked, "Was it difficult to meet with General Sadaqat?" I told her that it hadn't been easy, but patience had prevailed. She then asked, "How did you get him come over to the Compound?" This was clearly a question with an agenda that was yet to be revealed so I simply responded, "It really wasn't an issue." She flabbergasted me by saying, "Good, because you can't travel anywhere in

Quetta unless it is in an armoured vehicle. So he'll just have to get used to coming to you."

I just couldn't believe it! Fuck me; I was on the brink of securing a force that would make some of the U.S. taxpayers money well spent and she was worried about who went to see who!

I'd spent a military career on covert operations and effective risk mitigation. Was I not sitting in front of her? Had I not arrived back safely? Did she have any idea what it took to get a meeting with this General? I reflected that, for the good of the programme, I had actually offered to stand outside a shithouse listening to the General defecate. All of which would very likely provide her with future glory and awards from her Ambassador, and all she was worried about was if I left the damn compound without an armoured convoy.

Although festering inside, I calmly repeated, "Like I said, Dorothy, the issue was never raised, so I don't see it being a problem in the future." And I left it at that. I had now concluded that she looked for negative comments in anything I said unless she thought they held ambassadorial or political sway.

I attempted to finish on a high note and explained that I thought we'd had a "red-letter" week from which we could build real operational capability. She replied, "Good, that's great." So why did I leave her office feeling deflated?

I concluded time would tell, but for now it was time for an "Ice Cold in Alex" moment at the Happy Hour. Fortunately Jerry, Tom , Curtis, Keith and Brian were all there so one can easily imagine the laughter over the "In his office or in the toilet?" anecdote. Being able to bounce any and all frustrations off these guys was a huge help.

I called Paul in the U.S. to update him on the week's events. His response was night and day from Dorothy's and I could

119

practically taste his enthusiasm through the phone. Ever pragmatic, he warned me not to push it too hard and to be careful how I handled the "embassy folks". Before closing with Paul, he anticipated my final question, "How are the weapons coming along? We are exposed without that protection." He fully understood and updated me on the latest step in that convoluted process. I just wished they'd hurry up.

Over the weekend I started to draft my report for Sadaqat. My work was punctuated by going to the Embassy to take a run and lift some weights. I also needed to prepare for a Toga party to be hosted by Ellis of the FBI on Saturday night.

He lived a convenient two-minute drive from where I lived. Had it been any further, I would have felt more circumspect about driving though Islamabad in a pair of boxers and wrapped in a ridiculous toga.

As might be expected, the FBI put on a great party. Experience had taught me that law enforcement types always seemed to achieve wild parties primarily because there was no fear of being raided or arrested.

The combination of togas, booze, Huka (Sheesha) and exaggerated anecdotes made the party a late one. The result, beyond a monumental hangover and aching cheeks from laughing, was the formation of the "Sheepherders Club."

To be honest, I can't recall whose idea it was but one of our number categorised those who served in the Embassy as either "Sheep" or "Sheepherders". The difference being that the Herders were those personnel who, in the execution of their work, had at sometime in their career had to bear arms for their country. The comparison in mindset and attitude was obvious yet remarkable and from that moment we resolved to have a "Sheepherders" meeting (with beer) once a month. Any men or women who had borne arms for their country were welcome to attend.

The following morning I was skulking about the house when a call came from a number in the United Kingdom. "Howard, it's Alan." said a pristine Eton accent on the other end of the phone. Alan and I had got to know each other in Northern Ireland many years previously. I hadn't heard from him for years and asked how he was doing and how he got my number.

He explained that he had heard that I was out here working for the Americans and asked if I had yet run into any "old friends". I told him I hadn't. He said, "I thought it would be of value for you to touch base with a mutual friend." and provided a local mobile number.

He asked how many aircraft I had at my disposal. I told him nine in total, to which he responded, "You lucky bastard, our guys have to drive!" He'd just given me the reason for the call but I didn't mind.

I was aware the UK's focus was stemming the massive quantities of narcotics that were reaching the UK through Pakistan and were doing whatever they could locally prevent the process. I would do what I could to help.

By Monday, the effects of the Toga party had worn off but the laughter in the office over Jerry's outfit was still plentiful and evidential photos were in abundant supply on the Sheepherders email circuit.

My priority that morning was to lock in on the DoD guys. I needed to get a result in order to get a SOF training team to the RIF.

As I appeared round the door, there was a welcome, "Hey Howard" from a couple of them and I wandered over to the Special Forces desk. The swarthy young captain with copious amounts of badges on his uniform was leaning back with a mug of coffee in his hand; I asked how he'd got on with the Training Team request.

121

He took a big sigh and explained that it didn't look good. He had spoken to the guys at SOCOM in Tampa but, as predicted, they said they were completely stretched with Iraq commitments. He added that Pakistan was low priority in comparison.

I couldn't help but think this was just staggering. "Pakistan, Al-Qaeda Central, a low priority? What the fuck was going on?" But I knew I'd be shooting the messenger if I reacted adversely to the Captain, so I asked, "What time scale does 'low priority' mean?"

The answer was about as bad as it could be, "Well they reckon they could get a couple of guys out here to do a recon in about six months."

"Jesus Christ," I replied, not thinking about any American evangelists in the room, "Six months just to take a look? That isn't going to work."

I sighed and said, "I'm going to have to work out something else; I simply can't wait six months."

What I really meant was *America* couldn't wait six months but I knew I'd be seen as dramatic if I said something like that. "Let me have a think and I'll get back to you, but thanks anyway, I appreciate your effort for us."

I wished him "a nice day" and walked out of the room towards the theatre coffee shop. I needed a cup of tea to get over the shock of the strategic perspective and time to think this through.

As I sipped my Lipton's Yellow Label tea I instinctively knew what I had to do - but the question was; should I do it? If any part of the programme failed because I became a stretched resource beyond my portfolio, I would be opening myself up for massive criticism and would be deemed a failure. If, however, I didn't do it then I'd be safe physically and professionally because the programme would invariably meander on but be forever mediocre and have very little impact on the enemy.

I had never "played it safe" so I was going to have to push the envelope. We, let alone America, couldn't wait six months on a wing and a prayer that a couple of reservists may or may not come to train the militia.

Things were about to get very busy. It was time to 'man-up'.

That evening, I told Paul that I was putting a training programme together for the RIF that I would integrate them with our air assets. I explained that DoD had no teeth in Pakistan because of the U.S. Government's emphasis in Iraq and, in any case, everything they did was monitored by the ISI.

Although we were apparently in plain sight, we could fly under the radar by using our own resources, no-one would expect that, and we certainly wouldn't ask permission. So while the left hand didn't know what the right hand was doing I could make hay. It would mean I'd have to spend a lot more time in Quetta but I added my own caveat that I saw no reason that I couldn't keep the various agencies happy, and what the ISI didn't know about it couldn't meddle with so "fuck `em". I summarised by reiterating, if we wanted the RIF on board, then we had no choice but to do it our way.

To my amazement, Paul agreed and reassured me of the reasoning. "It's not like you didn't try to get a training team and you know what? It'll probably be better this way because at least we'll be in full control of the programme." He was certainly right about that. If DoD had gotten involved they would doubtless end up consuming the programme and, with that, the decision to get my boots dirty again had been made.

For the remainder of the week, I completed the assessment requested by the General and created a Phase 1 training schedule for the RIF. When I met with the General, I would need him to agree with me on all matters and essentially handover control of the first batch of twenty-five of his best men for helicopter assault training.

For much of the week, I stayed at home rummaging through my old counter-insurgency notes and figured out where I would need to blend in basic techniques with specialist skills. I needed these men to understand the benefits of standardisation and would have to start at the lowest denominator then steepen the learning curve to try to develop a basis for a truly effective night fighting unit. During the follow on Phase 2 training the entire training would be at night.

I made Dorothy aware that I would be ready to fly down to Quetta on Monday. I thought it best not to dwell on the expansion of my duties. After all what she didn't know she couldn't be blamed for.

It was Thursday when I called Alan's friend, Robert, in the British Embassy. We agreed to meet for a coffee in the Jinnah Supermarket area later in the day.

It turned out Robert was a rugged diplomat and not part of the British military. He was involved in anti-narcotics operations and liaised with the Anti Narcotics Force (ANF) and the British military to try to stem the constant flow of refined product from Afghanistan to the UK.

He gave me an outline of their activity and said that they too fell under the authority of the Ministry of the Interior (MOI). I told him that I was aware of the links and commented that it was strange how the UK and U.S. seemed to be operating separately when there should be a unified effort.

Robert explained that, while they had good relations with the likes of the DEA, they hadn't been able to establish a horizontal with NAS. He had also heard that NAS had a lot of 'internal issues'. I nervously reassured him that I thought they were over. He asked about our aircraft assets and how he could get access to them.

When I went suggested the best way to tackle this was simply for him contact me directly, he asked, "Well supposing we need to move people or equipment to or from Quetta, would you be able to help?"

I explained that our guys and equipment would have to take priority but there was no point in flying empty seats when there was a war going on.

The allied deal was done and we'd had a meeting of minds; Robert invited me to dinner at his house the following evening.

By the time I left work on Friday, I had finished the preparation for Sadaqat. We were now a week into December and I didn't intend to stay in Quetta for more than three days; I needed to get back to Slammy to organise the equipment for the training programme. My fixer, Saadi, in the Annex was about to get busy attaining equipment from any source available to him before I'd be able to head home for ten days over Christmas.

Dinner with Robert was excellent and by the time I left his house, we had bonded the resources to a point where the Brits would provide us with equipment that we couldn't procure for ourselves through the State system. We would help them with "space available" logistic and operational support. We'd also make ourselves available to emergency evacuate any Brits deployed in the 'playground' if the shit hit the fan down there.

By Monday morning at 0945, Dorothy would have been thoroughly pissed off to know that I was sitting in HQFC in Quetta, Balochistan drinking tea in Colonel GS's office.

During the conversation, he then let slip that the General was excited to receive my report and plans. He expanded, "I don't know what you said to the General the other day, but he is very enthused." He added, "I hope you have something good for him." I was confident I did.

The General's door was open and he welcomed me like an old friend. We sat down to drink tea and the General lit up a cigarette. During the small talk, he revealed that his family was in Karachi.

At this stage, I had not yet been to this infamously dangerous city of fifteen million people, but knew that the elites of Pakistan lived very well there. The General then asked me how I had got on with his men and I took the report from my folder and handed it to him.

The General was riveted as I went through the document and explained the logic behind each requirement. I added that I knew the equipment and manning scales would not be cured overnight but that we should do our best and improvise where necessary.

I then moved on to describe Phase One training programme itself, which was a fifteen-day programme that would take three weeks to complete *if* the Pathans could meet the learning curve. It started with absolute basics and then introduced tactics and doctrine along the way. I explained that Phase One would concentrate on training tactical disciplines during daylight. Once they were mastered we would take a pause before moving to doing it all again at night on NVGs.

By the time the General had finished his review of the report and the proposed programme, he could not hide his enthusiasm.

He admitted, "I thought this was going to be good, but I didn't expect anything like this."

I smiled and reminded him, "You heard it from me, General."

He responded, "Indeed I did, Howard, indeed I did." He paused, "So when do they start?"

"January 12th, General. That will give NAS and Colonel GS enough time to procure a reasonable amount of initial equipment levels and I do need to take a ten day break over Christmas to see my children."

"Sounds perfect. If there is anything you need or if anyone from my organisation doesn't deliver, you must let me know."

He pressed his buzzer. In less than a minute, the Colonel was with us in the General's office. The General took command. "We are pushing ahead with the special training for the RIF. It will commence on...." Then General looked at me,

"January 12th General," I prompted,

He continued as if he'd said the date, "I want full support for Howard and anything he needs, please make sure he gets it."

The Colonel squeezed in a "Yes Sir."

"We realise that not all the equipment is readily available, but you will need to coordinate with Howard that which we can procure and that which will have to be left up to NAS. Also, make sure Major Wajid and Major Javed are fully briefed and that they know this has my full attention."

The General looked at me and asked, "When are you going back to Islamabad?"

I told him I planned to do so on Wednesday.

"Good, then I suggest you guys get your heads together on this tomorrow." I looked at the Colonel and we nodded to each other.

He then volunteered, "I will come to you Howard."

The General once more reiterated that I should keep him informed and thanked me. I told him it was me that should be thanking him and I walked with the Colonel back to his office where we discussed the timings and issues. Now we had momentum!

Once back in the compound, I called the DynCorp team together and briefed them on the events. Their response ranged from genuine enthusiasm to "I'll believe it when I see it." I supposed they must have seen many an initiative fall on its face over the years. However, with the programme in front of them, they became animated and started to discuss what would have to be done when from a maintenance point of view. This interaction was truly something I hadn't seen before.

Each specialist contributed input and took notes, it almost seemed like they could suddenly see purpose for being there. These specialists were instinctively driven to be ready for the task and their morale would be proportional to the progress climb.

By the time I boarded the Caravan back to Slammy, it seemed that I had hardly been in Quetta. The past three days had been an absolute whirlwind of organisation since the General's go ahead. My priority was to get the procurement machine rolling and I'd have to tap into several entities to do this.

I quickly ascertained with Saadi back in Islamabad what he could get through official channels and what he couldn't. Thankfully, some of the big-ticket items like NVGs weren't a problem, however, items like smoke grenades, field dressings and Meals Ready to Eat (MREs) certainly were problematic and I would have to ply some imagination and persuasion elsewhere to get these.

Colonel Wahid back in Quetta had agreed that FC would procure the required weapons, ammunition and ordnance, but I would pretty much have to rustle up the rest of the requirement from NAS or elsewhere.

Saadi listed the equipment he could buy locally and that which he would have to reach Stateside to acquire. When we ran the numbers we were satisfied that we could get it done within budget without it seriously impacting any other part of the NAS programme. Where there was paperwork to be done, I sat in Saadi's cramped and cluttered office and helped him fill it in. It was a process that actually helped to spread the word within the Annex staff of what was going on and I could feel the enthusiasm amongst the locals who were Saadi's work colleagues.

For what I suppose are obvious reasons, the State Department's procurement index did not run to MREs for soldiers or Pakistani forces.

I could not conceive an operation when they would be on the ground for more than seventy-two hours but we needed reserve rations.

My concept was that the RIF would carry forty-eight hours of rations (2xMREs) when in Marching (backpack) Order and twenty-four hours ration (1xMRE) when in Fighting (belt equipment) Order. I would need at least 100 MREs as a basic requirement. So I doubled it and pitched it to one of the supply colonel's in the Embassy who seemed like someone who could help. He explained that there were absolutely no MREs in that quantity in Pakistan and that they would have to look for them in Afghanistan.

The obvious mode of transport would be to use the Ambassador's KingAir aircraft the next time it was on a routine trip to Kabul - if, that is, we could find a supplier. I sat at the colonel's desk with him as he made the call to one of his buddies in Kabul; he explained he needed 200 MREs (no pork) for an initiative here in Pak and could they help? Clearly the troops in Afghanistan had tens of thousands of MREs, so a quantity of 200 was a drop in the ocean and the deal was done.

Next stop was to call on the U.S. Navy in the shape of "Crazy Captain Mike" upstairs who flew the Embassy's KingAir. I explained the situation and asked if we could sling the MREs on his next flight from Kabul and added there would be a couple of beers in it for him. As a navy pilot this was all the sweet talk Mike needed to hear. We looked at the schedule and he could bring them back next week.

The Smoke Grenades, however, would require some imagination to procure; they were necessary as a marker for helicopters when they were trying to find us in daylight or, in an emergency. They can also provide you cover from view on a bug-out from the enemy.

I phoned Robert the Brit and gave him the good news regarding the "fare structure" for that available seating down to Quetta - two seats, round trip, economy class in a Cessna 208. The price placed on account was one case of Smoke Grenades. To his credit Robert, didn't even miss a beat and replied, "What Colour?"

This was going very well so far. The Medical Clinic in the American Embassy was the next stop.

The challenge of the Clinic was that I actually didn't know anyone who worked there. This would be a cold-call and I'd have to see what kind of response I would get. This could swing either way. I figured truth would be the best policy but I'd have to pick my moment.

I wandered in at about 2.30pm and found the place deserted. I stood in the reception area and studied the gruesome photos on the wall of infected limbs, sores, gum disease and the like and at messages telling me to watch my diet and so on.

My thoughts were interrupted by a "Can I help you?" I spun round to see a cute woman in her late thirties who was obviously a nurse. My training as a Navy Pilot had confirmed that there are only two certainties in life, "Death and Nurses." However, I needed this one to be a certainty from a different perspective to my previous approaches.

Pouring on the British accent that inexplicably seems to soften up American ladies, I said, "I wonder if you can help me?"

I explained my problem regarding the team that I worked with down in Quetta and the complete void of any medical first aid equipment. I told her I had tried to procure basic dressings and materials but the State Department shopping list just didn't run to field dressings or Band-Aids. I added that, if I couldn't find the basic essential, I would have to buy the stuff myself.

She asked if the beneficiaries would be American and I told her, "Some of them," which was slightly true. She then asked what I needed; I pulled a piece of paper from my back pocket and handed it to her.

She looked at it and smiled at me. "I'll tell you what," she said, "We might not be able to do everything but I think we can do most of it."

I sighed with relief, "You have no idea how much we need this stuff."

"Oh, believe me, I get it." She said, "If you don't have this stuff, it's inevitable you will need it. It's always the way."

She told me to give her twenty-four hours and she would put a box together for me but added that fifty dressings might be a stretch; she'd do her best.

I asked her name, and she told me it was Anne. I told her, "Bless you for this, Anne. What colour wine do you like?" She answered "Red" and I knew what I had to do. The very next day I received a large box of medical dressings and supplies and Anne received a bottle of Chateaux Neuf de Pape.

By the time I was ready to depart on my Christmas break, my office in the Embassy had more of the air of an operational storeroom than an office. There were boxes of ad hoc supplies stuffed under and on top of every desk, with Curtis and I just doing what we needed to do in-between all the clutter. Suzanne appeared at one stage to ask what it was all about and I explained that these were supplies we needed for the programme from outside the procurement chain. She asked who was paying for it and I told her "Dorothy!" and laughed. I then correcting myself said, "Actually it's her Uncle Sam. After all, it's *his* programme, just different sources." I assume she said nothing to Dorothy because the subject never came up from that direction.

Everything was staying under the radar and falling nicely into line, nonetheless I checked with Saadi and Colonel Wahid on a daily basis for updates on the procurement process. Paul, back in the U.S., was kept informed and seemed genuinely amused that we were making it all happen without bureaucracy getting in the way.

Unfortunately he could not achieve the same in regard to the weapons and thought it would be February before they finally arrived. Everything had been approved but it was the final packaging and placement into the diplomatic delivery process that was taking the time.

I made two phone calls - one to Ken, the RSO, and the other to my supplier of Mr. Makarov.

My meeting with Ken was actually the first time I had an extended conversation with him outside of the bar. He was very experienced and knew the ground and his job as well as any.

During the small talk I provocatively commented on the extremely diverse selection of personnel within the Embassy. He read between the lines very quickly and said, "The way I look at it, Howard, is that this particular type of Embassy draws three kinds of people in some shape or form." He paused for effect. "Misfits, missionaries, and mercenaries."

It was a profound description and I couldn't help but agree and was quickly classifying myself to the closest category. Ken continued, "Once you get over that fact, then you can forgive anyone in the Embassy almost anything." He paused again. "Keyword, *almost!*" He smiled and I knew exactly what he was trying to tell me. Ken was a man of immense logic and not easily worried or flappable.

He listened intently as I explained the weapons approvals and he concurred that he had seen all the paperwork and signal traffic confirming the permissions, something Dorothy had never told me. He was aware that the best guesstimate for the weapons arriving was February and that there were six "longs" and six "shorts" in the delivery.

I explained that Pete, Caz and I would increasingly be flying over hostile territory from 12 January and it would be crazy for us to do so unarmed - not only from the perspective of a threat from the known enemy but also from our own heavily armed RIF personnel whom we had yet learned to trust. Ken nodded as I spoke.

I showed Ken my State Department firearms proficiency certificate, paused, and asked if the RSO could substitute three of our weapons pending their delivery.

Ken checked the paperwork again, leaned back in his chair in brief thought then called Tom into the room to explain that we had all the required clearances for carriage and they needed to loan us three rifles. Tom responded that the only "longs" they had were low velocity M16, 9mm SWATs; he had no spare high velocity weapons.

Ken looked at me and asked, "Would they do?" I nodded and said, "They'd be fine as a stop gap." To which Ken added, "Well, they're certainly better than nothing."

As Tom walked out of the room, Ken added, "Loan them three pistols as well."

We were all set.

That evening, President Musharraf left the Presidential buildings in Islamabad to head for his favourite residence, the "Army House" in Rawalpindi. The President's affection for this "remote" residence meant that a daily vigil would include his road trip to and from his residence.

His security blanket tried to offset the risk of creating a pattern by running false presidential convoys and employing electronic jammers in the convoy itself. Naturally, the main threat was thought to come from Al-Qaeda's Number Two, Ayman Al-Azawahiri, who had announced his intent to have Musharraf killed, but on this occasion the threat was actually to come from within the Pakistani military itself.

As the President's convoy crossed the Jhanda Chichi Bridge in Rawalpindi, a massive radio-controlled bomb was detonated.

The perpetrators had used inside information provided by one of Musharraf's officers in order to get close to their target. Fortunately, the radio jammers in the convoy did their job and it wasn't until the last car had passed the bomb that the initiating radio signal was permitted to reach its receiver.

Musharraf's car was lifted off the ground by the explosion but he survived. The perpetrators must have known that the ISI net would quickly close on them. Unbeknown to all of us was that the attackers would be more expeditious to make another, more desperate attempt on the President's life before his henchmen caught up with them, and next time they wouldn't rely on a hi-tech attempt at detonation.

Concurrent to the whirlwind of activity in the wake of the assassination attempt Brigadier Shafiq in the MOI called a meeting and announced that we would now need to support the impending South Asian Association for Regional Cooperation (SAARC) conference.

I had seen the various posters and flags in Islamabad boasting that it was to host the Conference but had not really paid much attention to it on the premise that any visiting heads of states would be way above my social or professional interest.

Shafiq explained that Islamabad would be in virtual lock-down during the event and that they would require our helicopters to fly special police overhead while the visiting heads of state were in transit on Islamabad's roads. They would also require the Caravan's FLIR to watch for any suspicious activity.

We agreed that two Hueys backed by one Caravan with the FLIR would suffice.

It would be practically impossible to identify any suspicious activity prior to an attack and the FLIR could act as a poor-man's satellite. If an attack occurred, the FLIR tape could then be run in reverse in order to backtrack the attackers source location. This technique has been put to good use in past operations and it was now standard practice in just about every major city in the world.

Following the meeting, I briefed Dorothy, then Caz and Pete separately. Dorothy was about as enthused as I had seen her regarding the air assets and was clearly busting to tell the Ambassador regarding the "high-level operation."

I left her office thinking, "We were really cooking." The SAARC mission tasking was a clear indicator that our capability was actually being recognised at the highest levels *and* that we were trusted to conduct a high profile task. This was mostly thanks to the unwavering support of Brigadier Shafiq and the dedication of Caz and Pete to bring the Pakistani pilots up to the highest of NVG flight capability.

The other significant occurrence that was overtaken by events was the email traffic from a former corporate aviation client in Connecticut. They had offered me a senior executive position on completion of my contract in Pakistan and had invited me to Fisher Island for contract discussions. They offered their private aircraft for my entire family from our local airport to Fisher Island where we would spend two days in the luxurious Argent Centre. I had called Shellie excitedly to let her know. I packed my bags two days prior to my departure in a psychological attempt to make the time come sooner.

It was my first flight home since deploying.

Islamabad Airport was predictably shambolic and remains the only one where I ever saw a live rat in the departure lounge. Keith, the DEA special agent was also outbound to see his family in Miami.

About twenty minutes into the flight, I looked across the aircraft to see that Keith was also wide-awake. He nodded and got up to walk around to my seat and asked, "Do you reckon they'd give us some wine?"

No sooner had we made the suggestion to the cabin-crew than the cork was popped out of the bottle and, for well over an hour, Keith and I stood in the galley and chatted with the Flight Attendants about everything and anything. I think they sensed how grateful we were for female conversation and they "played her crowd." It certainly did no harm that their uniforms were tighter than any womanly apparel we'd seen for months. "This was going to be a great Christmas."

As ever, the line to get though Washington's Dulles immigration was long and slow with at least two officers barking military-style orders and desk numbers to the travel weary passengers coming to the front of the line.

I walked forward and gave the immigration officer my diplomatic passport; he swiped it, looked at me and smiled. "Home for the holidays?" I nodded. He handed me my passport and simply said, "Welcome home and happy holidays."

I walked through the opaque doors into Arrivals and the barriers channelled me to the right for one of the most precious moments I would ever experience in my life.

The two little girls holding a sign saying, "Welcome Home Daddy" were no longer concerned with aesthetics. They had probably seen me a fraction of a second before I saw them and my youngest daughter, Constance, had already ducked under the barrier and was in the equivalent of an Olympic sprint towards me. Her elder sister, Olivia, who was a bit more socially aware, suddenly realised in a moment that etiquette was not on the agenda. She dropped the sign and went in hot pursuit of her sister with the intent of beating her to me.

I released the grip on my bag, dropped to both knees, and opened my arms. I don't recall which daughter reached my arms first, but I do recall the word, "Daddy" being shouted as they sprinted towards me. In an instant, they were both in my arms being kissed and hugged. This moment; these two or three seconds, amount to being part of the most precious seconds of my life.

As I walked to Shellie, she held her ground and elegantly opened her arms. She simply and gently said, "Let's get you home," and we walked to the car with two excited little girls chattering about everything to do with Christmas and not truly realising the life-long value of the moment they had just given their father.

I was home for Christmas having survived the first phase in Pakistan and life was the sweetest flavour.

On Christmas day, amongst the all the joys in our house the bad news from Pakistan was that another attempt had been made on Musharraf's life, the second attempt in eleven days. This time they had not taken a chance with radio control; they had attacked the convoy with suicide vehicles on exactly the same road to Army House. By the action of some incredibly brave men, however, Musharraf survived, although fourteen people died. On hearing the news, I recall thinking, "Someone will hang for this." And in 2005, five men did.

My ten-day leave was from the 20th to the 30th of December and it was a relief not to be in Islamabad during those disruptive events of Christmas. Prior to my return to Pakistan, I was to travel to brief the unit headquarters in Florida. On the 27th, however, it was time for the family to go to Fisher Island in Florida to negotiate my next position as an Executive offered by Argent Funds Group. We were picked up by private jet and flown to Miami.

The next thirty-six hours were spent on Fisher Island in the most idyllic sumptuousness one could ever imagine. My thoughts were repeatedly drawn back to Sergeant Moussa's chai hut and trying to figure out which was reality. Was it the abject austerity of Balochistan or the lavishness of Fisher Island? The extremes of conditions were almost beyond comprehension.

Argent's CEO, Bruce, entertained Shellie and me to dinner and, the following morning, we sat down to discuss my future with his company. It was agreed that I would commence work as Senior Managing Director for Argent Financial Group and McMahan Securities upon completion of my tour in Pakistan. Now all I had to do was survive Pakistan.

In the evening, we were whisked away in a limo to the waiting jet, which was to take a short flight to Melbourne Airport in Florida. I was probably the only State Department Advisor to travel to my meetings in the US in a private business jet. The following morning, Shellie and the girls were bound for the beach. I headed to the base for the extensive back brief.

On arrival at the offices, Paul and Sharon greeted me and I was taken to the briefing room where the operations support staff had already gathered to partake in the coffee and donuts. The audience was given a detailed brief on all aspects of the developments.

I described the hurdles and bumps in the road, created by the departmental verticals and that many of the barriers to progress were not erected by the enemy but, rather, by the compartmentalisation of the departments within the various departments. Each with its own agenda, closely guarded budgets, and staffed by individuals whose career path was dependent on the apparent effectiveness of its own department rather than focus on the joint strategic goal. The room was a free flow of advice and as each specialist made comparisons to overcoming similar problems in Colombia and Peru.

Sharon had also received feedback from Steve Schrage who had returned to Washington touting that the Air Wing was holding down the eastern flank of American interests in Pakistan. Mr. Schrage had championed the programme, considering it to be a real opportunity to disrupt and distract the enemy.

He had enthused that his visit to Pakistan had shown him where taxpayers' money *should* be spent. Air Wing, Pakistan had been given the adrenaline shot in the arm it deserved and Sharon could now work closely with Steve to maintain his attention and momentum.

I could return to Pakistan knowing that the Command and Support of the Air Wing was committed to the provision of additional resources to enable "Sadaqat's Fifty" to bring value to the money that had already been spent and enable them to dislocate the enemies' expectation in the drug and Narco-terror infested border area of Balochistan.

The following morning was New Year's Eve and my family boarded Bruce's jet at Melbourne Airport. We headed home and bid goodbye to 2003, looking forward with much hope and anticipation to challenges that awaited in 2004.

The Christmas break had been as good as could have been for all of my family. My marriage was strong; I had a fantastic job to go to at the end of my duty in Pakistan.

I boarded the British Airways flight to Islamabad and braced myself for what was going to be a gruelling next few months from any perspective.

2004 was an election year for George Bush and this could have far reaching consequence for the latent capability of some fifty brave Pathan Militiamen and the example they would set across the verticals of U.S. governmental departments in Pakistan.

Train to Task

My arrival back in Islamabad coincided with the Bush administration announcing to the world that in the ultimate act of placing personal greed before consideration for humanity, Pakistan's scientist and nuclear pioneer, Dr A.Q. Khan, had sold the country's nuclear weapons technology to Iran, Libya and North Korea.

Another two weeks would pass before President Pervez Musharraf admitted that Pakistani Dr Khan had "probably" sold nuclear weapons designs to other countries for personal profit.

At the time of the initial announcement, I couldn't help but see the accumulating irony of the entire situation that seemed to have been lost on the rest of the world. The US and UK had invaded Iraq based upon the premise that Saddam's regime was developing weapons of mass destruction (WMDs), which, as it was later learned, was not the case. Meanwhile, Pakistan had developed its own WMDs in defiance of the United Nations and the world and was the host to Al-Qaeda's leadership.

Now the Pakistanis had been caught red-handed proliferating nuclear weapons for profit, yet Pakistan could neither be invaded nor sanctioned nor even given priority regarding counter terrorist operations when compared to Iraq. The aces in the pack for Pakistan remained their possession of Osama bin Laden and America's mission creep into Iraq.

Paradoxically bin Laden provided Pakistan with the ultimate bargaining chip, more powerful than the nuclear weapon itself. While he remained at large in their country the U.S. would have to pour money and resources into their nation in a vain attempt to contain Osama's movements and activities. The price tag worked out to be about $14 Billion in funds directly to the Government of Pakistan.

Curtis picked me up at the airport and I was thrown straight back into the fray. The SAARC air patrols had gone like clockwork and the aircraft were being prepared for their return to Quetta.

Curtis sarcastically added the big news in the Embassy was that Ambassador Nancy Powell had given Dorothy yet another award. By now Dorothy's repetitive awards from the Ambassador were drawing more than just passing attention within the confines of the Embassy.

The much more important news, however, was the announcement from Capitol Hill of a "snap" Congressional visit.

The past few months had taught me that, with Congress controlling the purse strings for all global programmes, the competition between the numerous U.S. Embassies for funding allocation was intense and verging on no-holes-barred in order to get attention. These visits provided verbal pitch opportunity for an increased allocation of funds from Capitol Hill and, if a picture paints a thousand words, then an increased allocation of budget was almost entirely dependent on the "spin" that could be achieved during such visits.

While I was in transit back to Islamabad, Paul had emailed to say that Sharon and Steve Schrage had requested a conference call with Dorothy and me.

During the call, Steve informed us that a John Mackey would be the main visiting personality upon whom we should concentrate. John was the Republican Investigative Counsel for the House Foreign Affairs Committee. The man was legend in appropriation of funding to fight crime and illicit narcotics.

He handled oversight inquiries and investigation, as well as issues of international terrorism, narcotics control, and global organised crime. Mackey had, in summary, played a major staff role in sticking it to "Narco-terrorism."

More importantly, from my perspective, he had previously served as a Special Agent in the FBI. Mr. Mackey was a "Sheepherder." This man would understand operational wavelength.

Much to Dorothy's chagrin Steve Schrage insisted to Dorothy that I be included in the briefing with Mr. Mackey. He made it quite clear that, if I wanted more equipment, then this was going to be our best and, very likely, our one and *only* shot.

The following day I sat in on the brief with John Mackey and my initial impression was that Mr. Mackey's aim was to intimidate everyone, he was tall and lithe, about sixty years of age and had a gruff but broad American accent. He was aggressive in manner, did not smile or suffer fools gladly. His body language pushed his presence across the table, however his tone softened markedly when he spoke to those he recognised as former cops.

Dorothy provided a brief on NAS activities, which informed me just how much she hadn't told me of what was going on elsewhere in the department. John Mackey gave her a rough ride over several issues much to the amusement of the former cops in the room. I wasn't sure if he was playing the crowd or whether she simply irritated the shit out of him. I suspected a little of both.

During the meeting, I elected to say very little except to emphasise the allocation of the militia and that the commencement of their training was just three days away. I didn't feel inclined to say much more.

Unbeknown to many in the room, I'd been invited along with the former cops to meet Mr. Mackey in the bar after the official briefing specifically to discuss our aircraft and their optimum use. It was this chat over a beer with John that really brought clarity to the entire situation.

He was keen to see the aircraft handed over to the DEA and wanted me to go with them. I countered by saying that it was more important to maintain the current momentum and to develop capability rather than confuse and decelerate progress at that critical stage of development.

Furthermore, given that the DEA was linked to the Pak's Anti-Narcotic Force (ANF), which was controlled by the MOI, there should be horizontal tasking across the board. This was exactly why the Paks earning operational control was not such a bad thing. We (NAS) had the Frontier Corps under our wing and the DEA and the Brits had the ANF under theirs. It should be a slam-dunk to achieve effective operational tasking.

John listened intently so, while I had his attention, I took Steve Schrage's advice and made the pitch for more assets (funding). I explained we were bringing fifty-specialist militia online and a single lift capability required six serviceable Hueys. I also needed the option of an additional Huey equipped as a gunship. We were averaging sixty percent serviceability, which meant I currently needed ten helicopters to achieve six on hand for a fifty-troop launch. Anything less meant either a reduction in range (less fuel so that we could increase payload) or half my force would be exposed to tremendous risk since their strength would be significantly reduced during any "shuttle" phase as a consequence of too few helicopters. If we were to be attacked at the wrong time in the shuttle process we'd be fucked. At a minimum, I needed three more Hueys immediately.

John Mackey got it completely and, with Keith from DEA there to agree, I think he felt reassured. During the discussion an assistant repeatedly reminded him that he was late for a dinner at the Ambassador's residence, to which he eventually snapped, "Dinner can wait! I need to talk to these men!"

It was obvious he knew he was getting situational truth from the men who were present. Not least of all because, at that moment, with beer in hand, he wasn't just one of the most influential men on Capitol Hill, he was a Sheepherder amongst Sheepherders.

That evening, I called Paul and Sharon to update them on events and reported that John Mackey's visit had gone well. It was now up to me to bring the capability to a point where we could demonstrate the need for the extra helicopters. That physical process would start just thirty-six hours later in Quetta, Balochistan.

As I exited the Huey at Quetta's Belili Military Camp, Major Wajid and Captain Pervaiz greeted me. They must have reflected that my appearance was radically different than during my last visit.

My combat jacket and trousers were worn as I would have worn them when in the military and it would have been obvious to the astute soldier that the pockets on the jacket were now fully utilised.

Around my waist was my belt order which contained my knife, water, a holstered 9mm Beretta pistol, a GPS, a first aid package, signal flares and glow-sticks, and a couple of snack bars. In my right hand, I carried an M16 - 9mm SWAT machine gun. If it looked like I meant business, that was precisely how I wanted to appear.

We walked across the parade ground to where the twenty-five armed militiamen were gathered. By any measure, they were an intimidating group of armed Pathans. As we came within thirty metres, I could feel my pulse increasing from nervousness, but I could not let it show. I understood that if first impressions were important, then that moment was here to grasp.

"*Asalamaleikam.*" I smiled and scanned the rugged looking audience that sat in front of me. I hoped these men were as hard as they looked; some of them looked more like the Taliban than the Taliban itself. They quickly responded "*Wah Aleekham salaam.*" Major Wajid would now interpret my words into Pashtu but I knew I had to get the tone and content right on the mark.

"My name is Mr. Howard and I am a former British special forces officer."

I would try to keep each sentence short and sharp so that Wajid could convey its full meaning. They were locked on to me. I had their complete attention.

"I am in Pakistan to develop a programme that is funded by the American government." I didn't know what they would think of that but I had to be sure they knew who was paying for all of this.

"Over the next few weeks, you will be introduced to the equipment that has been provided."

I looked over my shoulder to the Huey that had shut down on the Helipad.

"And you will have the opportunity to be the finest soldiers in its use."

It was time to raise their expectations of themselves. I continued.

"The reason that I stand before you and I am not speaking to any other soldiers is because you have earned the right to be trained and to operate this very expensive equipment. As RIF, you are considered the finest soldiers in the Frontier Corps."

I paused for Wajid. "It is now my task and privilege to provide you and one other platoon with the opportunity to become the most elite and highly trained soldiers within the RIF. The elite of the elite."

There were twenty-five pairs of dark brown eyes locked on me.

"Over the next few weeks, we are going to work together. I will train you to become the Helicopter Assault Force of the RIF. You will become known as the HAF and, if you are successful in this training, you will be awarded Assault Force Wings."

I recollected to myself that Napoleon had said a soldier would march 1,000 miles to gain a piece of ribbon for his uniform.

"Your training will start off with simple matters and gradually become more complicated. You will be asked to do many things you haven't done before and there will be times when you will have doubts about yourself and your abilities." I smiled. "Don't worry because, when you do something new, you won't always get it right first time. We will practise and practise until the entire platoon does get it right." But they needed to know it would be a test.

"It is my hope that, by the end of your training, all of you will be HAF. But understand, too, that perhaps some of you may not be right for this job and, should any of you fail this training, you should not take it personally."

Of course, I knew they would. "But accept at the outset that there are some things in life you are meant to do and some things you are not meant to do. Those who do pass the training must know that each man to their left and their right is as proficient as he is..." I paused. "Because your life will depend on it. I can promise you that you will use whatever you in learn here in combat - and we *will* go into combat. That is a certainty."

I needed to emphasise that statement. I wanted them to know it was a given.

"During the early days of training, you will perhaps be asked to do some things that make no sense to you and you will think, why is Mr. Howard teaching me this, is he crazy?" I heard Wajid punctuate the Pashtu with my name and then some of them smiled.

"I will need you to trust me because, although the reason might not be apparent to you when you conduct the task, it will ultimately become very obvious and you will suddenly know when that happens."

Another pause for Wajid, "And I can only promise you two things right now."

They looked as if they were willing the words out of me.

"I will never ask you to do anything that I wouldn't do myself."

Which they may have already assimilated; my very presence in Quetta was no great assurance to a hazard free existence.

"And no matter what happens, for as long as we are working together, if you are alive you will never be left behind on the battlefield."

I paused then reiterated, "Even if it leads to my own death I promise you those two things." I absolutely meant it, and they could see that was the case, but now it was time for me to close.

If the golden rule of speeches is that a man should never speak for longer than he can make love, then I knew my speeches had to get shorter with age, but I knew these tribesmen related teaching in stories so I felt compelled to use that cultural tool.

"I want you to know it is a privilege for me to be asked by General Sadaqat to train you."

I needed to reinforce that their commander and paymaster had sent me.

"And I want to tell you a story about something that happened about eighty-seven years ago."

They continued to listen under the deep blue sky that was their classroom's ceiling.

"There was a town on the coast of Arabia. Behind that town was a desert that had never been crossed by anyone. So no guns in the town pointed towards the desert. The guns all pointed towards the sea because that was the only direction from which an enemy could ever attack. But there was one English officer and fifty brave Muslims who believed that they could cross this impossible and undefeated desert. Everybody thought they were crazy but these fifty-one men rode through the desert against the sun, sand and heat for three long weeks. They then attacked the town from behind and, not only defeated the town, but then caused an entire army to fall."

I knew I was being simplistic but the message was hopefully clear.

"The town was Aqabar in the country of Jordan; the Englishman was called Lawrence".

I doubted they'd ever heard of Lawrence, but continued. "Now I don't know if we can ever achieve what Lawrence and the Fifty achieved, but I do know that we now have an opportunity to try. And that's exactly what we are going to do."

I had them nodding in agreement.

"So let's start the training and find our own *Aqabar*!"

As they gathered into a school circle for their very first lesson, Wajid looked at me and said, "They clung to every single word." I smiled and knew we were off to a good start.

The next two days I was true to my word in regard to starting with basics. I showed them how to standardise their kit so that each man's equipment was packed in a similar way.

I ensured there was a thorough understanding of layering equipment and concentrated on attention to detail in regard to the exclusiveness of ammunition pouches and the need for the equipment to be snug and to not to rattle during movement. I taught them techniques for using bungee cords to achieve this.

We went through basic first aid and ensured the only item in any man's top left hand pocket was his first field dressing. If a man was bleeding like a stuck pig you didn't need to be looking for something to jam on the wound, so this is where any man would search to start the process of "plugging him up."

We covered the fundamentals of how to eat an MRE. These troopers had never seen one before and we reviewed the importance of weapon cleaning and of dry working parts in the desert.

During these first few sessions, I could tell that these men were like sponges. They wanted to learn and I was acutely aware I had to use a building block method to get them to where they needed to be. I kept the teaching environment casual but informative, I wanted them to be relaxed and ask questions.

With Captain Pervaiz now translating, each day's event would become more complex for them as they assimilated new skills and became acclimatised to new standards and tasks. The steepness of the learning curve would remain constant.

From my perspective, they had developed no bad habits or ideas because only one of them had even flown before, so they would naturally perform as trained. Additionally, it became rapidly apparent that, not only were these men were as hard as fucking nails, they were also very bright. By the end of just the second day, we had achieved the briefings on the danger areas of the helicopter and had mastered the tactical and non-tactical procedures for mount and dismount.

In the evening, Suzanne called from the Embassy to let me know that she needed to prepare the Measure of Performance (MOP) since they were going to advocate for an increase to ten helicopters for Quetta. I reflected that the Mackey visit had really energised focus and I knew that Steve Schrage and Sharon were largely responsible for the sequence of events.

Suzanne also reminded me that Dorothy and the Ambassador were due to arrive in Quetta the next day. "Shit," I hadn't even thought of it until Colonel GS called inviting me to a highly publicised drug burning ceremony that was to take place at Belili, which was to demonstrate the effectiveness of Balochistan's drug capture programme. I reflected that the compound and the aircraft ramp would be a hive of activity. With the increased security, my armed and brutal looking militia might make the bullet catchers (bodyguards) a little nervous, so I reluctantly cancelled the training for two days.

I asked Caz if he fancied taking a Huey up to the ceremony and snagging a free lunch, because we wouldn't be able to go by road. He jumped at the opportunity and our own VIP transport was in the bag.

The positive aspect of Ambassador Nancy Powell's visit to Quetta was that every man and his dog from various agencies were there, and the opportunity to network across national and international departmental verticals was just too good a one on which to pass. One such opportunity that arose was with Robert's team and, after a good conversation regarding better integration to combine efforts against the narcotic convoys, the Ambassador's visit also gave me the first-time opportunity to talk to Dorothy outside of the formality of her office and we had fairly in depth discussion. She was concerned that rapid tactical development could detract from the political agenda. Whereas I debated it a simple extension of politics by another means and it was better to have such a unit in the political arsenal for use, or not, as the powers see fit.

I quoted Winston Churchill, "If you want peace, prepare for war." She listened carefully and nodded, probably never having considered this perspective; perhaps I was winning her over.

Dorothy and the Ambassador stayed in the luxurious Serena Hotel that evening, which was permanently out of bounds to our team.

The following day, I arrived at Belili by helicopter with my insurance policy discreetly tucked under my shirt. I reflected that the event would be a high profile target for the bad guys despite the considerable security. Not only were the authorities about to burn tens of thousands of dollars worth of drugs and moonshine, they were also about to veritably gloat over the matter.

I purposely loitered towards the back of the viewing area. As I did, Major Javed came scurrying over to enthusiastically inform me that General Sadaqat had arranged for my seat to be directly behind the main VIPs. I knew the General meant well by this gesture but it was all I needed.

I explained to Javed that I really did not wish to sit there, but he absolutely insisted on it. He also added that he had put me next to a "very beautiful woman" who turned out to be the very talkative Colonel Cheryl of U.S. Army Intelligence. She was petite and certainly not unattractive but she was a married woman, and a Colonel which, if not for the unusual but welcome smell of Chanel No5, should have been more than enough deterrent for the flow of natural desires (even in Quetta).

She was asked who was who and openly snapped away with her camera. My seat was right behind the VIPs, so I'd put on my sunglasses and baseball cap and offered Cheryl my seat to give her a slightly better view.

Thankfully, she took it before interrogating me about my activities. She was clearly an overt intelligence gatherer and, quite unashamed of the fact, she asked to meet with me for a brief on my return to Islamabad. I explained that it would probably be three weeks before I saw Slammy again, which seemed to impress her.

We watched the lighting ceremony and, as the huge pile of drugs went up in smoke, I sat there hoping to be down wind to get a gratuitous whiff!

That evening, I returned to the safe house on their invitation to meet with the Brigadier T who ran the Anti Narcotics Force in Quetta. This powerfully built officer had been a classmate of Sadaqat and I knew they were social and hunting friends. However, there was clearly an intense professional rivalry between them they were both always careful not to be

ASK FORGIVENESS

drawn into conversation about each other; I sensed they had mutual code of loyalty.

The Brigadier was former SSG and a soldier's soldier. He was clearly a tough and operationally focused individual who was wholly concerned with achieving drugs interdiction, provided it didn't interfere with his daily game of polo. He had a personality that was affable but one suspected that he could be abrasive just for the sake of being so and, perhaps, this was why he was operationally effective but under-promoted. He was living proof that, in modern (or modernising) armies, brigadiers and colonels are not promoted to the rank of General if they cannot be relied upon to be diplomatically inclined even when they have the urge not to be.

The Brigadier was focused on the use of our Cessnas' to support his own operations and I assured him I would work closely with Robert and pull the strings that I could to ensure he got use of the aircraft; I also offered to train the ANF troop drills with the Hueys. We were expanding his and our reach,

The following day all the VIPs were long gone so the RIF took their first flight in a helicopter. This was cause for considerable excitement and it noticeably gave the aircrew significant satisfaction. The gulf between officers and their men in Pakistan is outrageous by western standards. The additional chasm between Army and Militia is another giant leap. So it would take time but it was a mould I had to break.

The day's events finished with more first aid training and topped off by a call from Dorothy to say that she was going to try for twenty helicopters. She was now on a roll! I could hardly believe my ears and could only think of the memorandum she had written a few short months prior proposing to close down the programme. The tactical enablement now seemed to be driving the political initiative. That evening, I climbed into my sleeping bag with my machine gun feeling very content about the events of the past seventy-two hours.

The next few days were spent getting the RIF used to flying in the rear of the Hueys and all the procedures that go along with refining efficiencies. In the sands of Balochistan, no sooner did the Huey come into ground-effect, than fine, brown dust would envelope the entire aircraft causing brownout.

For the pilot, this effect served to completely fuck up all the visual references and was, therefore, extremely hazardous. The only two options the pilot had during brownout was to maintain a gentle descent until the skids kissed the ground or to pull power to get away from the dust and ground. The latter was useless in regard to getting his troops on the ground. We had to ensure achievement of the former every time and at night too.

Once on the ground, the troops must clear out of the helicopter at break neck speed to reduce its period as a "sitting duck" to the minimum. Our aim was a 4.5 second touchdown to take off.

Any lack of coordination would at best result in broken bones or at worst death. Our first few drop-offs and pick-ups would have no time constraints but we would gradually pick up the pace to achieve the target time-lines by day and by night with multiple aircraft.

Following the initial training flights, the troop seats were removed from the Hueys and would never be replaced. Each aircraft would carry between six and eight fully laden troops and seats were more hindrance than help. We installed lap-straps on the floor through which each trooper could put one limb to try to ensure he didn't fall out of the aircraft during flight. We would also typically shut the doors of the aircraft until we were two minutes out from the drop off point to prevent any of the men from inadvertently leaving the Huey while still in flight.

As the efficiencies increased, the confidence of the men also grew. Their absorbance never ceased to amaze me. With each evolution conquered, another was immediately introduced and mastered. We commenced day patrolling in the Pishin, north of Quetta.

This area is a brutal but stunning geographical feature. It was effectively a massive, flat-bottomed bowl with undulating dried up riverbeds and hills. On one side, it was fringed by breathtaking 12,000-foot mountains and, on another, a puzzle-pattern of small hills that were almost impossible to penetrate and cross. This terrain was not dissimilar to the Badlands of South Dakota. The remaining two sides were bordered by 300 foot sand cliffs; these were passable by means of climbing steep goat paths.

Although only Bedouin inhabited Pishin and we were effectively on exercise, I was only too aware that we were in broad daylight just a few miles from the Afghan border. The surrounding area was considered as "unfriendly" so there was no such luxury as an "exercise" in Balochistan.

All of our practice patrols were armed, carried full ammunition scales, and were conducted with weapons loaded.

Thankfully the area was devoid of population in those early days and, because our patrol routes were never disclosed prior to an event, I was fairly confident our operational security would not be compromised.

During these initial days on patrol we couldn't afford to run into an ambush. We simply weren't coordinated enough and we would get torn to shreds if a competent Taliban or Al-Qaeda team attacked us. I knew it was vital to work fast in order to ensure the patrol methods and techniques were quickly honed.

For some reason the RIF were weak in their patrolling discipline, so I asked Jim to assist me. His experience as a US Army Ranger was invaluable to ensure the Pathans concentrated when I wasn't in line of sight and he would watch my back during the early days when these guys were an unknown quantity in the trust department. After all, with their loaded Kalashnikovs it would only take one minor Jihad incident to ruin my whole day.

The anti-ambush drills were practised over and over again with Captain Pervaiz being given the options of holding ground and flank or breaking contact and flank.

It was vital for this small force that no elements of it became isolated. With just twenty-five men, standing ground and slugging it out against any kind of ambush by the Mujahedeen trained locals, would be undiluted madness.

Suppressive fire techniques using the light machine gun would either form interlocking fire towards an advancing force or keep the heads of any enemy down (or off) if we identified their firing location.

It was up to each man of the section closest to the danger to help put the gunner onto the target. None of the other sections would move to break contact until fire was being laid down.

Terrain and position of threat were never constants, so I walked the men through the drills before gradually speeding up the command and response. Once they had mastered patrolling, ambush and anti-ambush drills during the day, I would have to make them do it all again with similar proficiency at night.

The silence in the area was eerily intimidating, no cars, no human noise except when we would come in ear range of the Bedouin. Apart from these transient people, we could be sure that anyone we bumped into on the rapidly undulating plain of Pishin had no reason for being there except to harm us. It was the perfect "real" training ground but it would also be the perfect killing ground for the enemy.

These first two weeks had been intense for the RIF and they had worked their arses off. Each day concluded returning to Quetta tired, soaked in sweat and covered in dust. Every evening was spent preparing for the day ahead and cleaning weapons and equipment. I hoped the men were sleeping as well as I was. I tried to break up the substantial physical strain on our bodies by everyday introducing something to do with field-craft, first aid, or just advice.

These men who had been suspicious strangers just two weeks earlier were now warm to my presence. I recalled reading of Lawrence that, during his time with the Arabs, he psychologically adopted the rank of whomever he was sitting with or talking to.

Although I think my Pathans had initially been confused by the fact that I would use equal politeness and respect whether I was addressing a colonel or a trooper, they had by now began to accept that style. I didn't have to pretend that I respected them; I really did.

I never subjected them to any unnecessary physical training or military style bullshit. So far as I was concerned, they were specialist troops and I would treat them as such. I had learned long ago that if you treat a soldier like a man you have the best hope of him acting like a one. These soldiers were far from teenagers or boys and, by the age of twenty-five or thirty, with the life expectancy of the average Pakistani male being just sixty-three years, most of these guys were already at or past the halfway point in their lives.

Such had been their progress that the time had come to now subject them to real snap vehicle checkpoints. With that mastered, we would then switch to fine tuning and perfecting the night-time manoeuvres.

The use of "soft stop" vehicle checkpoints (VCP) was merely to dislocate the enemy. The term "soft" referred to the intent of bringing the vehicle to a stop without force, i.e. a patrol simply forming a very temporary road checkpoint. A "hard" stop, on the other hand, was when a vehicle must be stopped at all cost and would, if necessary, be brought to a halt by an aggressive ambush.

It was explained to the Pathan troopers that the likelihood of finding anything illegal was remote but the fact that this highly professional force was suddenly popping up, seemingly out of nowhere, would undoubtedly reach the ears of the Taliban and the Narco transporters. They would then be forced to adjust their modus operandi if they wished to reduce their chances of running their valuable cargo into this well-trained force.

It was the art of having the enemy worry about us even when we weren't there. The tactics employed were straight out of conventional operations in Northern Ireland (and the ancient Chinese strategist, Sun-Tzu).

We would drop off well away from the point on the road where we intended to establish the checkpoint. The actual point would be selected where there were no junctions or obvious slip routes for a vehicle to evade the stop. The other crucial elements were the cut-off sections.

They would be secreted about fifty metres on either side of the check point group so that, by the time the driver saw troops on the road indicating for him to stop, he would already be trapped by the cut-off group he had already inadvertently passed. If he chose not to stop for the main group, then the cut-off at the far end of the checkpoint would have pulled the tire shredders across the road. In either scenario, he wouldn't be going very far. If there was any sign of armed aggression from the vehicle, then it would be engaged with gunfire. In all cases, the advantage would be ours.

I explained to the RIF that the psychology of operations was as important as the tactics themselves. I also imparted that courtesy and kindness was crucial to those who meant no harm. The idea was to be nicer to the general public than the bad guys but totally severe to those who meant us harm.

Shortly before day break the drop off went perfectly. The four Hueys were not on the ground more than a few seconds, although it wasn't as short as I would have liked it. The swirling dust took our visibility to nil as they headed back to Belili, which was just a few minutes flight time away. The pilots and aircraft would stay there at "Alert 5," meaning at five minutes' notice, until the Caravan, which was also our communications relay, called them forward to the pick-up grid of our choice.

The Caravan was at 10,000 feet where Matt, who by now had become our volunteer expert and instructor on FLIR, would pick out 4x4s and radio their position using a moving spot code we had transposed on to the route.

We patrolled in through concealed gullies in VCP order. This deliberate formation meant that when we came along-side the road we would be in precisely the formation needed to deploy a 100-metre trap.

The entire concept was about linear depth. The patrol worked uphill keeping to the dead ground until we could see and hear the vehicle movement on the road. Once we had the road in sight, we held firm for a few minutes just to ensure the activity on the road looked normal and to ensure there were no pedestrians to notice our approach.

All the men were acutely aware that a tip off to the wrong people in this area could bring the wrath of the Taliban or something worse on us. Every hut along this smuggling route might not have running water but the chances were it did have an AK-47.

We drew alongside the road and were now in dead ground with traffic passing just a few feet above us. The "exit" cut-off team stopped where directed and readied the tire shredders. Each section also deployed one man as a rearguard sentry. The rest of the team worked along the gulley, hugging close to bank, to maintain our discreet presence. The Caravan's crew were viewing us through the powerful camera in the belly of their aircraft and told us we were "Looking good." I recall looking up the steep bank and thinking, "Oh really? You should see it from here."

The "entry" cut-off, Light-Machine-Gunner edged his way up the steep bank to site his weapon, his Number Two, with the bulk of his ammo, was alongside him like a Siamese twin. I glanced behind me to the other cut-off. I couldn't see the gunner so assumed he was already lying behind his gun having joined another fifty rounds to the link of thirty held under its top cover.

Both cut-off section commanders gave the thumbs up and I looked at Pervaiz and whispered, "You ready?" He nodded. I pressed the transmit button on my VHF radio and told the Caravan, "Falcon One is open for business," to which Pete replied "Roger that, looking". Now we waited.

Long minutes went by and I was starting to wonder if all the 4x4s had gone to a four-wheeling convention elsewhere when Matt's voice came up. "We have a white, will you accept?" He was saying he had a yellow 4x4 or truck heading towards our position.

I replied, "Affirmative."

"Roger that Yellow One is outside Blue Three." We had allocated a position three kilometres out as Blue Three.

"Yellow One is approaching Blue Three." Matt paused. "Yellow One is at Blue Three towards Blue Two." "Approaching Blue Two." One in three guys in the Platoon had radios. As the calls came in, they would relay the information to those troopers who were without communications.

These men couldn't speak English two weeks ago but now they understood all the necessary hand signals and the codes and key words spoken in English. I smiled to myself as I watched them ready themselves to make their move. I could feel their excitement.

"Yellow One is at Blue Two towards Blue One" meaning the driver of the 4x4 was two kilometres out and had no idea that his every move was now under intense scrutiny and had the undivided attention of thirty soldiers (a team of twenty six on the ground and four flying above in the Caravan). The stop team pulled their maroon berets from their pockets and put them on. They needed to be recognised as legitimate soldiers once they got on the road.

"Approaching Blue One." I saw the main stop group becoming the human equivalent of a coiled cobra and reflected that I would probably shit myself if I was confronted with a VCP of guys that looked like this.

"Yellow One is at Blue One towards the Table." This was all the information the team needed to know. The stop team went up the bank like it didn't exist and stood on the side of the road. To an onlooker, it appeared there were just four soldiers.

"Yellow One is halfway to table."

He was 500 metres out and we would see him as he rounded the bend about 100 metres short of the stop group.

"Approaching Table"

I replied "Roger." as I saw the team move out onto the road when the 4x4 rounded the bend. The driver could now see a soldier on the road in front of him holding up his hand with another soldier, with his weapon ready, but not pointing at the vehicle. The driver would also see another two soldiers kneeling down at the side of the road with weapons ready.

As he passed the entry cut off, four soldiers moved out onto the road If the driver looked in his rear-view mirror with any idea of turning the vehicle around, that thought would have quickly disappeared. Some fifty yards further down the road he could now see another four soldiers moving onto the road. All were heavily armed, all were wearing U.S. style combat clothing, and all wore maroon berets and the insignia of the Frontier Corps.

Whatever he had just driven into, there was clearly no way out. Word of this would doubtless spread.

The vehicle was totally surrounded in depth. The Senior NCO informed the driver that they were Frontier Corps and conducting routine searches of vehicles. He then asked if the driver would mind if he searched the vehicle. The Driver, who must have felt helpless but was by now psychologically reassured that he wasn't going to be shot, gave his permission. In reality, he knew he had no choice.

He was asked to switch off the engine, which would ensure he was going nowhere and that the vehicle wasn't hot-wired (aka stolen). He was asked to open the bonnet and the back door. There were two other male passengers in the car. They were asked to get out and had their IDs checked while the search went ahead. I remained in the gulley and took photographs of the event as it unfolded.

If there was a shortfall with the team that day, it was that they didn't direct the other traffic effectively. This was partially my fault because I had assumed common sense. However, I had forgotten that it was anything *but* common in this autocratic system.

As predicted, nothing was found in the vehicle, but that was not important. I was certain that the message would get through to the Taliban. If you were driving a 4x4 in Balochistan the chances were you didn't win it in a Toyota lottery.

The men in the vehicle were permitted to proceed. The troopers retired back into the gulley and the team in the Caravan, who had been recording everything, asked if we wanted more business. I told them we did and we repeated the process with a covered pickup truck, which went flawlessly, including the direction of the other traffic. It was then time to get the hell out of there.

I picked the next valley from our position and gave the coordinates to Pete, which I heard him relay to Caz. He then reported back and told me "Figures ten"; we had ten minutes to get to the pick up point for a tactical extraction.

We moved at pace and were in position by the time the four Hueys came up the valley in a rapid deceleration towards the smoke grenade that was pouring red smoke and giving Caz the best of wind indication.

On the way back to Belili, Pete swooped the Caravan down and slowed to the same speed as the Hueys to join the tactical formation. This wasn't exactly planned but it was as much fun for me as it was for the RIF. I mused that the Pathans must think this must be "normal flying."

Overall, the team had done fantastically; not only did they absorb the tactics, they also understood the doctrine. The pilots had likewise done a great job and they knew it. For the first time, I could feel that all participants shared a sense of achievement and knew we had worked well as a team.

What was most important about this day, however, was that word would now spread in Balochistan about this new force. We had successfully conducted our first fully integrated operation. If I could have gotten hold of a beer in Quetta, I'd have drunk one.

The following day brought a "Dances With Wolves" moment. During the afternoon, I had briefed the men on how NVG and FLIR worked and explained the differences in their technical tactical use. NVG enhanced what little light there was at night by using it to stimulate electron plates. FLIR simply used technology to turn heat to light for the viewer and, because everything had a heat signature, it created a picture.

We had not yet received the NVGs for the RIF, so we used a spare set of goggles acquired as back up for the pilots.

After dark, we went out to the airfield and allowed each trooper in turn to wear the NVG's and look through the FLIR. The only comparison to their reaction is the scene from the Dances with Wolves movie where the American Indians look through a telescope for the first time.

The response of the Pathans was one of complete disbelief, just like the Red Indians, as they looked through the device then literally jumped back in total astonishment and laughter, going through process again and again until the fascination overcame something in their minds that they never thought possible. They could actually see in the dark. Little did they realise that this ability was about to become their world.

CHAPTER 8

A Pig and a Poke

Following a day's well-earned rest, Jim and I had gone ahead on the first flight to Pishin to set up the shooting ranges. We discussed that this could be high risk because it was the first time we had seen these troops discharge their weapons. In the unlikely event that one of them had a "Jihad moment," they would be able to turn their gun on us in the blink of an eye.

I told Jim that, if he wasn't carrying his M16 SWAT, to make damn sure he had his Berretta pistol unencumbered. I reflected that, although I trusted these guys not to shoot me, the only person you can really trust is your mother, and even she'll let you down every now and again.

As the day progressed, five rounds at a time, each trooper saw his group get tighter and closer to the point of aim. Jim and I could witness the growing satisfaction and confidence in the men. They'd suddenly realised the importance of being zeroed and in their technique.

We could coach most of the wayward few by watching them shoot and either Jim or I would see where they were going wrong: snatching the trigger, wrong positioning, wrong sight picture.

I had to push the troopers through the Close Quarter Battle (CQB) lane where we had erected five concealed targets in a dried up streambed.

As I followed each man down the gulley, I had my right hand on my holstered pistol. If any man turned towards me with his weapon, I would have to react in the worst way. We had placed some of the targets out of the thirty-degree arc of natural view, so the exercise required significant concentration on the part of each trooper.

The highest scorer would be at the front of the dinner queue that evening.

The following day, I flew up to Belili to chat to Pervaiz. He was of slight build but had grown a thick black moustache in a feign attempt to conceal his youth; his English was fluent but his accent strong from Pashtu. I needed to have what seemed to him a casual chat to him about leadership and explained that, if he looked after his men, there was a strong chance that, when he needed them most, they would look after him.

He listened intently as I told him an officer should invest as much in his men as he can, even when he doesn't have to. For when the time came for payback, that man's loyalty and its extent could mean the difference between his life and death. I encouraged him to constantly ensure that his men were not hungry, thirsty, or exhausted except when he was equally so. I told him never to eat or sleep before his men and always ensure that they know that their welfare comes first.

I reflected that culturally he came from a society with a veritable gulf between the wealthy elites and the normal citizen. As an officer, he was considered the former, so his men never questioned him. There was absolutely no insubordination penetrating the class system, either in or out of the military.

Pervaiz was a quiet but determined man. That he had been the only officer to survive the initial RIF training spoke for his stamina, even though he smoked like the proverbial chimney. I reflected that dichotomy must be a privilege of youth. However, as he puffed away that day, he clearly got the message and he admitted that he wanted to set himself apart from his peers, if I could show him how.

We finished some small talk and meandered across the parade ground towards the Colonel's office. Tea was served and the Colonel said he wanted to make sure matters were organised for the General's pending visit to the RIF. The visit was a couple of days away, so I hadn't yet put my mind to the preparation, but I was glad Sadaqat was itching to see how we were progressing. The Colonel then confided that the General had made his enthusiasm known regarding a Memorandum I had sent him just two days previously. It read:

> *Dear General,*
>
> *I'm immensely pleased to report that phase-one training has gone exceptionally well. Although I approached this programme with great optimism, this was tempered with realism of what I might, or might not, achieve with these troops. It is to their very great credit that they have surpassed all expectation.*
>
> *They have worked exceptionally hard during the training period and endured long, dirty days in extremes of temperatures. At no time during the training did they complain or let conditions affect their performance. Their retention of intricate (and some-times) unconventional tactics has been outstanding. The selection process for RIF must, therefore, be deemed to be effective in its recruitment and basic training. During phase-one HAF training, besides developing the platoon's helicopter assault skills, I have gone to great efforts to instil the use of common sense in given*

situations, and am confident that their reaction and "situational awareness" will result in taking control of most given situations. They are without doubt ready to move on to more complex training and tactical use of technical equipment (NVG) whilst increasing deployed sustainment and soldiering confidence beyond exercise areas.

Throughout the training, I have applied the doctrine of specialist operations with these troops and view the tactics of "Lawrence" to be highly applicable to RIF. I believe our tactics should be <u>tip and run: not pushes, but strokes. We should use the smallest force in the quickest time at the farthest place</u> to undermine and confuse our adversaries. Furthermore, you will note the equipment list attached to the Phase-Two programme. I view as top priority that these soldiers be suitably equipped and, again, come back to paraphrase Lawrence: <u>The equipment of the raiding parties should aim at simplicity; with nevertheless, a technical superiority over the (adversary) in the critical departments</u>". (In our case, night vision, stealth, over the horizon capability, and deployable sustainment)

I look forward to your review of 1 Platoon, RIF this coming Thursday and to discussing the ways in which we can forge ahead. I believe your vision in creating the RIF has formed the foundation of building a formidable specialist force within the FC. I am immensely honoured that you have permitted me to take part in assisting with the development of this initiative.

Yours Aye

Howard

I made a point of using English and not American spelling in all correspondence with Pakistanis.

On the morning of 28th January 2004, the deserts of Balochistan were soaked by torrential rain. This served to turn the entire desert into three-inch deep mud, so training was confined to the classroom for camouflage and concealment techniques and covert observation post drills.

Towards the end of the day, I opened up the floor to "any questions on anything." The Pathans responded with a plethora of queries regarding the USA, including, "Is it true that there are posters in the U.S. with big targets painted on Pakistan?" and "Does Israel control the USA?"

Their final question was regarding the capture of bin Laden. I was asked if it was true that the USA had offered fifty million dollars for the capture of the leader of Al-Qaeda? I responded that it was indeed true.

One of the Pathans then explained that this proved that the Americans were liars since there was not fifty million dollars in the entire world. It suddenly dawned on me that, in the world that these men knew, such a dollar figure was completely unbelievable and beyond their comprehension. They had worked out that such amount represented 3,250,000,000 Rupees (3.25 Billion). Given that their monthly wage was only a paltry seventy dollars for risking life and limb, it seemed inconceivable that there could be *that* much money in the world.

To this impoverished culture, this amount simply could not be real and, as such, represented another lie perpetrated by the West. The U.S. had inadvertently demonstrated a gross misunderstanding of those people who could actually deliver bin Laden. I reflected that if the bounty were fifty *thousand* instead of fifty *million*, then perhaps the man would have been betrayed by now.

Later that day I jumped in one of the crappy Corollas with Moussa and we drove through a very mud-soaked Quetta to see the General who was energetic and enthused about the progress with the RIF and told me there was a real job brewing. He asked if they were ready.

I explained it would depend completely on the type of job but, regardless, we would need to rehearse the operation in some depth to ensure that they were prepared. The General confided that it would be a kill or capture operation and I told him that wouldn't be a problem provided the opposition's defences weren't significant and that the enemy would be totally surprised.

I reminded him that, if the RIF were to be used in direct action, they were a raiding force and dictated by their numbers. Furthermore, in the words of Sun-Tzu, *"A small force that obstinately fights will be inevitably captured by a larger force."* So we should never obstinately fight. The chances were we would be outgunned in anything we encountered, so en-route to our target, stealth was everything and speed was nothing; on the way out the opposite would apply.

The flight back to Islamabad in the Caravan was notable because it was entirely in cloud. The aircraft was mercilessly tossed around and I was always concerned about the mountains. We sure as hell didn't want to be in a cloud with a rock solid centre.

The main priority, however, was to chase Saadi for an update on the Phase 2 equipment, gear that would permit the RIF to fight at night. I then went to the Embassy to cash a sizeable cheque for some serious weekend shopping.

Robert from the British Embassy had invited me on a trip to Lahore. He offered the opportunity to go wild boar hunting, so what could I say? I enjoyed a couple of beers with Jerry on

Friday evening and got up early for the four or five hour drive down the M2 Motorway that links Islamabad to Lahore.

The police who patrol it were apparently trained by British Traffic Police and proudly maintain their standards. If you speed you *will* get a ticket, it is as simple as that. Neither rank nor bribery will get you out of it. The M2 is jokingly said to be the only place where the law exists as it is intended in the entire nation of Pakistan.

About ninety miles south of Islamabad the M2 drops off the plateau at the Khewa Salt Range and the traveller experiences crossing the highest pillared bridge in Asia. This might explain why the road is one of the most expensive ever built and in many sections straight, smooth, and wide because it is designed to permit Pakistan Air Force fighter jets to use it as a runway in the event of a conflict with India.

As we entered Lahore, the sights and smells overwhelmed me. We had arrived just two days before Eid Al-Adha, which commemorates the willingness of Abraham to sacrifice his son as an act of obedience to God.

In memory of this event, each family in Islam that can afford an animal is obliged to sacrifice a sheep, goat, cow, or camel, by slitting its throat and bleeding it to create Halal meat. The meat is then divided into three equal parts to be distributed to others. The family eats one third and another third is given to relatives or neighbours. The final third is given to the poor as a gift. Needless to say, if there are 6.8 million people in Lahore, then there must be 1.5million families and, from what I could see, there were about that many live animals for sale on the streets that day.

The commotion and atmosphere was breathtaking from an emotional and pungent perspective. One could hardly comprehend that all these animals would have their throats

The author.

No.1 Platoon Heliborne Assault Force (HAF). My first group of 25 Pathans – 'as tough as the land that made them'.

The mountain profile of the 'Sleeping Lady of Quetta' greeted me every morning.

Welcome to Quetta!

HAF team in a Huey still in Peru Police livery – for whom they were originally allocated.

Pete (centre) and the Caravan Aircrew.

Our eyes in the sky – the Caravan – which watched over us (night and day) while we were operating on the ground.

We often operated around the mountain Road from Chaman to Quetta.

Ready to go. Six man sticks about to board their helicopters.

Hueys flying in tactical formation.

Egressing fast from a Huey was an essential HAF skill.

Luxurious living conditions on patrol. My bed in a wadi.

The 'Badlands' of
Balochistan.

Daylight rehearsals for a nighttime 'snatch'.

Inside our eye in the sky – the Caravan.

Each operation was carefully pre-planned so everybody knew what they had to do.

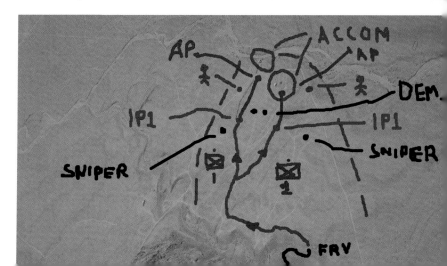

*After the discovering
the illicit drug
crop – Caz (centre),
Colonel, Brigadier
and some poppies.*

*Prisoners from the
illicit poppy field.*

The captured drugs were burnt in a formal ceremony.

Training day – I explain while Tanveer translates

Jim – ever watchful of my back during training.

Spot the snipers. There are two camouflaged Pathans neatly hidden in a fire position on the ground just to the left of the standing figure on the right.

Concealed in the mountains, observing a village down in the valley so we could feed information back to HQ in Quetta.

Whilst the observers watched the village we had to have all sides protected – our vigilant rearguard with two Light Machine Guns (LMG).

General Sadaqat addresses his HAF troops.

Waiting to exit from a patrol with Tanveer

Very definitely not Osama bin Laden – but one of my fifty Pathans bore a striking resemblance. His nickname by all, including his fellow Pathans, was 'Osama'!

HAF Wings – the badge of honour which was hard earned by each one of my 50 Pathans.

Our noble Huey crewchief, NK Muhammad Iqbal Butt, Killed in Action, July 24, 2004.

'A Vehicle Check Point on the Chaman Road. I had to remain hidden while my HAF team ran surprise road checks which kept the enemy on their toes.

The one and only time I wore a suit in Quetta – presenting General Sadaqat with his commemorative plate at our goodbye lunch.

Nearly home. My last day in Quetta.

slit within forty-eight hours or the amount of blood that such acts would generate.

We picked our way through the teaming streets and, fortunately, Robert knew his way through the city to the Pearl Continental Hotel, a.k.a., the "PC," a veritable haven of tranquillity compared to what we had just witnessed. I presumed Robert was 'carrying' and asked him how he intended to get through security with a gun. He said, "Just walk through. They won't stop you unless you stop."

I had explained to Robert that I needed to meet a friend of a friend and he understood. All I had to do was find the McDonald's Restaurant in Lahore, which after three weeks of surviving on Quetta cuisine, proved to be a welcome culinary sight and respite.

My friend was on time, to the maze that is the old walled city of Lahore and he led me down an alley lined with small shops on either side. We entered one of them and I was taken into the back office. The gentleman to whom I was introduced had the air of a former army officer and, after the niceties and tea, he asked me what I was looking for. I confirmed that I needed a SIG 228 pistol and a decent assault shotgun.

This was information he had already received a couple of weeks previously. He spoke to his colleague in Urdu and within minutes he appeared back in the room with a small carrying case. He opened the latch to reveal a brand new SIG Sauer P228 with two magazines and explained that he had an additional magazine for me.

I handled the 228 carefully and asked if it was real or locally produced. He reassured me it was definitely the real thing and I believed him. We then moved onto price, which was slightly shocking. He explained that the pistol was fully licensed and legal and, most importantly, that it worked. We agreed on the price and by that time his assistant had returned with four assault shotguns. The seller politely asked, "Do you want it for show or do you want it to work?"

I smiled and told him, "The latter would be nice."

He responded by suggesting that, if that were the case, we should just look at the top of the range and he wasn't kidding. At his instruction, the assistant pulled out a large white cardboard box that contained a long thin object.

He laid it on the table in front of me. The salesman looked at me, smiled wryly, and said, "Open it." He knew that whatever was in the box would sell itself. I pulled out the lips on the lid and used my thumbs to push the lid away from its restraint. What I saw in the box was better than I could have ever hoped for. Still in its packaging was a Benelli M3T Tactical 12-bore shotgun with a folding butt stock. I just couldn't believe my eyes. In terms of shotgun quality, it just doesn't get any better than that.

I picked it up, flicked out the butt that swung into the locked position, and worked the pump action. It was perfect.

Eventually we struck a price that included ammunition for both pieces of hardware and the cash was handed over. The boxes were wrapped in newspaper and my friend and I walked back the car. I arrived back at the PC for dinner in the exquisite Thai restaurant where some friends of Robert's had joined us.

The following day, it was time to head north and go shoot a wild pig or maybe die trying.

The Punjab is a far cry from Balochistan. It was peaceful, pleasant, green and tranquil and about two hours north of Lahore we entered a village and drove up a steep hill to a compound where the ANF guide instructed us to park. We walked into the outer entrance area of what was a very modest home and were made incredibly welcome with tea and spicy biscuits. It was explained to us that we would have to wait until after dark to go try and find a boar. In the meantime, we were treated to a Punjabi curry.

With full stomachs we went to the vehicle and prepared the hunting equipment. I pushed six LG shotgun cartridges into the Benilli. These would take down a man or a pig so should do the trick. I holstered my Sig under my jacket while Robert remarked that I had gotten a heck of a deal on the shotgun.

We drove slowly around the area with the guides using spotlights to try to pick out any movement. With the clock ticking towards 2.30am, we decided to dismount the vehicle for a third and final time for the night. Robert and I were at the front of the party with two guides behind us carrying large flashlights (torches).

We patrolled along the riverbed with Robert on my right and, as we approached a large, looping bend, I heard movement in the undergrowth to my left. I whispered to the guide who was already positioning himself with his light. As he hit the light switch, we saw the rear-ends of three wild boars scurrying into the undergrowth.

We needed to get round to the other side of the bend to cut them off. We moved quickly and silently to the far side of the riverbed so as not to spook them again. One of the guides, using his mobile phone, whispered to the driver to bring the vehicle to where we had seen the pigs enter cover and, on his word, to turn the lights on full beam.

At the far side of the bend, we moved towards the undergrowth. We were approximately twenty-five metres away when the driver must have thought we were ready. We were not.

We could see the glow of lights from the far side of the river bend. My guide turned his hand-held spotlight on and was shining it over my head. Without warning, the three boars broke cover and came hurtling toward us out of the undergrowth.

The Benilli was already up on my shoulder and the safety catch was off. I had a line on the lead pig now rapidly closing on me. The guide, in a moment of abject terror simply dropped his light and ran. I was now entirely in the dark with three angry wild boars just metres away.

From behind me, I heard Robert recite the world's most commonly stated last words, "Oh fuck" as I squeezed off the first round.

Instantly there was squealing not more than five or six metres in front of me. I snapped the pump of the MT3 back and forward in a fraction of a second and squeezed off another shot, sending the LG shot directly towards the noise and the squealing abruptly stopped. Erring on the side of extreme caution, I pumped one more time.

By this time Robert had picked up the fallen light and, with no movement in front of me, I was now edging toward where the pig must be. Robert was behind me saying, "I think it's had enough."

I said, "If it hasn't, it's about to get some more."

The adrenaline was coursing through my veins and every nerve ending in my body was alive. The shape of the boar lying on its side became obvious. There was no movement and, thanks be to God, no sign of its herd-mates.

The beast had taken a hit to the throat, presumably my second, that had finished him off. I congratulated myself that this was pretty good marksmanship, considering the shot was aimed on sound alone.

Robert and I gutted the pig and put the pork into an icebox while our hosts, who would not touch pork as a matter of religion, looked on.

It had been quite a weekend and, during my phone call to Shellie, I recounted the adventure and that it had been twenty-seven years to the day since I had joined the British Military. Quite a life it was continuing to be.

It would be another week before I would get back to Quetta. There was no point in leaving Islamabad unless I had all the equipment for Phase 2 training. There were two highlights during that week and the first came from Brigadier General Stone.

He called me in for a coffee and explained that they had heard what was being achieved with the RIF and, coincidently, Donald Rumsfeld had ordered the DoD to enable Pakistan to assemble a battalion size helicopter assault force by June.

I asked how they intended to achieve this assault force and the General explained that DoD would fund the purchase of twenty-seven Bell 412 Helicopters. Beyond that it seemed little thought had been given to manning their team with the appropriate skill sets. I offered my help and told the General that he would need my company of RIF and 50 Squadron as the lead element to accelerate the training process of both the other pilots and the two companies of military assault troops.

He responded by asking if they could look at our training programme to see if there was a fit. I told him I'd be glad to help.

That evening, I called Paul and told him what was happening and he pragmatically sighed, "Howard, you are more likely to achieve cooperation between the U.S. and Iran than you are between the State Department and Department of Defense!" Given the very public rift between Colin Powell and Donald Rumsfeld, he was soon to be proven correct.

As I locked myself in my bedroom later that night with the proven Benilli propped up against the bed, reality again set in. It was time to turn all my attention the next phase in Quetta and take my boys to the fight.

HAF

CHAPTER 9

Near Misses

The first stage of the journey to Quetta for the Phase Two Training involved transporting the operational equipment to Qasim Airbase and cramming it into the Cessna.

I had given Pete the nod that we should keep passengers to a minimum because we would very likely bulk-out on cargo. I think even he was surprised, however, when I turned up at the airport with two 4x4s and a van.

As the equipment was unloaded from the vehicles, Pete was grinning from ear to ear and scratching his head. I couldn't help but laugh as I reminded him, "I told you I had shit loads of kit! I then quickly followed up, looking for reassurance, "Do you think we'll get it in?" to which Pete replied, "I guess there is only one way to find out." He then asked, "What the hell have you got here?" I smiled and handed him the list:

8	Daytime Scopes	1	HF Radio Back Pack
24	Night Vision Binoculars	1	VHF FM Base Station (with telescopic antenna)
16	Night Vision Goggles	16	Motorola Handset Radios
24	Hand-held GPS	16	Motorola Handset earpieces
1	Thermal Imager	50	Meals Ready to Eat
40	First field Dressings	35	Rolls of Masking Tape
4	Spike Strips/Tyre Shredders	12	Laser Pointers
80	Landing site/strip marker lamps	16	Compasses
10	Motorola Radio Ear Pieces	210	Bungee Rubber Cords (1m)
35	Strobe Lights	50	Triangular Bandages
105	Cam-lights	50	Sand Goggles
35	Personal Locator Beacon (PLB)	2	Section Medical Kit (Including Morphine & Snake bite kit)
35	NVG Personal Locator Lights	10	Maps, Balochistan 1:50,000
1	Roll of Parachute cord	5	Maps, Balochistan 1:150,000
70	Tie-Wraps (Plasti-cuffs)	35	Shemagh, (camouflage colour)
4	Pocket flares	35	Sheath Knives
16	Binoculars	30m	Scrim cloth
9	Laser Range Finders (Commercial Hunting Type)		

"How the fuck did you manage all this in such a short time?' Pete asked.

"I didn't; Saadi did!" I smiled, "With a bit of creative coaching."

Simply put, where there was a will I'd found a way and Saadi had ably helped me to apply that will across the spectrum of his contacts either for local purchase or the State Department procurement process. For my part, when Saadi couldn't find a way within the system, I would acquire from elsewhere.

Without doubt, the NVGs were occupying most of the space in the aircraft. I was being extremely fussy about their fragility and didn't want to risk any equipment stacked on top of them, even though the NVGs that had been provided were veritable antiques.

The west was paranoid about technology transfer to Pakistan, which was rather akin to shutting the stable door after the horse had bolted with a nuclear weapon on its back. Hence some joker in the Department of State's procurement chain had somehow found fifty sets of obsolete NVGs that must have been waiting for disposal in a warehouse somewhere in the states since the early Eighties. They were unused but more than twenty years old.

I'd had mixed feeling of disappointment and amazement when I opened the first package in front of Saadi, but quickly decided they were a lot better than sod all, and my Pathans would know no different anyway. We would just have to make them work for us. My only hope was that neither Al-Qaeda nor the Taliban had later models.

As the Caravan climbed into the light blue skies, I looked back at all the stacked boxes in the Caravan's cabin and felt a glow of satisfaction. We really had made the procurement system work and at break neck speed. To her credit, Dorothy had not interfered, even though she must have had her sources keeping her up to date with what was going on and my full utilisation of the budget.

I was now six months into my year's deployment and step-by-step we'd come a heck of a long way but now I was itching to get in the fight. The DynCorp mechanics had worked against the elements to keep the Huey's serviceable and impart their skills to their Pakistani counterparts. Gerry, Jay, Frank, Mark, Jason and Ed had worked around the clock and against all odds to ensure the aircraft were prepared for the imminent increase in operational tempo. They were going way and beyond their contractual obligations and I knew it took more teamwork patience and perseverance than these guys were ever selected (or paid) for. Meanwhile, Curtis had worked the phones and supply chain in the U.S., hassled Pakistan's stunningly obstructive imports bureaucracy and not accepted the answer "no" in order to get the much needed component parts and tools to his team.

To the credit of the entire DynCorp team, they figuratively dragged the Pakistani mechanics kicking and squealing to the required standards and, once they had got them there, continued to try to instil the attention to detail that is so vital to helicopter maintenance. The emergence of visible progress and a defined role for these men was becoming apparent and this became an incentive to get all-else achieved. Additionally, Caz had spent most of his nights with a Huey strapped to his arse training the 50 Squadron pilots to new levels of NVG proficiency. Thanks to Caz, they were by now, indisputably the finest night flying pilots in all of Pakistan.

Pete clearly lived for flying, (in-between his odd conjugal breaks in Bangkok), and he too had been working tirelessly on the backside of the clock to bring the Pakistani fixed wing pilots night flying skills to a place where they could provide the top cover we'd need.

For his part, Matt, our unofficial, unpaid FLIR operator, had continued to embrace the techniques and technology and was becoming a veritable authority. He passed this skill on to three junior Pakistani officers who, initially, were not enamoured with their role as observers but who had quickly assimilated how crucial their skill was to the guys on the ground. They were our eyes over the horizon and our risk management ace in the hole! They made an otherwise impossible mission possible because, through them, our tiny force could know what was over the next ridge or round the next corner. Simply put; without the FLIR operators there would be no operation.

Phase Two training commenced with the issuance of equipment and training of how to operate, carry, and maintain. Having rehearsed night patrolling on the airfield, we conducted our first extended NVG night patrol in the Pishin area. The massive and undulating plain looked as spooky as shit in the two-dimensional greens and blacks of the goggles.

I'm not sure how many miles we patrolled that first night, but it was a test of stamina to ensure the Platoon maintained their drills at night even when tired. This kind of patrol also served to get the Pathans used to the goggles and to iron out any problems in their use. Wearing them would have to become second nature.

The Section Commanders in the Patrol were introduced to the use of laser pointers to direct attention or fire, as well as to the use of NVG visible cam-sticks, tape and strobes in order to identify friendlies from the enemy in the dark. The drone of the Caravan's PT6 engine overhead and the FLIR operator's reports of heat sources, be they goats, dogs or humans, helped us to rehearse patrolling clear of any contact with anything that was alive and above the ground.

Most of the Pathan's took to using the goggles like ducks to water. These mountain men never failed to amaze me. In a few short weeks, they had transitioned from unguided enthusiasm with no technical knowledge whatsoever to honed troops. I reflected they would be formidable and savage against anyone who tried to take them on - and I was soon to be proven right.

On my third day in Quetta, I was invited "for tea" with General Sadaqat. These invitations were a far cry from the early efforts that I'd had to make to attempt a shit-house meeting with the General just three months previously.

Sadaqat was already concerned that word was getting out about the potential of our capability and that he might lose control of the assets if higher command decided to "steal them." He was also opposed to letting his troops be led by any DoD-sponsored or Pak Army force. He explained that, no matter how good his RIF proved themselves to be, the Army would still view them as cannon fodder.

He was uncomfortable that an impetuous Army commander who didn't give a toss about the militia might throw them into suicidal "bayonet charge" where he would not send his own Army equivalents. Sadly, the General's view was one of wisdom and, therefore, I concluded that he was probably right. We needed to protect these warriors even from their own side.

During the afternoon, we conducted our first demolitions (explosives) training. This was one of the first skill-sets I had been taught in the British Military as a Clearance Diver responsible for Explosive Ordnance Disposal (EOD) or "Bomb Disposal," as it more commonly known. I had achieved EOD2 standards as a Leading Diver by the age of twenty-one and this understanding of explosives was later honed during other specialist training. I was not, however, prepared for what the RIF had in store for me.

We were casually standing by one of the trucks when a trooper who had been tasked to bring the issued explosives wandered up to our group and unpacked his backpack. He pulled out a bunch of detonators that had been tied together by their electric wires and laid them on the bare metal tail-gate of the truck. He then pulled from the same bag two packs of plastic explosives. The man was a walking bomb!

I moved everyone back from the truck and handed the explosive to him. I told him to put it in the bag and lay it in the shade about twenty-five metres away. I then turned my attention to the detonators. As I delicately unravelled their wires and separated them, I gently placed each detonator on my Shemagh, which I had taken out of my jacket pocket. As I did so I explained how dangerous and unstable these seemingly harmless looking items were.

If a detonator were carried in a trouser pocket, it is quite possible for body heat to cause the detonator to explode.

If, additionally, detonators were bunched together as these had been in the same pocket, they would probably blow your leg off if you were lucky and your balls off if you were not.

If this had happened in our trooper's backpack, it would have certainly caused the plastic explosive to detonate and this Pathan would have been instantly vaporised and meet his maker by his own inadvertent doing. I stressed to the Pathans that death does not excuse incompetence. In fact it generally eats you up for it.

With a stern, "Don't fuck about with these," demonstration I rigged one of the detonators into a coke can and, via electric cable, used a battery from my torch to set it off. The can was instantly shredded, ably demonstrating the damage a detonator would inflict to your hand or, worse still, your testicles. The Pathans got the message and the explosive carrying trooper had paled at the thought that he had been lucky not to blow himself sky high.

That night, Gerry the Spanner made me an alloy detonator box where each detonator was housed in foam in its own hole. The RIF's detonators were stored safely from there on. Gerry was a former US Marine; he understood the gravity of the situation and did a great job helping out with the improvisation. I harboured no doubt that Gerry's detonator box would save a Pathan from badly injuring or killing himself due to the careless handling of one of these detonators.

The same evening Dorothy called to say that the Ambassador had requested a briefing on what was being achieved in Quetta and Brigadier Shafiq called to say that he and I had been invited to go to Washington DC to justify the allocation of additional Hueys. I guessed that the two calls were somehow connected and that either Steve Schrage or John Mackey were ultimately behind both phone calls. Regardless, my glow of contentment was growing. I felt like we were getting somewhere.

Two nights previously, we had rehearsed Night Standing Observation Post (NSOP) drills, which basically use cover of darkness to observe a target from close range. Each NSOP would typically consist of two men lying head-to-toe in shallow cover. One would view the target area, one would view the rear to make sure no one surprised or stumbled on the team without being challenged.

It was an all night exercise with each section deploying three NSOPs just one hour after dark and extracting from their positions one hour before light. During the course of the night, the teams would see individuals or vehicles come into their vicinity (either Jim or myself) and they were required to keep a timed log of the event. Pervaiz later translated these into English. So, after a day's rest, if there was a day of "almosts," then Friday, February 27th was that day. During the morning I flew out to an abandoned village to plan that evening's exercise.

On the way back, Caz, who was piloting the Huey, noticed two men in the mountains watching our every move through binoculars. In the rear of the Huey, Jim and I were armed. With us was Captain Bahtti, who was attached to the Frontier Corps. Caz asked me what I wanted to do.

By now, I was using my binoculars specifically trying to identify whether or not they were armed.

Only the previous week, we had received intelligence reports that local insurgents intended to shoot down a Pakistan International Airways (PIA) airliner using a MANPAD (Man Portable Air Defence System).

From their vantage point, these men could easily loose off a Stinger when an unfortunate Boeing 737 just happened to fly by on its approach to Quetta. One of the individuals was wearing a camouflaged jacket, so we had no choice; we had to check these guys out. If we didn't a planeload of innocent men, women and children might pay with their lives.

I told Caz to "Take her down" and to try for a landing spot in dead ground if he could find one close by. I briefed Jim and Bahtti. Jim and I would spread out to triangulate the two men with our weapons and the Captain would move forward to ask them questions.

My primary target would be the guy on the left unless the other produced a weapon; Jim's primary would be the other guy. I told Bahtti to stay close to me until I told him to go forward. He was then not to get any closer than ten metres. If they produced a weapon, we would shoot to kill and, if we did so, he should hit the deck and stay there until I instructed him to get up.

The signal for Jim to open fire would be when I opened fire and vice versa. As one would expect of Caz, he had his shit together and brought the Huey to rest in a small bowl about 200 metres from the target individuals and in a place where they didn't have line of sight to the Huey. But they sure as hell knew we had landed.

As soon as we were out of the helicopter, Caz took it airborne. As instructed, Jim broke off to the right moving at pace in the dead ground; I went left, with the Captain almost up my arse.

I came up over the ridge and could see Jim do the same with his weapon trained on the area where the men were loitering.

By now, these men were only too aware that we were approaching with them in our sights. I stopped about forty metres from the two men who were, by now, standing up in an attempt to look harmless.

I dropped to one knee with the left of the two men squarely in my sights; Jim mirrored me. I told Bahtti to move towards Jim and then, when halfway between us, turn hard left and approach the men. This way, he would never be in our line of fire.

He did exactly as instructed and, as he turned towards these men; my thumb pushed the safety catch of my M16 to the vertical, single shot position. If either of these suspects pulled a weapon, I'd put them down. Overhead, Caz circled the Huey, as he monitored the situation from about 500 feet. He'd also radioed back to Quetta that we were potentially closing with an enemy.

Captain Bahtti followed my instructions to a T. I'm not sure if it was because he was naturally precise or because he was shitting himself. I suspect that it may have been a bit of each. At the moment he reached ten metres from the two men, he stopped and presumably asked what they were doing.

If they were going to go for it, now would be the time. One of them reached into his breast pocket. My finger was on the trigger; I exhaled slightly and stopped the breath. I'd got the shot if need be. The target pulled out a coloured card of some sort and held it out to Bahtti who moved forward.

"Now it could get tricky," I thought.

However, no sooner did the Captain have the card in his hand, than he backed away to read it. He was acutely aware that, if we opened fire on the two individuals, the distance between him and the two men, was his best friend.

He looked at the card for a few seconds and then turned to give us the thumbs up. He went forward, gave the guy his card, and spoke to them both for about another minute. As he did so, my thumb pulled the safety catch on my M-16 to the horizontal "safe" position.

Bahtti walked back towards me, wisely staying out of my line of view/fire. He explained that they were forestry personnel looking for poachers. It was incredulous, but true.

We returned to Quetta laughing in disbelief about the whole incident and still amazed that these two men were where they were doing what they were doing. We *almost* had the first contact of the day and it wasn't over yet.

Back in the compound, the work continued for the evening patrol when Colonel Wahid called. He asked if the RIF were with me yet, and I told him they were not. He explained that a bus with several civilians on board had been snatched by a group led by Jalil Jaffar (aka "J.J."), an individual who terrorised Balochistan, and that we needed to react.

He said I needed to put an operation together and brief the RIF when they arrived. He didn't know how many hostages, how many terrorists or even the location of the bus, just that the bus was headed out towards Sibi. He explained he had his intelligence team working on finding the location. He added, "Howard, we will need you to lead this." I told him I'd do what I could but, in the back of my mind, I knew it would be a high-risk operation. If we had to do it as an "immediate action" in the daytime, there would inevitably be casualties.

I briefed Caz and Pete and they brought the 50 Squadron pilots to immediate stand-by. We would have to brief on the hoof. I called Moussa and told him to get us a bus, any bus, and bring it into the compound. He didn't ask any questions. He could sense by the tone of my voice that I wasn't fucking about. I went to my room and donned my kit for the operation. I'd need my low velocity M16/9mm to limit the penetration of fire in a bus; I'd also need the assault shotgun.

I checked my equipment, conscious that I should not trade speed for attention to detail. I made my peace with my God and asked him to give me the strength to fight bravely and to please look after Shellie and the girls if anything happened to me. I closed with an "Amen" and walked out into the sun to face my men.

The RIF had just arrived from Belili, so I briefed Pervaiz. The Pathans lightened their equipment. We'd be travelling light except for ammunition, comms and water. Then Moussa turned up with the bus; God bless him.

We ran through the take-down drills as best we could. It was likely we would be heavily reliant on our two best shooters as snipers to take out the terrorists during the initial moments of our assault and we identified their optimum positions relative to the bus. We then went over the three entrances to the bus, the main door, the back door, and the driver's door and practised getting into the vehicle using a trooper as a step where necessary for the rear door. We discussed the need for absolute speed when the time came but that we would try to wait for as long as we could through the night to tire these bastards out.

We'd also work to disable the bus as soon as we located it and we discussed the various options, including the deployment of the tire shredders. When we'd covered just about everything I thought possible, we moved out to the Hueys where Caz, Pete, Matt and the pilots were lounging on the flight line much akin to a scene from a Second World War movie. Meanwhile Mark, Gerry, Jay and Ed were doing last minute checks on the aircraft just to make sure everything was buttoned up.

Under the heat of the day, the rest of our entire team found shade, sat and waited ... and waited. The behaviour of men at times like this is always something to behold. Some are quiet and some just try to sleep, others nervously joke around, others just talk quietly and smoke. I sat with Pervaiz and we tried to go over every permutation. It would be difficult to make a precise plan until we got to the assault area.

My phone rang; it was Colonel Wahid. I could see every guy within earshot looking over to see my expression for some sort of clue as to what was about to happen.

Colonel Wahid said succinctly, "Howard, they've found the bus, but it's empty. We don't know where the hostages are, but we are working on it. Stand down for now." He added, "Please come to Headquarters immediately, we need to talk to you." In order to broadcast my response, I simply said "Roger that Colonel, stand down. Give me forty minutes to be with you." The second *almost* was a clear signal; operational tempo was about to get busy but now it was time to go and take off my kit and head across Quetta in the Corolla.

We potentially still had a patrol to perform that night, so I told Pervaiz to prepare the men for that. Unbeknown to all of us that afternoon, J.J. had just created an appointment with the RIF and his clock was running.

This first taste of a potential operation for my militia served them well and, if any of them had any doubts that they would be going into combat, all such feelings were by now dispelled. I arrived at the HQ in Quetta to discover the hostages still hadn't been located. Both the General and the Colonel were now keen for the RIF to "go operational."

I explained that if there was an "immediate action" operation where there was a window of opportunity to save life then, of course, we could do it. It could, however, prove costly in lives and, if we had a choice, we should try to start the platoon off on deliberate operations. Just a few more weeks of training could make all the difference. I also commented that a lot would depend on who was leading the operation.

Captain Pervaiz was a good man but he still had some ways to go in order to assume the kind of responsibility this type of operation demanded. Colonel Wahid responded. "Howard, you're one of us, you lead them." I explained that the powers that be might have something to say about that but I was willing to 'ask forgiveness not permission'. I was also aware that the Colonel had probably just served me one of the best compliments I would receive in Pakistan. He had referred to me as "One of us."

That night the concentration of the patrol during the evening's mountain insert and the covert search was second to none. The coordination between the aircrew and the ground troops continued to be ever more slick. These guys were getting to be good at what they did and they knew it; and as their confidence continued to rise in themselves and each other they were becoming combined and cohesive in effort. To use a modern military term they were rapidly evolving into a "composite" force.

The following day, the platoon revised hostage rescue techniques. I knew I would have to refine and accelerate the hostage rescue capability. The Shi-ite festival of the tenth day of Muharran would occur that weekend, so practical training would have to wait until this event was over.

Up to now the city of Quetta had been deceptively peaceful so I settled into the compound for a weekend of mission planning, report writing, equipment cleaning and general recuperation. We had all been working long hours on the back end of the clock and the pace involved constant physical exertion. I was forty-five years old and my body was tired and bruised but I actually felt in great physical condition. I had dropped in weight from my usual love-handled laden waist at seventy-eight kilos down to a lean seventy-four kilos.

I surmised that I was having the equivalent of my mid-life crisis but without the sex. However, the lack of western food and booze was doing my body a huge favour and the physical exercise, whilst not high impact, was all at altitudes above 1,500 metres above sea level. My body had fully adapted to operating at this altitude and it was clearly having a great effect on my overall fitness. I felt so alive.

Dinner that evening in the compound was the lull before the storm and coincidentally the corporation that had sold the FLIR to the State Department for use in the Caravans had sent a technician to Quetta to assist Jay with the upgrade and servicing of the equipment. The tech-rep would also provide advanced operator training for Matt.

The representative had come straight from the States so the culture shock must have been enormous and he was a duck out of water if there ever was one. He sat at dinner; eyes wide open while the DynCorp guys took the opportunity to provide anecdotes of terror and hardship on this rare and captive audience.

The next day all hell broke loose in Quetta. The Shia formed their Muharran procession and, while beating themselves with chains, moved from their partitioned community on the hillside towards a central gathering square in the city. As the procession was passing through the city's shopping district, three Sunni radicals rained hand grenades on the crowd from a hotel roof.

When they'd dispensed of all their grenades, they used AK-47s to fire indiscriminately at the crowd. When they had finally run out of bullets, one of the attackers made his way to the confused and panicking crowd, some of whom were tending the wounded, and detonated the explosives he had wrapped around his body. Forty-three Shi-ite Muslims were killed and hundreds injured by the attack. One could only reflect with abject sadness that the attacking radicals had surely not read the Holy Koran *(In the Name of God, the Compassionate, the Merciful)* wherein it is written in *Women 4:93: "He that kills a believer (a Muslim) by design shall burn in hell forever."*

After these killings, groups of angry Shias seeking revenge attacked shops, vehicles, and government property before security forces fired shots and tear gas to disperse the crowd. Unbelievably, and in an act of determined demonstration of hatred of Muslim against Muslim, one of the original Sunni attackers managed to slip through security and was actually apprehended trying to get into the hospital in order to shoot dead the Shia wounded!

Meanwhile, we could see the city was burning and on the brink of descending into total anarchy. I gathered my kit and my weapons, once again pledging to myself that the only way they would kill me with my own gun was to beat me to death with it because I would have dispensed all bullets. I told Pete to make sure the Cessna was ready to go and directed all the men in the compound to load their "run bags". If the rioters breached the Cantonment, we would have about ten minutes to get out of there and make our escape.

All the run bags were loaded into the Caravan. We were ready to bug-out in all respects. I ordered Moussa to keep me informed if any trouble hit the cantonment; he did just that. Colonel Wahid called with an update and told me the RIF had been deployed in town to rescue several policemen that were trapped in a building by an angry mob.

As smoke continued to rise over Quetta, I called the Brits and told them we were preparing to move out. Robert asked if we had room for three. I told him we'd make room and hung up, having agreed to let him know if we decided to bug out. He would then have three minutes to decide whether they would tough it out or come with the only currently reliable transport away from the city. I then received a call was from Paul in the US who was just "checking in" and completely unaware that the shit had just hit the fan. He asked, "Howard, why does it sound like you're hiding behind a rock in the desert; what's going on there?"

I replied "Well mate, it's very likely because I'm actually behind a wall watching Quetta burn and destroying itself".

He got the message and using his inimitable calmness, simply said, "Roger that. Call me when it's sorted."

My mind was racing. Had I thought of everything? Could we get everyone in one aircraft? Would the weather let us get to Islamabad or did we need to look at an alternate destination? Then, as ever in these situations, came the icebreaker. It was the visiting FLIR technician; he approached me as I stood by the truck with my rifle cradled by my right arm and sheepishly asked. "Excuse me, Howard." He paused, "If you guys are leaving, do you mind if I come with you?"

I paused and looked back to the increasing smoke rising over the city and said without looking at him, "I promise you we won't leave anyone behind."

I then got a jolt of reality, glanced at him and laughed, "How could you think I would leave you behind?" to which he replied.

"Well, because I came PIA, I thought I would have to go back PIA."

"Sod that," I told him, "You'd get hacked to pieces before you got anywhere near the airport."

Colonel Wahid called again to say that a curfew had been put into force so the Cantonment should not be threatened by the mob. He also reported that the RIF had performed perfectly. They had rescued the trapped policemen and arrested seventeen people suspected of holding them - and with no injuries on our side.

I decided at that juncture that the threat to the Cantonment and to our compound had somewhat subsided and during the next few hours gradually wound back to our normal routine. The events had proven our evacuation plan could be quickly implemented.

The feedback from the States was one of great satisfaction. Our entire force had really started to make a difference and, as if to emphasise the fact, a Huey was dispatched the very next day to evacuate a young Pakistani army officer who had lost his leg to a land-mine planted by the subversives of Akbar Bugti the Balochi warlord of Dera Bugti. Judging from the amount of blood in the helicopter, I could only hope it looked worse than it was.

I reflected that there were battle lines in all directions but having come off the back end of a real riot, it was time to concentrate on the potential operation regarding the hostages taken by J.J. and to work the 1st Platoon through a covert hostage snatch exercise. The planning, coordination, and actual execution of this mission was about as complex as the Pathans were ever going to be asked to experience.

Out on the ground we would have to ensure stealth and, once unleashed, unlimited aggression to overcome anything we came up against. Everything we did out in the mountains to prepare was real, the elements and that we were in bandit country meant we would have to deal with both whether we were rehearsing or out for the real thing.

My Pathans were blooded killers but it was up to me to get them to the target and make sure they worked as a raiding team to get what we needed out of the operation. They were now on the brink of being tested by the enemy time and time again.

CHAPTER 10

Operation Broken Finger

By now, it was the first week of March 2004 and we were actively patrolling areas of interest. Following one particular patrol I grabbed about three hours sleep before being called into Quetta to debrief the General.

Feeling dazed, I met Sergeant Moussa by the cars with my SIG 228 pistol down my trousers and tucked my M16 machine gun under my jacket. The Embassy, in their wisdom, had continued to dictate that we should always travel in "bullet proof" vehicles while in Quetta. I knew, however, that the deskbound moron who had made this rule had probably never even been to the city.

In my view, the only difference between an inconspicuous vehicle with a westerner in it and an armoured, conspicuous vehicle with a westerner in it is at most one Rocket Propelled Grenade (RPG) round. The logic being it takes just one RPG to destroy an ordinary vehicle, while the armoured variant, might take two rounds. In Quetta, an armoured 4x4 vehicle would be the only one of its kind in the city so would stick out like a dog's balls and be an RPG magnet.

In our shitty little Toyota, no one took any notice of me as we drove inconspicuously through town. Provided our OpSec held this form of covert protection combined with an irregular pattern of movement it was a far better defence than any armoured vehicle.

When I arrived at the HQ of the Frontier Corps there was by now always a bit of a flurry. Major Javed who, by now, knew I was becoming a confidant of the General, made a seemingly ever-increasing fuss over me in the hope that would carry some favour.

Ever gracious, General Sadaqat offered food and drink and, even if I didn't want them, I got them. The crustless cheese sandwiches always came with ketchup on the side, which, I assume, is some sort of screwed-up hand me down from the days of British rule. As we sipped chai, we chatted about the RIF, our progress, the way ahead, the further equipment needed, the issues of the U.S. Embassy regarding extra Hueys, and the military's intent regarding their planned procurement of twenty-seven Bell 412 helicopters.

He then moved to his map and pointed to a village deep in the mountains well to the north of Quetta. He showed me that there was just one road/track in or out and explained that his intelligence team was certain that something was going on in that hamlet.

It was extremely remote and they had received an intelligence report of unusual activity, an ideal location for the enemy. He went on to explain that there was a 4x4 SUV that had recently entered that village and that neither the identity of the men who drove it nor the vehicle's purpose were known to the security forces.

This vehicle had no logical reason for being there other than for some sort of illegal or subversive activity. He explained they really needed to know who was driving it but needed to protect his source. With information on the occupants, he could put together an intelligence picture to ascertain the organisation that was behind the operation of the vehicle and, from that, deduce the focus of its activity. From this description I guessed Sadaqat's source must be a villager otherwise we could have mounted an overt stop on the vehicle.

This village was deep in bandit country; if we got captured out there we would get skinned alive. We would have to try to break contact and hide in the mountains until help arrived in the form of the Hueys. I explained the risks and asked whether the information he needed was worth it.

The General looked at me with solemn expression, pursed his lips and simply nodded.

I studied the map. The track out of the village followed the base of a valley that emerged on to the road to one of the main roads to Quetta. Shortly after the track joined the main road, there was a permanent vehicle checkpoint. If we could determine the make and colour of the 4x4, by timing we could almost certainly identify the time it would pass through the checkpoint. In order to do this effectively, however, he had to know when the vehicle left the village.

The terrain made the village stunningly remote. There was a range of mountains that almost formed an upside down "U," with other ranges forming the valleys around that "U".

I quipped that the terrain looked ridiculously hard going for a guy of my age but we could likely get "eyes-on" the village from the ridge. We would have to patrol in and out completely undetected so the Hueys would have to drop us off deep in the mountains about ten kilometres from the target. We could then stick to the high ground that appeared on the map, to be uninhabited.

Sadaqat asked when I could do it and I told him we could insert in the early hours of the day after tomorrow if I could achieve fly-past reconnaissance within the next twenty four hours. The General instructed, tell no-one the full extent of what we were doing. "Just let me know when that damn SUV is on its way."

I explained I would have to use VHF communications into the communication centre at headquarters. The General said he'd arrange a round the clock frequency watch but warned, "Don't tell them it's a car."

I looked at the cheese sandwich on his coffee table and told him, "*Sandwich.*" You let your signallers know that you are awaiting a report on sandwiches. We'll call in when the *sandwich* is on its way."

And with that simple instruction, the process of planning the operation was to consume my next two days.

The day of a patrol always had but one singular focus and the intensity would increase as the day progressed. The clock would countdown from the moment I woke, with each stage of preparation timed hour by hour on precisely what needed to be achieved and when.

I woke up knowing that it would probably be another three nights before I got back into bed again. The large tatty and dusty room that was my bedroom was an abysmal greeting to each day. My M16 machine gun was in my sleeping bag with me and my SIG 228 under my pillow, my shotgun was on my desk with a set of body armour over the back of my bedside chair, carefully arranged to give maximum protection if the miscreants of Quetta came calling.

Solely for my own amusement I would more often than not wake up and mutter in paraphrase Martin Sheen's opening line in Apocalypse Now, but substitute my Quetta for his Saigon. "Quetta... Shit; I'm still in Quetta."

It was in this godforsaken room I had spent the previous day pawing over the maps to figure out the optimum avenues of approach, drop offs, pickups, and rendezvous.

This particular morning some of the DynCorp mechanics were in for their second coffee of the day and as I joined them for my first cup of tea I reflected that the level of profanity amongst the team who were isolated in Quetta was at one I had honestly never experienced throughout twenty years in the military.

The ability of the guys to actually split up a word to include the word "fuck" was a source of some amusement to me. It was indicative of what happens if men live in total isolation from the formalities of social or disciplinary pressures to moderate.

To their credit, my vocabulary was expanded to words such as, "infuckincredible, absofuckinlutely, helifuckincopter and awefuckinsome." I do still find myself muttering such expressions under my breath when the moment takes me.

After the profane breakfast it was back to studying the maps and aerial photos just one last time and I used tracing paper over each poster size visual aid to indicate our drop off point, the alternate drop off point, the emergency rendezvous, the route to target, the form up point, and the route onto target. Front to back, minding every detail and point of vulnerability or potential cock-up.

We'd be most exposed to being compromised on the way to or from this village. If the Cessna was not on-station, we'd have to make damn sure we weren't on the move. The aircraft was our sole communications relay station to the Hueys. They would have to go back to Quetta while we were in the mountains simply because there was nowhere else they could land, shutdown, and be secure from attack. While the helicopter crews rested, we'd be isolated from any back-up and I knew for sure we would have to fight our way out of any compromise but I also knew that if we were caught deep in these badlands so far from support, we'd likely be decimated.

I'd already told Pervaiz that the men should carry Marching Order (back packs), which would permit carriage of sleeping bags, warm clothing, and plenty of additional ammunition.

I'd also need to rehearse the platoon through break from contact drills to make certain the procedures were as honed as possible. If we were compromised, we'd have to strike a careful balance between standing our ground and risking envelopment or a tactical withdrawal. The foreign fighters in Al-Qaeda, especially the Chechens who were lunatics, would interpret a break from contact as a retreat. This would likely cause them to pursue us with even more resolve.

So while we were in these mountains, we'd have to break contact, flank and hit the bastards as hard as we could in the hope that the opposition would realise they were going to get slugged if they came after us. As in all aspects of life, it's always what you don't prepare for that kicks your arse. So I opted for the military equivalent of "that which is most rehearsed is seldom used in anger."

Given the scale of this operation in terms of distance and risk I'd asked Jim if he would come along. He wasn't morally or contractually obliged to do so but he knew I needed back up and it spoke volumes of his courage that he immediately agreed, so I chatted through the plan with him. He and I would remain at opposite ends of the patrol while we were on the move and stay close to each other once we were static. If I was asleep he'd be awake and vice-versa.

By early afternoon, I was content that the mission plan was complete from start to finish, so I concentrated on the preparation of my own kit. My emphasis that day was to prepare in the same way I did every single time. I tested the batteries of the radios at least twice. Communications were our lifeline and I packed twice as many batteries as I anticipated we would need. I then turned my attention to my weapons.

I cleaned my dependable SIG 228 pistol and unloaded and reloaded the magazines to exercise the magazine springs with the 9mm Parabellum rounds. I favour these rounds because, although they are not the most devastating round when they hit a body, they are the most reliable for a feed from magazine into the breech. The pistol was my last line of defence (apart from my knife). If I was forced to use my pistol then it would be as a last resort, shit or bust situation, so these less damaging rounds minimised the chance of a stoppage that, if it occurred, would undoubtedly cost me my life.

The M-16 rifle had the similar cleaning drills and I'd zeroed the weapon over the weekend. With the weapons clean and ready to fire, I checked and double checked my Russian-style combat vest, my medic pack, night sticks, camel back and emergency water, ensuring I had spare batteries for my NVGs.

Check, double check, triple check.

I ensured each layer of my equipment so that if I did have to dump kit, I'd still be left with equipment that would permit me to survive and fight. The most vital were my radio, ammunition, and water. These combat commodities are the currency of the desert.

With that complete, Caz and I walked out to the flight line to see what the mechanics were up to. Gerry and Frank were beavering away on the Hueys just making sure we'd have 100% serviceability for those aircraft that were needed for the patrol. Jay, Ed and Matt were tweaking the equipment on the Caravan to make sure the operator tests were up to snuff. We only had two FLIR aircraft so the serviceability was crucial.

Tonight the Cessna would loiter over the area of drop off for about an hour ahead of the Hueys. By using cover of darkness many thousands of feet above us, his task would be to scan the area for any heat sources (humans). If he picked up any heat source, I would then have to decide whether to switch to the alternate drop off point or to abort the mission.

Even at this late stage in planning, the circle of knowledge of our precise destination was still extremely tight. The biggest risk to our lives on patrol was an information leak to the enemy, so no risks were ever taken. The closed circle of knowledge and the mitigation of such risk set us apart from other units in Pakistan.

None of the Pathans would know the objective until they arrived in the briefing room and their mobile phones were switched off and in a bucket. For them it was simply another patrol, for the General and me, however, it was a deliberate operation.

Following the walk back from the flight line, I tried to take an hour's rest but, to be honest, there was no chance of sleep with so many thoughts whirling around in my head.

I ate my chicken curry supper early, which had doubtless been prepared on the filthy, concrete kitchen floor by the chef, Cha-Cha; I then grabbed a pre-patrol shower.

That last shower before entering the mountains is always a weird experience. I was acutely aware that, when I turned the shower off, unknown events awaited me prior to my next shower.

However, it was now time to carefully review the orders one last time before the Pathans arrived. I made sure I was in the briefing room, waiting for them while characteristically and casually sipping my mug of tea when they arrived. I made a point of being upbeat and cracked a few funnies with them, also checking to see whether everyone was okay. We couldn't afford any ailments at the outset and they knew, with me, it was no shame to have to sit it out rather than come along as a "passenger".

Capt Pervaiz translated the orders into Pashtu and we worked through in deliberate steps that would typically take an hour to dispense, ensuring each and every element knew their precise role and task. The ability of the Pathans to comprehend the orders procedure and understand what was needed of them was second to none.

Following the mission orders, some of the Pathans smoked, others prayed, or both. They also conducted their final kit checks. They completed the "jump test" to make sure nothing rattled and then each man was left to his own rituals.

I went to my room and donned my own equipment, all the time thinking of last minute checks. I did my own jump test to ensure my equipment made no noise. I took a deep breath and dropped to one knee.

I am not typically a praying man but, prior to going on any op, I've always asked God for just two things before walking out. "Please help me to lead bravely and, if anything should happen to me, please make sure Shellie, and our daughters, Olivia and Constance, would have a good life." With that done, I walked out to the boys and asked them if there were any more questions and if everyone was happy.

They were always upbeat before going into the mountains but you could almost taste the nervousness in the humour. However, from this moment life would become very serious indeed and, as I looked at them lined up in front of me, I simply said, "Let's go to *Aqabar*".

As we approached the flight line, the din of the Huey-UH1 Helicopters drowned out any chance of last minute conversation. In the helicopters, illuminated by the faint glow of the cockpit lights, the pilots and crewmen were visible conducting their final checks under the Huey's thrashing rotor blades.

We lined up at the one o'clock position to each aircraft. Each section commander ordered his stick to "Load!" and the Pathans pushed a fully loaded, curved magazine onto their AK-47 Kalashnikov rifles and checked that it was secured. We were now on one knee waiting for the signal from the crew-chief or pilot to mount up. The wait sometimes seemed like an age with the noise of the helicopters negating all other communication.

I walked my line of troopers to do a last minute check. No loose articles, no twisted straps. Meanwhile, the other stick commanders did likewise. It was all part of the reassurance in leadership.

Then, all too soon, the thumbs-up came from the crew-chief and we walked in line to the helicopters. Four men went to each side of the Huey to mount up. As I got to the door of the helicopter, 50 Squadron's lead crewchief, Iqbal, gave me a broad smile from his bearded face.

He was a kind man who, I'd noted, tried to help the Pathans with their heavy equipment as they loaded up on his aircraft. He would always have water ready on our return. He was steadfast and highly professional and would regularly choose to be in the lead aircraft. In the not too distant future, Al-Qaeda would make him pay with his life for his leadership and courage.

Iqbal handed me a set of headphones and I positioned myself between the pilots. Tonight I was in the same aircraft as Caz. He would lead the three other helicopters in tactical trail formation through the difficult terrain to our drop off point. No sooner were we in the aircraft as I felt it coming light on the skids and pulling itself into the air.

We climbed towards the intimidating mountains that were shrouded in darkness. Some of the troopers in the Huey cabin had their NVGs down and were adjusting the focus, some not.

As for me, I took the view that, if we were going to slam into a mountain, then I'd rather see the one that was going kill me and every pair of eyes looking forward could help avert that event. As an experienced pilot, I had the privilege of being able to judge flight profiles and the prevailing light conditions from an informed perspective.

NVGs in extreme low light (no moon) conditions become extremely grainy and depth of vision becomes a very real challenge. Our pilots were magnificent; never did they fail to drop us off. Much more importantly, however, they were *always* there for pick up.

Getting stuck deep in the mountains on the border by sandstorms or aircraft unserviceability would leave us stranded and exposed to the elements and the enemy. Our biggest vulnerability was that we had no back up and no quick reaction force to bail us out of a sticky situation. With just twenty-seven of us on the ground we would most likely be out numbered and out gunned so only ruthless skill and guile would help us survive. If we were compromised deep in these mountains some of us would be dead by the morning.

The pilots gained altitude as the four Hueys wove through the mountain passes in order to shield and confuse the noise of the aircraft to those on the ground. We crossed the mountain ridges at an angle of forty-five degrees to avoid being pushed into the mountain by deadly downdrafts. The flight through the mountains on this evening took about fifty minutes.

When the four Hueys were two minutes out from the drop off, the Cessna had cleared the zone as "Cold," meaning the area contained no heat sources. The only way that we would be compromised at this stage was if we were unlucky enough to land in a tunnel area, where Al-Qaeda had dug in, or if our operational security had been compromised.

So we were a "Go" and Crewchief Iqbal held up two fingers and shouted "Two minutes!" All troops in the aircraft returned the signal and shouted "Two minutes!" (Thus ensuring all on board would hear the call). The immediate sound, thereafter, was of the working parts of the Pathans AK-47 rifles collecting a round from their magazines and slamming it into the weapon's breach. This could even be heard above the racket of the aircraft's main gearbox.

With weapons loaded and ready for action, the guys pulled off the floor strap across their laps, which went some way to ensuring the men would not slide out of the "banking and yanking" aircraft. The two open side doors became packed with four men each side and I could feel the adrenaline being released into my system. The sole intent of each trooper was to get out of that helicopter as soon as it landed because, on its approach and landing, it was no longer just a helicopter. It was now a bullet magnet.

Caz knew how important it was to get us on the correct ridge and I had selected a small bowl feature that was just below ridge level. It was a difficult approach by any measure. The clarity of the grainy NVGs made the identification of the landing site occur quite late and Caz had to get his aircraft well forward in the space in order to permit the three aircraft in trail to also get into the zone.

It didn't go quite as planned with the last aircraft missing the zone and having to "go-around". So, as we poured from the helicopters, a major concern was that the last aircraft could actually land on top of one of the men already lying in the drop zone.

Thankfully, the pilot knew what he had to do and, despite him having the most difficult and steep approach, he nailed it. Then, having spent just four extremely tense seconds on the ground to dispense his valuable cargo, he nosed his now nimbly light, aircraft into the air to accelerate down the re-entrant, popping over the ridge in urgent pursuit of his wingmen. I imagined he would be desperately keen to rejoin his pack for what would be an equally challenging flight out of the mountains by a different route from whence they came.

From the moment the last aircraft disappeared over the ridge, an eerie silence descended on the twenty-seven men now lying prone in a circle of defence on the mountain. Silence - absolute, brain-numbing silence after the apparent commotion and intense noise of the dismount.

As the dust literally settled, I tried hard to control my breathing and to listen for any sound, just anything above the pounding of my heart. The key was to try to identify any noise that might be a human sound and not to move. NVG's are great for what they are but, if you are flat on the ground or even in the slightest cover, an onlooker is unlikely to see you (provided you don't move) and, more to the point, nor you him.

I slowly cocked my head to one side and opened my mouth slightly to provide my sense of hearing the largest sound cavity available to the human body. During the minute or so we lay statue like, in absolute silence on the landing zone, it was difficult to imagine that my heavily armed Pathans and Jim were in such close proximity. It's funny how a man's focus to keep still is so honed if he knows an enemy sniper might be out there just looking for movement.

After a minute or so, when I had convinced myself that we were alone, I came slowly up to one knee and slapped my chest twice. This was the signal to move out and the signal would be passed down each line that had been automatically formed by our all-round defence.

The narrow paths formed by goats or the flow of water would only permit patrolling in single-file, which was always a bit nerve racking. If we got bounced, we would be spread out and, in order to flank the enemy, we would have to rely on the part of the patrol that was not in the ambusher's "kill zone." Response is very difficult in mountainous terrain because extreme geographic features channel everything and the chance of accidentally shooting at each other in the chaos of a night firefight is increased exponentially.

I knew that the ridgeline would guide us round to the north and then ease to the west as we got close to the position. Here we would have to insert the Observation Post (OP). However, the snag was that my position on the map, according to the GPS, didn't match the surrounding terrain.

In such instances, it is very easy to talk yourself into making the terrain match the mental image that the map is portraying. However, experience, and getting lost a few times (at the right time), soon reinforces the importance of trusting your map and the unwritten rule that, "terrain *never* lies".

The ridge undulated constantly, which was a real pain in the arse, but I managed to pick out paths that kept us on the blind side to the target valley. There was no permanent population up in these mountains apart from goat-herders and cutthroats, so if we were to bump into anybody without a goat, we'd try to evade but if compromised we'd have to kill or capture whatever we came up against. We simply could not risk our position being betrayed.

On this occasion, because we were at high altitude, I could hear the faint whine of the Cessna's Pratt and Whitney PT-6 engine somewhere in the distance. In 2004, there were no Unmanned Aerial Vehicles (UAV) Predators in the area and the local population took no notice the dull humming sound that one's subconscious would register as a distant, passing aircraft. The FLIR operator, as always, was giving useful commentary. He reported he had eyes on the patrol and that the route ahead appeared clear of heat sources. He also reported that the target village was quiet with no unusual activity. We clearly hadn't been seen or heard so far.

The rocks on the ridges gave way to gritty plateaus or paths and small, shrub-like plants lined our route even in this unforgiving and arid terrain. The images and the landmarks looked imposing and surreal through NVGs and the shadows, combined with the enhancement of reflected light, caused a remarkable green and black image of these massive and remarkable protrusions from earth. The troopers would constantly have to re-focus their goggles for close up scrutiny of the narrow path to ensure the footing was good and then focus back to middle distance to judge the best route ahead.

The patrol was slow going; the terrain was unfavourable and treacherous by any measure, the small climbs were very steep.

I needed to push on to get to where we needed to be long before first light. If we failed to reach the target, we would have to hide during daylight and get to the observation site the following night.

In these mountains, only desperate men would move by day, so we would only move during daylight in an absolute emergency. The other factor slowing us was that we were above 8,000 feet. The air felt thin and the temperature was dropping like a brick. It was vital not to sweat in these conditions so a gentle pace could avoid becoming damp from our own body fluids, which would only serve to accelerate hypothermia when we eventually stopped moving.

Moving precariously along just below the ridgeline it took us about three hours to cover the ten kilometres into the Final Rendezvous (FRV). The patrol went firm, meaning it would hold this ground if we were attacked. I advanced with Pervaiz and two men to seek out a vantage point for the observation of the village.

We could see the faint lights in the village many hundreds of feet below us and we located a rocky outcrop that would give us cover from three sides. We then moved up the slope and, as luck would have it, there was a small bowl-like feature that was on a reverse slope and out of sight from the target and surrounding area.

I remained at the LUP with one man; Pervaiz went back to the patrol to bring them forward.

As they came in, each stick knew their position in order to form the defensive box around the LUP. This was our rear guard and flanking sentry. I showed them the boundaries and they went firm in the positions that they would occupy with minimum movement for the next two days.

The last stick in was the OP team itself. They passed through the LUP and I worked them down the ridge to the outcrop, a distance of about thirty metres. Only three men would man the outcrop itself, two observing and one sleeping. Each sleep cycle was just one hour. The three men to the rear of the OP party were tasked to watch over and safeguard the men by looking for any movement on neighbouring mountains. This counter-surveillance team would work the same sleep routine.

Each section formed one side of a three-sided defensive square and had four men sleeping and two men awake in the rear guard. This enabled the luxury of two hour sleep cycle as opposed to the OP's one hour cycle. Jim and I positioned ourselves behind the OP rearguard with both Pervaiz and the Platoon's signaller so that we could give direction to any part of the Platoon. It was a desirable coincidence that my Pathans also happened to form a defensive square around me.

I grabbed a quick catnap until twilight and planned to check the daylight integrity of our position as the sun came up. The time now was approaching 5am. This is just a horrible time of day in the mountainous desert winter because temperatures plummet well below zero and it's bone marrow freezing, and this was in March! Even though for this partic-ular patrol I'd stipulated that we'd carry sleeping bags it was still hideously fucking cold.

We were going to be at high altitude for two days and three nights, so the below zero temperatures combined with moun-tainous winds, savagely and ruthlessly sought to suck the warmth out of our bodies. It was no reassurance to think that if we survived it that night, we'd have to go through it all again the following night.

As usual, the Pathans were quick to get themselves sorted out without any noise. In fact, our patrols were devoid of human noise. That I couldn't speak Pasthu except to order, "stop," "go," "right, "left" or "straight" when I absolutely needed to, ensured that they relied almost solely on my hand signals and used the same mode between themselves.

Watching the sun come up when in a tactical position in the mountains is probably more gratifying than any other sunrise, not least because heat is on its way. Unfortunately for my body's core temperature on that morning in the moun-tains, I could see the sun's extremities light arriving above the mountains long before the photosynthesis and the heat it would provide arrived.

As the light spilled over the ridges, the blacks turn to greys and then the greys changed to introduce spectacular colour to the world. It was easy to be wooed by the way God "turns the lights on." However, for a soldier, this is a time to be wide-awake.

For in the world where men don't have night vision or NVGs, it is this time of first light (or last light at sunset) that an attack will most likely occur. The entire patrol had been woken and we were, "stood to" ready for an enemy's "bounce" if it came. With the colour and the light also comes the truth of whether the selection of ground during the night will hold effectively during the day. It soon became obvious that the outcrop would not offer as much cover as I had hoped, so the day team would have to brass it out on the outcrop all day. There just wasn't sufficient cover to move teams back and forth to the LUP, which was perfect in its location.

I also discovered that, unless we were going to be attacked by an all out Everest-type climbing expedition from our left flank, then only one of our flanks was truly exposed. This was along our original avenue of approach, so we sited an additional light-machine gun on that axis. All in all, I thought we were in good shape to hold off any attack, however, our escape routes were very limited.

The really good news brought by the daylight was that we could see the target 4x4 vehicle (our reason for being there) parked under its makeshift carport in the village. It would have been impossible for any aircraft to see the vehicle or confirm its presence. We could only hope that whoever was driving the vehicle would move in the next thirty-six hours. We would then be able to relay that news back to Sadaqat in Quetta. Beyond that timescale, we'd very likely be running short of water and battery power for our radios.

As the sun rose above the ridges, the bliss of lying in the middle of these mountains on a beautifully sunny day as the temperature climbed was almost enough to let me forget that I was in bandit country. I had to remind myself that I was one of the biggest pieces of human currency around and that the bad guys would relish the thought of capturing me.

But as my mind wandered to places such as home, my wife, my kids, my next beer (whenever that would be), I picked up an unusual and unexpected sound - the gentle hum of a Pratt and Whitney engine. Across the radio net, I heard Pete's voice calling for a "Radio-check."

I gave him a "Loud and clear," and asked him what he was doing.

He replied, "I just wanted to check that you guys were okay. We'll stay out of sight but remain in radio contact. We are here for you if you need us." He paused. "All part of the service."

The last quip was, of course, his way of pushing a sense of fun into the fact that he and his crew could not permit themselves to stay on the ground back at base while we were potentially in harm's way. This kind of loyalty amongst men is something that has become increasingly touching to me as I grow older, especially as it seems to be so utterly devoid in the business world. Anyway, with Pete watching over us, I could rest a little and dozed in the sun with my earpiece firmly in place.

It must have been about ninety minutes later when Pete came back on the radio letting me know he was going off station. I thanked him for being there and we agreed to "See you later."

Ironically, it was only about an hour after Pete returned to base that the OP reported movement of the 4x4. It was being reversed from under its hiding place and manoeuvring within the village. The OP team remained locked on it while the Platoon's signaller, with his backpack radio, began to raise Quetta ops.

With communications established, I knew that the signaller would have notified them to let the General ("Sunray") know that "Blue One" was on the net. I had visions of Sadaqat making his way to the operations room. He was an incredibly laid back man. It was actually difficult to imagine him getting excited about anything.

The 4x4 remained outside one of the village compounds for about thirty minutes. The OP then reported that two men got into the vehicle. Shortly thereafter, it left the village and joined the track towards Quetta. As it disappeared out of view, I told the signaller to tell the COMCEN that "White *sandwich for two* was on its way." This would surely be the only white SUV travelling towards Quetta from that direction in that time frame, so the fixed check points should get Sadaqat the information he required.

Our task was likely to be complete, but I would have to wait for confirmation that the checkpoint had conducted a "routine check" on the vehicle. This came later when Pete came back on station. I asked him to confirm with Wahid permission to withdraw. He came back a few minutes later confirming they had what they needed and that we could pull out. I knew Sadaqat must have received the information he required without anyone, except his inner and trusted circle, realising what he'd done or how he had acquired the information.

Naturally the Pathans were unquestioningly pleased that they would be moving out a day earlier than expected. We would, however, have to wait until the sun was well down before moving out. The timing for the egress was important. We couldn't arrive at our pick-up point too early and risk compromise. A 3am rendezvous with the Hueys would be perfect.

One hour after sunset darkness had descended and the area had been scoured for any evidence of our being there. The Pathans were under very strict instructions to leave no trace whatsoever of our presence. I had even taught them how to shit in a Ziploc bag and carry it back to base rather than leave human excrement behind.

As we formed up, Ali, the iron-man in my section, asked if he could go on "point" (i.e. lead the patrol). He was as hard as nails and one of the most steadfast men in the platoon. I'd noticed that although he had a stable personality all the other Pathans were wary of him. I figured letting him going point could only do good. The map indicated that the route would be quite simple.

We had to work our way west back along the continuing ridgeline that paralleled the track the SUV had used many hundreds of feet below. As we neared the edge of the mountains, we would take a re-entrant and descend to the track itself. We would then parallel the cover of a dried-up riverbed that formed the base of the valley. Our pick up point (PUP) would be where the riverbed opened up into wide, almost delta-like feature.

We had plenty of time, but the terrain here was much more difficult to traverse than the route in. The shear drops and climbs of between one and three metres along this track were perilously difficult to negotiate using only the two-dimensional images provided by the NVGs.

My instinct was to get off the mountain as soon as we could. Ali was doing a good job picking his way along the ridge and I reassured myself as I thought, "This was how he grew up for Christ's sake!" He was a mountain man. And, with that, I surmised that he'd be able to accurately read these mountains. Unfortunately, I was very wrong.

On my map I had picked out three possible re-entrants that would be suitable for our night descent. They all looked about equal in difficulty, but doable. As we came to the top of the first and largest re-entrant, I recall looking down and thinking, "looking good" and thought Ali would turn right to start the downward trek. Instead, he hung on to the altitude and chose a path around the top of the re-entrant.

When we reached the second re-entrant, the path along its side looked somewhat reasonable for a descent. Through our goggles we could see the valley floor, which was a good indicator that the slope was not too convex, i.e. steepening with descent. Ali paused and I was shoulder to shoulder with him as the patrol behind us had automatically gone to cover. This was standard procedure anytime we stopped moving. I told Ali I would lead the team down the mountain and took point.

We started down the perilously steep incline and it wasn't long before we found ourselves in a world of hurt.

As we drew to the bottom third of the slope, it became evident that it was almost sheer. We'd descended at least 1,500 feet but had another 750 feet to go. What remained of this natural drainage path was increasingly steep with more and more loose shingle; there was another dangerously steep drop to our left.

Keeping a footing on with NVG was very difficult and we had no suitable safety equipment. As I edged down the narrow goat path, the inevitable happened - the ground under my left foot gave way. Before I knew it I was flat on my back sliding uncontrollably down the shingle slope with no sign of stopping. I had to think quickly, Jesus Christ, I could feel myself accelerating as the shingle formed a mini-avalanche all around me. I had no idea if there was a sheer drop ten or thirty metres away or if Ali was falling with me. But I did know the ledge couldn't be far and, if it swallowed me up, it would all end right here.

I rolled over to my front and rammed the extended butt of my M16 rifle into the shingle in a desperate attempt to anchor my slide and within, an instant, had transferred my entire weight into that effort. Thank God I came to an abrupt halt.

I lay there for a second or two gathering my thoughts and then, in my loudest whisper, told Ali, "Go up, go up." He was some thirty metres above me and was also lying down, having likely slid as well. He instantly understood that we would have to now try the next re-entrant and the signal was passed up to our twenty-five-man team to turn around and climb back up the mountain. This was going to be exhausting.

I crawled up the shingle, using my rifle as an "ice-axe," and got onto the makeshift path back up the re-entrant. The steep climb was scattered with boulders, which posed a genuine trip hazard on any upward trek. I was now at the back of the patrol as we gently ascended. My goggles were focused slightly ahead for best efficiency. Then came the crunch; I stumbled on a rock and, as I fell, I pushed out my left hand onto the slope, which would meet me prematurely.

Falling forward, in what was a minor stumble, my right hand gripped my rifle and my left extended to steady me on the slope, but it didn't work. Another boulder, which I couldn't see through the blur of my goggles, was where my left hand reached out and my middle finger hit the rock square on, taking the force of my entire weight.

The metacarpus knuckle was the pivot and it instantly gave way, dislocating my middle finger through ninety degrees. I must admit that, after millions years of existence, this Balochi re-entrant was introduced to a couple of whispered, but ripe English, expletives that it had likely never heard before. The pain was excruciating, but I knew I had to reduce the dislocation immediately.

I grabbed my finger with my right hand, braced myself for the pain, and gave it a sharp pull. The joint, stabilized, but then immediately popped out again. - Shit! That *really* hurt! I grabbed the finger again and gritted my teeth. I knew I would have to fight my instinct that was telling me to limit the pain.

I exerted a rapid and aggressive pull of the finger while trying to ignore the additional pain that was now permeating up my entire arm. It worked; the finger popped in. This was progress. I pulled out my medpack and bound my middle finger with tape to my fourth finger. It would act as an ostensible splint. Jim moved down to check if I was OK, I told him it hurt like shit but at least I wasn't at the bottom of the gulley. I asked him to stay at what was now the rear of the patrol so that I could move forward and take point. He patted me on my arm and simply said, "I've got you covered." And I truly knew that he did.

With that short, unscheduled rest for the platoon complete, we made our way back up the re-entrant, cursing quietly like the sailor I once was. It was then when Pete's voice from the Cessna crackled over my earpiece, asking, "How's it going?"

I replied, "You don't wanna know. I'll tell you later."

The third re-entrant was kinder than the second but there were nonetheless numerous two and three metre sheer gullies to navigate, each offering the opportunity to break a limb or turn an ankle. We were now running short of time for the pick up rendezvous and I was concerned that we might not be there before the helicopters. At the bottom of the re-entrant, I must admit I've seldom been so happy to see a dried up riverbed.

I could tell the Pathans were exhausted. It had been a perilously dangerous patrol, not just because we were deep in enemy territory but because the terrain was so dangerous that even the enemy wouldn't think that we would use it. I guess the constant threat to us was always going to be one or the other.

The patrol along the riverbed was without incident and almost a respite after what we'd been through. As we came out into the delta feature, the ground was moist, which was a pleasant novelty.

The Caravan confirmed he had no heat sources in the area other than us so we were apparently still undetected and on our own. However, the overriding instinct was to get the fuck out of there.

We moved quickly and silently to mark the LZ with infrared strobes and cam-sticks. These are visible with NVGs but not to the naked eye. As soon as we heard the Hueys or received a two-minute call, the strobe would be activated to help the pilots land precisely where we were waiting.

Our sole purpose in life was then to mount the Hueys as quickly as we could. We selected cover in a position where we could get to the helicopters quickly provided he landed on his light. The last man on board would invariably be the section commander. He would recover the light prior to boarding the aircraft and calling the best words of any patrol. "Last man."

As the helicopters made their approach, it was akin to waiting for the starter's gun to sound in an Olympic hundred-metre race. The pick up was always high risk, and inevitably took longer than a drop-off. Each trooper, although alternately placed for all round defence, was preparing his body for the launch from cover and the sprint to the helicopter. This often happened through blinding sand. All the men had been provided with sand goggles, which were invaluable, but, due to the primitive design of their NVGs, were essentially useless at night. In these circumstances, it was often just a case of running blindly through the dust storm towards the sounds of the churning rotors, engines, and hydraulic pumps.

That night, as the troopers leapt or rolled with the weight of full marching order into the helicopters, the crewchiefs were tensely anticipating making the call to the pilot to lift off. We all knew we were incredibly vulnerable during the mount up. It was really the only time when an ambush would undoubtedly and fatally split the force.

In the confusion caused by the extremes of dust and noise, it would have been all too easy to leave a man behind. That never happened.

The flight back to Quetta meant one thing; water! Our Crewchief, Iqbal, opened the case of water and handed each man a bottle. Each dust drenched trooper either hugged a bottle to himself or shared with the man next to him.

Every man would now be feeling the onset of exhaustion caused by the cessation of the adrenaline rush in his system. We were all caked in dust with the fine sand even finding every gap in our bodies be it between teeth and even our buttocks, causing temporary irritation to both ends. For my part, two thoughts overwhelmed this discomfort; I was on the way to the shower and I'd survived another patrol but the throbbing pain of my finger was killing me.

The helicopters climbed to more than 1,500 feet above ground level. This put us out of threat from small arms fire and, with the aircraft lights off, the night provided a comfort blanket to let us feel about as safe as we could get in a single engine helicopter.

Upon landing, we walked out from the helicopters to conduct the last drill of the patrol. Each section lined up to unload their weapons. Once the "unload" was complete and each weapon was checked by the section commanders to be clear, we climbed onto the waiting trucks to go back to the briefing room.

The smokers who had been craving a cigarette since they'd last left the same room could now "smoke 'em if they'd got 'em". There was hot chai waiting for us and the first sip would seem like the best taste in the world.

One could feel the sense of pride amongst these men and the respect in themselves and their colleagues. Following the debriefing session, the Pathans were about to mount their trucks when my phone rang.

It was a sleepy sounding Colonel Wahid. He asked me to hold the Platoon at the airfield because the General would arrive in an hour. It was his intent to congratulate them and to present them with their Helicopter Assault Force wings. It was not what anyone really wanted to hear. We were all physically and emotionally spent and wished for nothing except quiet and sleep. I immediately told the team what was going on and asked Moussa to arrange some more Chai for the Platoon and to have the chef prepare a small snack for the General, should he want some breakfast on arrival.

We were exhausted from the overnight trek across the mountains but the Pathans took the sleep depravation all in their stride. It was always humbling to see how these truly brave and special men unquestioningly accepted whatever life dealt them.

I needed to shower the dust out of every orifice before the General arrived and I walked, dog-tired, to my room with my kit slung across one shoulder and my weapon low slung. I wiped the fine sand off my M16 rifle and put it back in its carrying case. Along with the shotgun and machine gun, it was locked in the metal chest under the full size table/desk by my bed. I quickly unloaded and wiped off the working parts of my SIG. I may have been obsessed with keeping this weapon clean but couldn't bear the risk a stoppage caused by the grit that had inevitably impregnated the working parts over the past few hours.

All the rest of the clean up could wait until after the General had been and gone and I'd got some sleep. I'd also have to figure out how I could get my finger fixed. As I looked at the considerably swollen and paralyzed digit, I wondered about the challenges of working through the injury during the next few weeks. But for now, it was time to get out of my dust soaked clothes and into that soothing shower.

I decided to call my mate, Dr. Bob in the U.S. to get some medical advice. I explained the injury to him and somewhat predictably, his sense of humour immediately kicked in. He promptly told me that the best treatment would be to stick the swollen finger deep into my anus and squeeze my butt cheeks together. If for no other reason, I would feel like I was back in the Navy and forget about the pain altogether!

He then added, I'd done all I could and to get to a place I could get it X-rayed. In a continuance of his delight at my minor injury the prick later emailed me a bill for $450.00 for this sage medical advice. If nothing else his humour did actually provide some light relief.

By 8am, the 1st Platoon of RIF had cleaned up and were fallen in three ranks on the flight line awaiting Sadaqat's arrival. The General addressed his men as any good leader would. He told them that he was aware of just how hard they had worked over the previous months and that they had achieved a capability far beyond any level previously achieved in the Frontier Corps or by any soldiers in Balochistan.

Then, in the presence of the 50 Squadron officers and crew and the DynCorp mechanics, I called out each platoon member's name. As each individual broke ranks and marched forward to the General to accept their HAF wings and certificate, I quietly passed commentary to the General on the man's individual performance and role within the Platoon. Breaking with Pakistani military tradition, the last man called forward for his HAF Wings was Captain Pervaiz.

The fact that he was the last soldier to receive his wings was not lost on the General or the men. He was a leader who now thought first and foremost for the safety and well being of the men in his command. The poignancy of this event was apparent to all who watched these men receive a qualification they had worked so hard to gain. The pride in the HAF themselves was matched only by the pride in the faces of the tenacious mechanics who had made it possible for our aircraft to fly, by the magnificent pilots who had so ably conquered the elements to deliver and retrieve the men, and by the FLIR team who had constantly and consistently kept us out of harm's way.

In the United States, the news of "the twenty-five" would quickly travel to the highest levels of Capitol Hill. The only operational unit of the Department of State in Pakistan had delivered for its Government the first element of a joint task force and a composite border assault team that was now capable of taking the battle to the Taliban and Al-Qaeda in their own backyard.

Following the ceremony, I drank tea with the General in the cookhouse in the compound. We had become totally relaxed with each other. I explained that I now had to travel to the U.S. to provide a briefing to the Air Wing and attempt to convince the powers that be to allocate more Hueys to the programme. The General told me not to be in the U.S. too long. He explained that they had a lead on the hostages that had been taken by Jalil Jaffar and were focusing on Lauralai to the northeast of Quetta; he added that the infamous Akbar Bugti had blown up the Sui gas pipeline again, and was forcing a show down.

I told the General that I hoped they wouldn't move until I got back but, if they got a window of opportunity, then Pervaiz and the team would be the best qualified to solve the problem. After we'd said our goodbyes, I packed my kit and grabbed an hour's sleep. I woke and called my sister, Angela, to wish her a happy birthday and headed up to Islamabad to rest my weary body. I looked forward to a well-earned glass of wine and getting treatment for my finger, which by now was completely paralyzed and very badly swollen. However my injury was put into perspective by a fellow passenger on the Cessna that day, it was the young Pakistani Army officer who had been blown up by one of Bugti's landmines and whose life one of our Huey's had saved a few days prior. He had been stabilised and was now headed to Islamabad with us to clean up his leg amputation.

In the news, Colin Powell announced that Pakistan would be a "Major non-NATO ally". I wasn't convinced this statement meant anything in practical terms or if it would have any affect on the future of our programme. However, I was leaving for Washington DC at the end of the week to ask for more Hueys, so would soon find out

CHAPTER 11

Congress and a Martyr

The next two days in Slammy were a whirlwind of activity heaped on top of sheer exhaustion from the previous week's activities in Quetta.

I reluctantly dragged myself out of bed on Friday morning and drove my Rav4 through Islamabad to the U.S. Embassy. Cheryl from Army Intelligence had asked for a brief on events in Quetta, and hadn't there just been a few since I'd last seen her. She frantically took notes as I brought her up to date.

These would doubtless be transcribed and be sent to the DIA's Bolling Air Force Base in Washington DC within hours of me leaving her office.

In the afternoon Dorothy escorted me up to Ambassador Powell's office in order for me to provide a progress brief and update on the events of the past few weeks. I must admit I was expecting the meeting to be solely with Dorothy and Ambassador Powell so was rather surprised when General Stone and representatives from the Embassy's other organisations were already waiting for me in the Ambassador's ante-room.

Nancy Powell was a career diplomat and had previously spent some time as an Assistant Secretary in International Narcotics and Law Enforcement, so she was certainly familiar

227

with what my counterparts were doing in Colombia and Peru. Her assignment as the U.S. Ambassador to Pakistan when the American emphasis was on military and intelligence operations must have been a challenge for her. Not least because she had to deal with the fact that male chauvinism in Pakistan was not only accepted but moreover, by religious dictate, traditional.

I'm not sure whether it was a conscious response by the State Department, or by Ambassador Powell herself, to demonstrate to the Pakistanis that the Embassy would bow to no such foibles of the role of the sexes within an Islamic republic.

I explained to the Ambassador the events of the past few months and how, with the help of General Sadaqat and Brigadier Shafiq from the MOI, we had moved rapidly to develop what I considered to be the most capable, integrated joint task force on the border. I emphasised that the training had been conducted at break-neck speed and stressed that all elements involved, U.S. and Pakistani, (I didn't mention the stalwart British support I'd received), had truly pulled together to make it happen.

However, "State" had been forced to shoulder the burden of training and equipping because we simply couldn't afford to wait for other elements (the DoD) to provide assistance or resources. My emphasis had been to develop an appropriate concept of operations that suited the capability of our force and sought to undermine the strengths of the enemy. I had then used proven British military counter-insurgency doctrine by which to implement it.

I moved on quickly to show the Ambassador the FLIR tape of the night assault and hostage rescue. As I gave commentary to the events unfurling on the screen I noticed General Stone lean forward as if to help his absorbance of what was unfolding in front of him. A discreet but wry smile came onto his face. He later provided the reason for the smile when he disclosed to me, "Howard, you achieved in a few weeks what all these other "experts" haven't in two fucking years!"

Other regional affairs experts who were in the room remained silent for most of the brief but at the close of the video one of them asked me when I'd have the second platoon trained. I told him by the end of June provided I got the additional Hueys. An apparently Arrogant Woman who I didn't know glibly asked, "Can we have a copy of the tape?"

"Of course," somehow emerged from my mouth.

It was then time for the Ambassador to round off the meeting and make her final comments or questions. Previous experience had imparted on me that when in a meeting or receiving an email it is often the last point that is raised that is the predominant reason for the communication. So I was about to find out why I had been squeezed into the Ambassador's schedule and she into mine.

"So you're leaving when for DC?" she asked.

"Sunday morning Ambassador."

"And who do you expect to meet in DC?" She had just asked me two questions to which she knew the answers, but she was in control of the conversation so I'd play the game to see where this was going.

"Well I'm not really sure Ambassador," I replied, "But first I have to go to Air Wing for a debrief and then my guess would be I'll go to DC to meet with whoever controls the allocation of Hueys."

I put the piece in about the Air Wing because I knew she wasn't the slightest bit interested in this part of the visit. I simply didn't want her to think that I thought the DC appointments were a sole emphasis.

"I believe you'll be meeting with John Mackey in that regard." Here was the real reason I was sitting in her office.

"I think it important that you are aware you should stick to the sole issue of the helicopters with Mr. Mackey, it is quite easy to digress in such meetings and I would advise against any dilution beyond the reason you are there."

Naturally, I agreed with her and, in fact, if she did have any concerns about me digressing she needn't have worried. My sole aim was to get the helicopters. I wasn't bothered about the internal politics of the Embassy or even the State Department for that matter. The meeting ended with the Ambassador thanking me for my time.

This meeting proved to be the only time she met with me or thanked me during my entire year. All other communications regarding our composite activity on the border would be delivered, received and filtered as Dorothy deemed appropriate but, as long as I got the job done, frankly, I didn't care.

That evening I went to the American Club with Jerry the Cop where we covered the whole sequence of events.

While there, I received two calls. One was from Paul confirming my meeting with John Mackey the following week. The second was from Pete letting me know that the Caravan had been tasked to provide video and FLIR coverage over Laurlai in the hunt for Jalil Jaffar. The noose on this brutal subversive was beginning to tighten and his clock was running.

My phone awoke me on Saturday morning; it was Robert from the British Embassy. He explained that a Pakistani ANF patrol had been ambushed on the border during the night. One of their troopers had been killed and five wounded. The patrol, which was about fifty strong, had somehow been compromised and they estimated that over 200 gunmen had attacked them.

Robert explained that the patrol had been attacked whilst covertly searching for a cache of narcotics. They had been on target for about twenty minutes when the first rounds came inbound. This indicated the opposition had managed to mobilise 200-armed men in as much time or had been informed of the patrol's target. It was probably the latter.

My mind raced thinking how we could avoid a similar calamity, but those thoughts were to be rapidly broken when Robert said, "But that's not the worst of if mate."

I thought, "What could be worse? They lost a man for Christ's sake."

After a short pause Robert said, "We've received a report that the reason they had so many gunmen ready was that they were looking for the U.S. led patrol."

He paused again, and just to make sure I'd comprehended what he'd said, he concluded, "They were looking for you mate."

I'd just been given notice that *my* clock in Pakistan was ticking.

I told Robert I was outbound to DC for a week and a half, and we agreed that it was just as well so that things could calm down a bit. I hung up thinking how I could use the information I'd just received to make damn sure these bastards didn't get me before my year was up.

The following day I rendezvoused with Brigadier Shafiq at Islamabad airport at 3am for our departure to the U.S. and discovered how real VIPs are treated in Pakistan.

Upon our arrival in Florida Sharon and Paul greeted the Brigadier and me at the Air Wing offices. We went through the gambit of current issues with Sharon referring back to the many update emails I had been sending her and Paul. We also received a message from Quetta that three Hueys had been tasked to Lauralai, I hoped that the HAF weren't going in just yet; I wanted to be there.

Sharon revealed that while we had been in transit Ambassador Powell had proposed that we meet with John Mackey next week. Whatever had been reverse engineered had effectively provided the illusion that the meeting was at the behest of the Ambassador, which was fine.

Sharon told me, "You're gonna love this," and laughed as she pushed a printed copy over to me. Dorothy had added comment to the Ambassador's proposal that I should only meet with Mr. Mackey "Under close supervision." As I read the words aloud all of us in the room broke into laughter.

The following day the Brigadier was dispatched to DC for the full dog and pony show that befitted his status in the programme. I was pleased Sharon had arranged this protocol. Brigadier Shafiq was an exceptional officer and a key element in ensuring Pakistan's Ministry of Interior and the State Department's aviation assets were a success. I spent the day completing my preparation of a presentation for the following day's Air Wing annual operational conference.

As might be expected Colombian operations took the forefront at the conference with Peru as a contrast. What the Air Wing had achieved in Colombia was nothing short of remarkable. Over a sustained period of years under John's command they had eradicated and prevented countless tons of illegal narcotics reaching the shores of the USA. If one had any doubts regarding the difficulty of their task then one only had to look at the number of rounds fired by the helicopter gunships, the hits sustained, and especially the actual losses of the spray aircraft and pilots.

When it was my turn to speak I had decided to paraphrase an introduction used during the Second World War by Lord Louis Mountbatten when he first addressed his troops after becoming Supreme Allied Commander of South East Asia. With Britain's focus on the war in France this part of British Army in Asia had been nicknamed "The Forgotten Army". Mountbatten has told his troops, "Some of you may have heard that you are called the Forgotten Army. I'm here to tell it's not true. You are not forgotten... because nobody has even heard of you."

My introduction slide read:

> *Department of State*
> *Air Wing*
> *in Pakistan*
> *"It's difficult to be forgotten when nobody has even heard of you."*

It was important to take full advantage of the expertise in the conference room that day.

In Colombia they played by "big boys rules." If they were shot down or captured over narcotic producing territory then they would most likely be taken hostage for ransom. However, when they were off duty, there was no concerted effort to hunt them down and the threat level was no higher than the normal crime rate. In Pakistan, however, the threat from extremists was always there whether on operations in the mountains or shopping; it was only the depth of threat that varied.

It was gratifying to have the Colombian operators keenly engage in questions and suggestions. The entire Air Wing was plainly cohesive as a unit and the different programmes were helping each other wherever they could. The unit was solely focused on operational effectiveness and devoid of glory boys. This point was pushed home when, at the end of the conference, Peru's Senior Advisor commented that he would not stand in the way of Hueys that had been allocated to Peru being diverted to Pakistan.

Most of the pieces of the jigsaw to gain the extra Huey's were now in place and the next day Sharon and I boarded a plane for DC to try to close the deal.

Once in Washington, we'd go to the State Department in the morning to provide a brief and meet key figures before going across to Capitol Hill for the meeting with John Mackay. I was once again thrust into a world of extreme contrasts from my work in Quetta but knew the next twenty-four hours would be crucial to maintain momentum on that distant and godforsaken frontier.

On the morning of Friday 19th March the taxi dropped Sharon and me at 23rd C Street. We walked through the various layers of security to enter the main entrance of the Department of State. Sharon knew the routine and corridors like the back of her hand so I just tagged along next to her as she pointed out numerous items or people of interest.

Eventually we arrived in a lecture theatre that contained an audience of about forty people. The Brigadier and Steve Schrage greeted us. It was good to see Steve again. This man had the admirable quality of channelled determination. His ballsy trip to Quetta, where he had put aside his own personal safety, had truly given him an indication of what we were up against and he was doing his damndest to ease our burden. This man was a patriot by his deeds as well as his words.

Steve made an introduction to the audience that, in the words of Churchill, "my father would have been proud of, but only my mother would have believed." I thanked Steve for his kind words before Brigadier Shafiq and I presented a progress report and update on Pakistan. Steve and Sharon's intent was to use our presence in DC to gain penetration within the State Department in the hope that, picking up on the

Mountbatten theme, the programme would one day have the opportunity to be forgotten.

That afternoon Sharon and I caught a taxi to Capitol Hill. As we passed the Smithsonian Metro station I looked over to the grass of the Mall where fourteen-years earlier I had landed a USMC CH-46 Sea Knight as part of the Desert Storm Victory Parade.

This spot of grass on the Mall was also hallowed ground from a personal perspective. It was the spot during the event of that parade that I met the lady that was to become my wife and the mother of my children.

As Sharon and I reached the top of the Mall I learned that all the work behind the scenes of the House of Representatives occurs, not in the famous Capitol Building itself, but in the grey stone buildings that line the right hand approach to the Capitol.

Again, Sharon knew where she was headed and we entered the building's security procedures. The interior of the building was spacious but sparse and as we walked along the wide corridor towards John Mackay's office I kept telling myself the worse that could happen was that he could say "No" but even so I felt nervous.

John Mackay swept into the room and although he was absolutely as pleasant and as courteous as any man could be, it was easy to see why those around him could be intimidated. He had an abrasive form of delivery that had served him well in life. I thought it very likely that only his wife and his grand-children had the nerve to challenge his naturally harsh tone.

He opened up by saying it was nice to see me again and reflected that Capitol Hill was a far cry from the bar in Islamabad. He also thanked Sharon for coming which I thought was gracious because, in truth, he must have known she had no choice.

Sharon gave a very quick overview and then asked me to bring John up to date on what had been happening in Quetta and the operational status of the HAF. This gave me the opportunity to use the unit's new title. John asked about the ANF. I told him we were now tied in closely with their team, the DEA and the Brits. I added that we would be putting the ANF troops through the helicopter drills upon my return.

I then explained we were about to commence the training of the next batch of twenty-five RIF militia and this would bring the ground strength up to fifty Pathans. This expansion of the ground force would require seven serviceable Hueys to make a full lift of troops. I needed an additional three helicopters to avoid leaving half the force stranded on the ground, exposed and unprotected deep in Taliban territory during a two-wave delivery or pick-up.

John listened intently. I didn't know which way this would swing, but I'd made the pitch as best I could. He asked, "Have there been any more issues with the Pakistanis messing with the aircraft?"

It was a clear reference to them being impounded in 2003. I explained that those problems were a thing of the past and went further to enlighten him that, such was the current level of cooperation, Brigadier Shafiq had even accompanied me on my trip to the U.S. on this occasion. I added that the Brigadier had co-presented a brief on the programme in the Department of State that very morning. I believed this was "a first."

John paused and explained that it was clear to him that the Hueys destined for Peru should be diverted to Pakistan. He said, "You are doing front line work out there Howard. You are up against it and I wish we could do more to support you."

I thought, "So do I" but I didn't say it.

He continued, "It will do Peru no harm to wait for the next batch of Hueys coming from the manufacturer and I've confirmed with them that can happen within a few months."

He had done his homework. "Also the fact that Peru doesn't permit us to conduct air eradication by spraying gives an indication of the urgency they place upon the problem, so I don't see how they can object." He had taken an angle I had neither considered nor had knowledge of.

All I knew was that I should agree with everything he was saying. John then explained that there could be some resistance from the US Ambassador to Peru, James Struble, but added that the Ambassador was new in post and reflected that the Ambassador would have to look to the global interests of the USA and not those of Peru.

Sharon and I walked out of the John Mackey's office having got everything we went there to get. We were elated and it was time for a beer before my family turned up at my hotel to take me home for five precious days. It also gave Sharon a chance to meet Shellie and my daughters who all arrived in the hotel bar looking stunning.

The next few days flew by but gave me a chance to get decent medical treatment for my finger, which was constantly painful and all but paralysed.

My return to Islamabad was all too soon with far too many loose ends left at home. Shellie was clearly struggling with the thought of the move from Pennsylvania to my next job in Connecticut and things seemed a bit tense between us. I managed to grab a few hours with my Mum and sister Sue while in transit at Heathrow and I reflected that my mother was looking very tired. The struggle through immigration in Islamabad was the cream on the cake in regard to a low-morale return to the now all too familiar pungent smell of Pakistan.

As ever, the term "baptism of fire" applied to my arrival in Islamabad. We'd had several aircraft tasked to Wana to provide casualty evacuation support. The Pakistan Army had decided to use a conventional "fix bayonets" approach to try to drive foreign fighters out of the tribal area and had been sucked into a trap of monumental proportions.

The subversives permitted the spearhead of the attack to enter and penetrate the area without resistance; the logistic tail of the force had followed bringing up the rear.

No sooner was this large but lightly defended logistic element in the "kill zone" that the insurgents opened up with an overlapping attack from mortars, rockets, heavy machine gun fire, pre-placed explosives and small arms fire. The logistic unit was decimated and the spearhead cut off.

The result was a rout so savage that the Divisional Commander had to disguise himself in civilian clothing to avoid being captured when Al-Qaeda overran his command post.

Sources involved estimated that some 300 Pakistani soldiers were killed, wounded or captured and the entire Division was operationally decimated. Many of the soldiers' who were captured were summarily executed. In one instance, five soldiers were hanged under cover of darkness in full view of an Army position. The unfortunate individuals had additionally had their tongues cut out.

Morale amongst the enemy must have been high until 2am a few nights later when a different force came into effect.

I was awoken by the uncharacteristic squawk of crows outside my bedroom window. Within seconds the entire house was violently shaking. I just lay in my bed thinking, hoping, the rapid shaking movement would stop at any moment but it didn't. The noise was of items falling over downstairs and outside so I decided it was time to get out of the house before it piled in on me and I leapt out of bed. Almost immediately the shaking stopped but then transformed into a rolling motion below my feet. I had to get out of the house but I always removed the key from the lock because I knew locks were easier to "pick" from the outside if a key were left in the lock so now could I find the key to the bedroom door before the house collapsed?

Outside there were car and house alarms sounding, birds squawking and dogs barking. I found the key, grabbed my pistol and went downstairs, at least everything looked intact. I opened the front door to see if my guard was okay and he was. My crisis was over but deep in the mountainous border areas, close to the epicentre of the earthquake entire villages and homes were destroyed and entire families killed. I simply hoped the bad guys were amongst them.

Before I headed back to Quetta, Dorothy, Jerry and I had a meeting with Assistant Secretary Agra of the MOI and Brigadier Shafiq. The addition of the three extra Hueys would mean the requirement for an increase in aircrew. In a stroke of genius the Brigadier proposed offering civilian contracts to former pilots from 50 Squadron who had now left the military. This would be cost effective and permit Caz to conduct refresher training rather than starting from scratch.

In order to ensure the support for the new Hueys from all sides we would also continue to embrace the ANF and would start with an operation to destroy a drug refining location near Girdijungal; this place turned out to be two towns with one name on both sides of the porous and ill-defined border. Our FLIR coverage would be crucial and it was agreed along with the approval of Brigadier Shafiq that we would support this.

Early the next morning I arrived at Qasim to jump on the Caravan and that afternoon I was called to the Headquarters in Quetta to find that General Sadaqat had gone on some leave. His Deputy Commander, Brigadier Ali Reza was keen to meet with me on an unannounced subject but one on which I could feel his excitement.

This was our first opportunity to chat in operational terms and I found the Brigadier precise and informative. Furthermore, I suspected that he was keen to have an operation happen "on his watch".

He explained that J.J. had murdered two of the women who he had taken hostage on the bus. It was the Brigadier's intent to commit the HAF, with other RIF in support, into an attack on the compound that had been one of the locations subject to the Cessna's surveillance, once he received 100% confirmation of Jaffir's presence.

The Brigadier pulled open a map that was on the side of his desk and indicated to me the probable location of the target and went on to make clear that the information was extremely sensitive.

If there was a leak their informant would undoubtedly be exposed and killed. I told him I'd tell no one and we could fake our preparation to look like something else to onlookers because both he and I knew J.J. had his paid spies in the police and in the FC. They would be looking for any unusual activity so we would have to make any preparation appear to be something else.

I'd start the preparations straight away and on the way back to compound I called Pervaiz to have him book the rifle range to zero our weapons and to bring the HAF to the airfield the following day for training. We would spend our day at the deserted village trying to cover every permutation of what could occur at the target compound.

The Caravan was tasked to Girdi with the ANF that evening so using it for an over-flight of the J.J. target was not an option. I spoke to Caz and told him I needed him to fly me past an area at an altitude of about 1,000 ft above ground level. It would be one pass so that any observer would just assume it was a military helicopter in transit. We studied the map and decided Caz could follow a road as a line feature. I needed him to put the area of interest "down-sun" so I could get a couple of pictures using the Nikon D-100 and the zoom lens.

I reiterated it would be just one pass and asked for normal speed; if we messed it up we wouldn't be able to return for at least twenty-four hours. Caz had notified the crew that we had a fastball and without revealing the reason or precise location we drove out to the flight line.

The Nikon D-100 with its 80-210 zoom lens was a fantastic camera and gave me precisely what I needed. The road that Caz had used as his guide gave us enough stand-off; I was confident I'd taken a first look at the target and no suspicion had arisen from any element, friendly or otherwise.

From the target area Caz flew us in a long race track to the east of the mountains and then to the disused village where I needed to ascertain if any of the buildings had similar layout to the potential target. Fortunately rural architecture in Balochistan is neither decorative nor creative. It is a culture that is dominated by Islam and the tribal chieftains, known as Sardars. In order for them to maintain an iron, and often-savage, grip on their people they have blocked almost all development and empowerment of the people.

The regrettable result is the area has been unimpeded by development and progress in design of rural structures has been non-existent. So I was able to pick out part of the village that was similar enough in layout to the target compound and determined, where there were differences, we'd be able to compromise.

The following day I briefed the HAF that we were required to perfect their compound take down drills. We remained at the village all day practising approach and siting of the main assault group and fire party and the cut-offs. If we were forced to stand off in a siege-like operation we would need careful siting of the snipers and the light machine guns.

If the bad guys decided to counter-attack the interlocking fire from two machine guns would ensure they would run into the protective fire. This precluded the need for the gunners to have to aim straight at and potentially miss multiple suicide targets running or driving towards them.

We also rehearsed several takedowns of the compound in case we were required to physically assault the buildings in order to attempt to free the hostages. This is an extremely high-risk procedure so it was my hope we would only be forced to do this if we had the advantage of total surprise. The other event that would force a takedown was if J.J. actually started killing more hostages in a siege situation.

By the end of the day the HAF were exhausted but I was content that when they were called upon to besiege or storm the compound then they could do so with minimal unwanted casualties on either side. We would meet the next day at the ranges, which were close to the Shi-ite settlements of Quetta, to zero our weapons and rehearse our arcs of fire drills.

By now it was approaching the middle of April and the air assets had become the victim of their own success. The Caravan was working in support of ANF, we had one Huey tasked to Waziristan for Casevac and one Huey on "Poppy Patrol" during which it would try identify fields of opium poppies. All these tasks were vital but our aircraft and crews were literally spread to the four winds.

To make matters worse we had one Huey that was permanently down due to its main gearbox shedding metal into its oil. Two other aircraft required parts that were held up awaiting the fickle and uncooperative clearance from Pakistan customs officers.

I was increasingly concerned that the HAF wouldn't have any helicopters if the compound takedown occurred imminently. However, all we could do now was wait for a confirmed intelligence report for one thing was for sure, it wouldn't do any of us any good if we hit the wrong compound. We had to know 100% that J.J. was there and this crucial necessity had to dictate the entire pace and conduct of the impending operation.

The ANF's operation in the west-central sector of Balochistan did not go well and would also serve to inject yet more caution for our own approach to events of the same week. Robert called me to let me know that the assault on the drug-refining compound had gone ahead but there had been an incident involving crossfire that had killed an innocent bystander. This was clearly a significant setback because it would doubtless cause the innocents in the area to become more hostile to security forces and lean towards the drug producers as their protectors and saviours.

It was exactly what we didn't need to happen. Robert said he needed to get down to Quetta soonest with his boss and asked if we had any aircraft running between Islamabad and Quetta. As luck would have it Tom from the U.S. Embassy was due to visit us for a "security review" so I told Robert to catch the same Caravan the following day.

That afternoon the call I'd been dreading on one hand but wanting on the other came. The compound was confirmed and J.J. was to stay there for the night. The problem was the HAF were now ready but we didn't have enough Hueys. "What shitty luck. Oh for those Peru birds now," I thought.

I decided I would have to be dropped at Belili and that the HAF would have to use their trucks. It was a damn shame but we had a window of opportunity to nail the operation and we had to get it done. I briefed the team on the mission and situation and went over the siting of our team. The HAF would form the main siege/assault group and first line of cut-offs. Beyond that line the additional RIF would provide reserve in depth.

I called Colonel Wahid and told him we were ready in all respects. He said the General was on his way back from Karachi but he'd ordered that the HAF were to deploy immediately. He added that we would have to challenge the compound and give the murderers the chance to surrender. Shit; there would be no surprise assault. This could cost us lives.

I re-briefed the new game-plan men and emphasised. "Stick to your drills. Do exactly as you have been trained. If you are told to move, move fast and totally overpower the enemy with speed and aggression. Do not hesitate!"

I repeated this, "Do not hesitate because *he who hesitates is dead*!"

I continued, "If any man goes down injured during an assault do not stop to help him, you have to keep going towards the target at speed. Don't let them break our momentum. None of you will be taken prisoner and none of you will be left on the ground, but we have to overcome the target before we tend our wounded. Any questions?"

The atmospherics were as serious as they could get. "OK stick to your drills." I repeated. "Stick to your drills and if told to move *do not hesitate*." I paused. "Let's go to Aqabar." They moved to the trucks.

On the approach to the target the HAF linked up with a trusted police guide who reiterated the need for giving J.J. the chance to turn himself in. The siege force moved in on foot from three kilometres under cover of darkness and, as always, remained completely undetected. By the time first light came the trap was set around the compound.

The main assault group was in positions where, if necessary, they could use cover to get up to the walls of the compound. The Light Machine Guns were placed where they could either concentrate fire on the compound or swing to pre-designated arcs to push out interlocking fire.

The cut-off groups were placed out of sight of the target but covered the channelled routes that came from the rear of the compound. The situation seemed to be sealed as tight as a nut and the rehearsals at the disused village had been worth their weight in gold in order to achieve this quickly and quietly with minimum noise. Every man knew his role.

Pervaiz had been provided with a loud hailer so it was decided the challenge would be made shortly after first light when the siege force had got their bearings and adjusted position where need be, which is precisely what happened. Unfortunately for J.J. when his wake up call came he was truthfully informed that Frontier Corps had surrounded him and that he should give himself up.

However, he made the critically incorrect assumption that the term "Frontier Corps" referred to the conventional and poorly trained border guards so his response was to loose off a few rounds from the compound.

The response in kind from the HAF was one of concentrated firepower by the three light machine guns each providing a long burst of fire into the point from which the rifle fire had been made. The multiple rounds practically demolished the wall that had protected J.J. so, in a rapid assimilation of his situation; he decided to take an early gamble on escape.

Under normal circumstances this represented his best option with the exception of giving himself up and being placed on a murder charge. However, the HAF had taken the all normality out of the situation.

J.J. and three of his gang members decided to make a break for it out of sight of the direction of fire. Perhaps he had figured out that the machine gun fire was only coming from one direction and that his attackers would not be shooting in the direction of their own troops, an assumption that was entirely correct.

J.J. and his group moved to the back of the compound and separated into two groups of two and try to flee under what cover was available to them. They could not escape directly to the rear of the compound due the steep terrain. So J.J. and one partner in crime worked quickly along a shallow gulley, which would have worked were it not for the cut-offs.

As J.J. and his accomplice came to a rise along the gulley they had unwittingly moved straight into the sights of one of the HAF cut off groups. The Section Commander who was in cover with his men at a range of about twenty-five metres called upon J.J. to *"Buss!"* (Stop!). To which J.J. idiotically raised his weapon to engage. He and his accomplice were cut down by accurate fire in an instant.

From the moment the high velocity rounds slammed into their bodies their wounds were not survivable. Each shooter placed well-aimed shots at the torso of their target and each of the four men in the cut off group fired no more than three rounds. This meant that the sheer transfer of kinetic energy from the bullets hitting the liquid form of a human body caused the murderers to be almost certainly dead by the time they hit the ground.

At the other end of the siege the second HAF cut-off group heard the gunfire, as had the other two runners. These murderers had also run directly into the kill zone of the other cut-off group but, fortunately for them, not as quickly as their leader.

They too were challenged. However, rather than die for whatever their cause happened to be on that day they immediately dropped their weapons and surrendered. Their war was over and it is to the immense credit of the Section Commander and his men that they maintained perfect control and resisted the temptation to open fire. They went on to affect a textbook arrest precisely as they had been trained.

The men were told to lay face down and to spread their arms and their legs. Two HAF moved forward to each man one with his weapon trained on the man on the ground, the other with plasticuffs and a sand bag. The men on the ground were told, "If you move, you will be shot." So having just heard the burst of gunfire from the direction of their compatriots in crime the guys clearly believed that these Pathans would follow through with the threat. An indication of their belief in their situation was amply demonstrated by the fact that, while lying on the ground, they had both pissed themselves.

The HAF handed over the two urine soaked prisoners to the Police. The contorted bodies of J.J. and his colleague were loaded on to a truck and covered with a tarpaulin. The HAF's job was done; they had just rid Balochistan of a gang that had terrorised the region for years. They had done it quickly and without fanfare.

The HAF had made their *shahadat* (martyrs) and taken no casualties, they had stuck rigidly to their drills so now it was time to return to Belili where an elated General Sadaqat would address another seventy-five RIF who had just completed basic training. Here the HAF would be hailed for the heroes that they were.

I reflected that J.J.'s last thoughts must have been very similar to the thoughts of the police as the HAF left the area, "Who the fuck are these guys?"

Back at Belili Tom who had flown down from Slammy joined me and I explained what had happened; he was elated. I also called Dorothy and Brigadier Shafiq with the news. I sensed there was a slight air of disbelief because for Dorothy the event had come out of the blue but her response was entirely positive and excited.

However, the news of these exceptional militia troopers would not stop there. Within the next few hours it would permeate the U.S. Embassy and spread across the globe to the corridors of power in Washington DC and even to my counterparts in Colombia.

Assistant Secretary of State Bobby Charles would be woken in his bed by a call from Sharon giving him the news and he, as a former U.S. Navy aviator, would react in the best of ways. He'd make damn sure we got more Hueys.

Coincidentally at Belili that morning, there was a graduation parade for new RIF troopers, which the General insisted I attend. I was dog-tired but the excitement overcame any feelings of weariness and Tom and I sat in the rear of the small grandstand behind the other guests.

There were some local journalists present at the parade so I was a bit taken aback when Sadaqat made his speech and spoke of the stunning success of past few hours. He closed by adding, "And it is all down to one man who is sitting over there."

I was hoping they would all think he was pointing at Tom and I assumed Tom was hoping that I'd be recognised as the subject of attention. I muttered to him without moving my lips, "Jesus Christ, I wish he hadn't done that!"

Fortunately the baseball hat was of some help. Also that the Press had been told they would only be able to take authorised pictures saved me from being plastered all over Pakistan's Daily Times.

Following the parade Tom and I took tea with Sadaqat and Colonel Shaheed. It was a very happy day and one that would have far reaching and positive impact on the programme and on the HAF. It was perhaps ironic that although J.J. had squandered his evil and wasted life, he had actually achieved something very positive for the forces of good by his death.

I spent the rest of the day showing Tom around Quetta and explained all aspects of our security measures and how we achieved them. I showed him the use of the Corollas so he could note how inconspicuous we were in transit. He agreed it would be foolish to use an armoured vehicle and he'd move to change the senseless rule.

I reflected to myself that Tom could not have arrived in Quetta on a more perfect day. Not only had the atmospherics of the occasion helped him see our relationship with the local forces at a peak, but also he would take a third party commentary back to Islamabad on what he had seen and felt on this precious day in Quetta. However, my schedule quickly changed when I took a call from Dorothy asking that I return to the Islamabad as soon as possible to provide briefings.

I'd have to accompany Tom back to the Islamabad that evening.

As I parked my Rav4 in the Embassy car park the following morning I didn't really know what to expect. I'd experienced fall out from such events during previous operations and knew debriefs could swing either way. The view would either be that of a job well done or an analysis of whether minimum force was used in the apprehension of Balochistan's most wanted. I figured I'd either be deported or decorated.

When I walked into the office, such was Jerry's welcome I thought he was going to kiss me on the lips, but thank God he didn't. He wanted a blow-by-blow account. However, I knew Dorothy was in her office within earshot so I was very vague and just explaining that we'd rehearsed our asses off and when the time came the boys stuck to their drills and achieved the operation with no injuries on our side.

Dorothy called me into her office and, having heard me chatting to Jerry suggested he came in too, to listen. I explained to Dorothy that this operation had been building behind the scenes with FC since the bus and hostages were taken, but we'd had very little to go on until the Pete and his crew in the Caravan had narrowed the search for J.J.

We had responded to the events in the only way we could by rehearsing potential scenarios and we were fortunate that one of them came to pass. So the men were prepared in all respects. We had used classic commando tactics and that there had been no magic to anything that had transpired. We had simply secured the target and sealed off all possible escape routes.

The three elements that were not foreseen was the lack of helicopters, (but at least we had used trucks supplied by NAS), that the operation was conducted in daylight, and that the target individuals would try to affect an escape so quickly in the hope that surrounding forces were disorganised.

Dorothy took notes, I surmised, for her morning brief with the Ambassador which I half expected her to invite me to, but that didn't happen. In fact I didn't hear anything from the Ambassador by way of comment on the programme for the rest of my tour; perhaps there was none or perhaps it was filtered away before it reached me.

As I sat in my cupboard of an office after the Dorothy debrief I wondered what the response would be in the

Ambassador's daily departmental meeting. I didn't have time to be deflated because Curtis had arrived and was excited to know what had happened and Jerry came in for a second dose of events.

Paul had emailed a congratulatory note and added that the timing of the event was perfect because Sharon was actually in DC for the International Narcotics and Law Enforcement Conference. She was perfectly placed to brief the powers that be on the operation and reinforce the urgency of the Huey requirement.

I reflected that the twenty five HAF troopers were probably still in their barracks getting on with their daily routine with no concept of how internationally famous and how talked about they were that day. That was until General Sadaqat went to them with some news, which was relayed to me by Colonel Wahid.

Such was the Governor of Balochistan's elation at the dispatching of J.J. that he announced the award of a bounty of two-million Rupees to the RIF and, in particular, to the HAF. General Sadaqat took the decision to match the bounty and in this one act, at a salary of $70 per month, each HAF trooper received approximately two years salary for his services to Balochistan.

I could imagine the elation of the troops and wished that I could have been there to see their faces at news of the announcement. I also reflected that these guys might now expect reward for any subsequent act so I would have to emphasize minimum force next time I was with them. However, now was not a time to ponder on what might be, I was simply elated and immensely proud of these good men.

As that day in the Embassy progressed there was a marked difference in response from the Sheep and the Sheepherders. I received calls from Keith in DEA, from the FBI and RSO and from General Stone inviting me for a celebratory beer in the Marine bar that evening; from any other quarter there was nothing.

Dorothy did not mention the matter again nor did she let me know the Ambassador's response to the news. It had perhaps been lost on the Sheep that only days before his death J.J. had brutally murdered, and doubtless raped, two female hostages. He had terrorised the innocent people of Balochistan for years and was beyond redemption, he had lived by the gun and his last act in life had been to try to kill someone, so he had died by the gun. The world was a better place without him.

The following day, which was Saturday 24th April, Sharon called to say that it had been confirmed by Assistant Secretary Bobby Charles that the Peru Hueys would come to Pakistan. In truth, the credit for enabling him to make the quick decision was all down to my twenty-four Pathans and one Punjabi of the HAF.

Sharon added that the official directive would be sent out on Monday and that she would leave it to me to give Dorothy the news, which I duly did. The official confirmation was received the next day. Curtis swung into action to ensure we would have enough maintenance support and additional spare parts for the aircraft.

We would have to rely on the DoD to deliver the helicopters by C-5 or C-17 airlift so I coordinated with the USAF representative in General Stone's team to ensure they knew what was going on. He in turn could coordinate with Paul's team back in Florida. It was quickly ascertained that the Air Force would use a C-17 out of Charleston South Carolina for the task but, due to Iraq commitments, it would probably be another month before they would be able to allocate an aircraft. Once again the Iraq operation had given the efforts on the Pakistan/Afghan border a good kick in the balls.

Curtis and I looked hard at what could be achieved in regard to training the second platoon given the level of tasking and serviceability of our current Hueys. We reluctantly ascertained that it would be wise to wait until the new Hueys arrived rather than attempt a programme pieced together with one or two aircraft.

The operational pace in Waziristan on the northern border of Balochistan was at full tempo and that we were in the middle of poppy growing season meant that the training must logically take second place. Frustratingly, I realised my place would have to be in Islamabad until the new Helicopters arrived; this was to be the longest period I spent in the town during my tenure in Pakistan.

The events in Lauralai had caught the attention of others in the Embassy and Tom had been asked by them to coordinate a meeting with them. The meeting included the "Arrogant Woman" who had attended my ambassador's briefing a few weeks earlier. She walked in the room, sat down and simply asked, "How the fuck did you manage that?"

I told her, "You're listening to it."

She frowned in confusion.

I continued, "My accent. It's my English accent." I paused between each sentence. "They trust my accent and they trust me." Another pause. "Also, I keep it small. We have just twenty-five men, which means our OpSec is better than that of any larger, parallel initiative." I smiled.

From there the meeting went well and Arrogant Woman's colleague Kevin seemed impressed with what had been achieved and offered help if I needed it.

On 4th May the HAF notched up another success when one of the aircraft identified an opium harvest occurring on the outskirts of Quetta. Led by Caz, the Hueys and the HAF were immediately dispatched and arrived at the sizeable field where twelve workers were harvesting the crops. The HAF arrested the dozen workers, one of whom was armed. With the area secured by the HAF, Frontier Corps soldiers were trucked in to destroy the crops by hand.

It was an opportune arrest but nevertheless one made possible by the rapid response and willingness of command to commit the HAF into such situations. It had been another daylight success and one that was reported back to the States with some satisfaction.

On the same day in Islamabad the Embassies went into virtual lock-down. Information had been received that a terrorist group had entered the city with the intent of attacking the British High Commission, the U.S. Embassy, the Australian High Commission and the US Education Centre. I immediately got hold of Robert to get the Brits' assessment and compared notes with Ken in the RSO.

If an attack was going to happen the place *not* to be was in the Embassy so I made my way to the NAS Annex to lie low and sort out remaining equipment requirements with Saadi; we worked well into the night.

On Thursday evening the dulcet tones of Amir announced "Commander Howard" as I answered my phone. Amir was not only a proven salesman of anything military but he was probably the social hub of Islamabad. Additionally, he had very quickly assimilated that my success could be his success. If I demonstrated what could be achieved he could take the initiative to sell additional assets to the U.S. Government via pressure from the Government of Pakistan. The result would be enhanced military capability and, for him, significant sales commissions. Amir asked me if I would like to join him for a drink that evening and added. "I want to induct you into a very special club."

I must admit I thought he was alluding to a nightclub because I knew there were a couple of happening, "undercover" clubs in the city. More so, Amir had once commented to me that the only people in Pakistan who didn't drink were those who couldn't afford to. So I knew wherever he'd be taking me that Johnnie Walker Black Label would be freely available. (For some reason this brand of whisky is more popular in than any other in Pakistan).

I asked no questions on the phone so as not to encourage any lies but was struck that Amir had invited me to his apartment very early in the evening. This was unusual so I concluded my 'insurance' should come along too.

That Amir was on time was an event in itself because he seldom paid any attention to the clock so by now I was intrigued. I jumped into his car and we headed south to the G-11 area, a part of Islamabad I hadn't seen before. The area was that of sizeable villas and as we progressed Amir reiterated that I was about to be inducted into a very special club and that I should tell no one at the Embassy about it. We pulled up outside a large white villa with a significant wall around it and unusually efficient guards.

Amir explained that it was the house of a retired Brigadier, who I had previously met. He had a personality that was larger than life and was a genuine hero of Pakistan's Army, having been highly decorated for once risking his life to save several soldiers from certain death in Kashmir.

The Brigadier's house was very tastefully furnished and civilian life was obviously treating him well. I was briefly introduced to his wife and then guided to his "I love me" room, where the walls were adorned with military paraphernalia and citations charting his military accomplishments of which there were many.

In this room he also kept his cache of Johnnie Walker and other suitable refreshments. As I sipped my first Murree beer I wondered if I should ask why the hell I was there, but resisted the temptation concluding I would find out soon enough. After about forty-five minutes the Brigadier left the room and I could hear him greeting some people in his hallway. The door opened and a diminutive man in his fifties entered the room.

He was wearing a leather bomber jacket, jeans, and cowboy boots. Another gentleman followed him. He was a bull of a man and was also casually dressed, although not as themed. One of them was introduced as General M the other as General K. There was some small talk amongst the gentlemen in Urdu as the Black Label was poured and the smaller General M who was clearly the most senior officer asked why I wasn't drinking whisky.

I explained that I seldom drank spirits because the hangover inflicted would stay with me for days. I therefore limited my alcohol consumption to wine and beer. I reminded the General of Oscar Wilde's quote, "A man who is tired of wine is tired of life," which he found amusing and then proficiently flowed the conversation around to military matters.

He said he had received glowing reports from Quetta and of the success of the HAF and that he wanted to know more about the doctrine that I had applied. I explained that the desert hasn't changed at all since Lawrence fought the Turks but we could now achieve much greater manoeuvre by using the Hueys instead of camels.

I went on to explain that we would never use the Hueys in direct action unless forced to do so. We were a tiny force so we had to rely on achieving stealth and shock action. I explained that if we didn't have surprise on our side then we had no place being wherever we were. My entire focus during a build up for a patrol was achieving operational security. Just one leak and we could all be wiped out.

Additionally, the use of the night provides us with technical superiority over the enemy and the FLIR in the Caravan served to hedge our risk. What might perhaps seem like extremely high risk operations actually weren't because the Caravan would ensure the drop zone was clear of heat sources and, once we were on the ground, monitor the heat sources in our path to keep us clear of any human or animal that might compromise our position.

It was a carefully selected combination of Lawrence, Commando tactics, Northern Ireland applications and a spattering of SF techniques that had permitted the HAF to reach the levels of competence they had achieved in such a short time. All the men in the room listened intently.

The General asked questions about the level of proficiency amongst the RIF when I had first encountered them. I told him that, in my opinion, these men were the cream of the Frontier Corps and that Sadaqat had nailed a concept that I had been permitted to enhance. The Brigadier kept the Black Label and Murree flowing as we discussed all aspects of what had been achieved, what could be further achieved and the limitations.

Every now and again the two Generals would mutter to each other in Urdu and nod. I had no idea what they were thinking or their aim. Regardless, they were certainly stimulated by the conversation. I took the opportunity to emphasise the State Department's commitment, the money already spent, the additional helicopters and provision of an integrated, composite joint task force unit. It was also important to stress the importance of winning hearts and mind in Balochistan.

I made the point that, in my opinion, the Pakistani military was missing a major trick by not giving aid and support to the remote villages and compared the concept to that of Malaysia in the 1950s. In this first defeat of insurgents in modern history the British demonstrated a newly written, textbook doctrine by implementing hearts and minds, deterrence and attrition in the right amounts to the right people.

With that doctrine imparted we adjourned to the roof of the villa where one of the servants had prepared bar-b-que'd kebabs.

As we devoured the third or fourth kebab, I engaged the powerfully built General K in conversation. He explained he was the commander of a Corps that was based several hours drive to the south of Islamabad. I asked him whether he was up in town doing business, to with he responded, "No, I came especially to meet you."

I was stunned that the level of interest had reached such peaks. However, what he said next was even more astounding when he explained he would soon be based in Islamabad as the head of the Inter-Services Intelligence agency. Jesus Christ. This man was soon to control the infamous ISI!

After about an hour on the roof Amir suggested we should be on our way, which was a clear indication the Generals interview was complete. On the way home I exclaimed surprise regarding the ISI announcement to which Amir responded, "You shouldn't be surprised, the other General is Musharraf's second-in-command. If anything happens to the President it is likely he'll take over. You've just been speaking to the *real* commander of the Army."

I drove back to my villa reflecting whether this had been the most surreal evening of my life that hadn't included a closet-nymphomaniac and had to decide what I should do about reporting the high level encounter. There was no way I could tell anyone in the Embassy for two reasons. The first was that they would surely over-react and screw things up by in advertently leaking that I'd called in the meeting. The second was that I'd given Amir my word that I would not tell the Embassy.

I decided I'd have to report the event to Paul, which is precisely what I did. He asked if I expected another meeting, I told him I had no clue. We both agreed he could feed the information upstream to Sharon and beyond but also, in this case, what the Embassy didn't know for now they wouldn't worry about. There was truly no identifiable upside to letting them know, so that is just the way it stayed.

The following evening, before heading back to Quetta, Keith from the DEA and I were invited to Robert's house. Robert had a video that he insisted was essential viewing. When we arrived he revealed that it was a video of the execution of Daniel Pearl who had been abducted in Karachi some four months earlier in January. Daniel's tragic story is now well known but as a Wall Street Journalist with U.S. Nationality and of Jewish faith I had already concluded that his biggest "crime" was that of gross naivety to believe he could investigate Al-Qaeda finances in Karachi and not die trying.

Furthermore, Daniel had perhaps not read the Holy Koran (*In the Name of God, the Compassionate, the Merciful)*, the book of Muhammad 47:3. "*When you meet the unbelievers on the battlefield strike off their heads.*" As a Jew, to his deranged captors, Daniel epitomised an unbeliever and, in Karachi, he had certainly entered their battlefield.

Robert warned that the video was extremely graphic but I took the view it was my duty to watch it. Anything else would be the equivalent of an ostrich putting its head in the sand. I knew if these bastards ever caught me I could expect very similar treatment. It was their ultimate insult to kill a man who they viewed as an unbeliever as they would a goat.

The video that I saw bore none of the latterly published PR images. It appeared to be an unedited version. Daniel spoke for about two minutes when a hand wielding a large knife came across the screen and simply slit his throat. The only blessing about any of this was that Daniel seemed totally surprised by the fatal event and, as he collapsed to the floor, we reflected that he must have only been conscious for very few seconds.

The brutality unfortunately didn't stop there. Daniel's murderers butchered his body including decapitating him and holding his head up to the camera while absurdly claiming the entire savage act had been done in the name of God. Daniel's body was recovered several days later in ten pieces.

Like any other civilised human beings Robert, Keith and I were horrified by what we had seen, but it was also an important lesson of what we were up against. I commented the video should be forced viewing for all U.S. Embassy staff in Pakistan.

I had long before decided that if I was ever forced into a situation where I was down to the last magazine in my pistol that I would count my rounds and save the last bullet for myself. Having seen the video I decided to save the last *two* rounds for myself just in case I miscounted. I would not, could not, let myself get taken alive by such men under any circumstances.

The following morning, I left for Quetta but on the way called into Jerry's house. He had been a dear friend and confidante to me in Islamabad and he would be leaving for a six-month assignment in Dhaka before I returned to Islamabad.

As emotional good-byes go it was not an easy one. For us two veterans of goodness knows how many conflicts we both knew it was unlikely we would see each other again. Some weeks earlier Jerry had derided British cuisine and described our love for the yeast extract, Marmite, as living proof the entire British nation was fucked up.

For his farewell present I had bought him the largest jar of Marmite that I could find in Islamabad. I also presented him with a framed passage that had been written by Teddy Roosevelt, which had, coincidentally, been adopted by my former specialist unit. It read:

> *To my friend and fellow operator*
> *Jerry H.*
> *It is not the critic who counts;*
> *nor the man who points out how the strong man stumbles,*
> *or where the doer of deeds could have done them better.*
> *The credit belongs to the man who is actually in the arena,*
> *whose face is marred by dust and sweat and blood,*
> *who strives valiantly;*
> *who errs and comes short again and again;*
> *because there is not effort without error and shortcomings;*
> *but who does actually strive to do the deed;*
> *who knows the great enthusiasm, the great devotion,*
> *who spends himself in a worthy cause,*
> *who at the best knows in the end the triumph of high*
> *achievement and*
> *who at the worst, if he fails,*
> *at least he fails while daring greatly.*
> *So that his place shall never be*

with those cold and timid souls who know neither victory
nor defeat.
You've never lived until you have almost died
And for those who have had to fight for it
Life has truly a flavour
the protected will never know.
Theodore Roosevelt,
It has been an honour to strive with you.
Your friend
Howard

Jerry was a man who had quietly and purposely served his community and his country for all of his life. As Jerry read the passage I could see the emotion in his eyes. Like me he'd been through enough in his life so that emotion came easier with the years. We shook hands and said goodbye. It was the last time we saw each other.

CHAPTER 12

The Clock Runs

The long stint in Islamabad seemed like a lifetime but from a strategic viewpoint, it was time well spent.

We were, however, about to discover we weren't to have it all our own way.

Sadaqat had identified a particular compound that was sourced as being frequented by a high profile target and he had deduced that a surprise attack on that compound by ground forces would unbalance the enemy and draw a particular response (that cannot be described here), which would help us identify who was where. On receiving the initial report I realised that this was potentially 'great game' changing stuff so I called Paul in the U.S. and he confirmed I should speak to Kevin within the Embassy.

Sadaqat had suggested the HAF insert a patrol to initiate an intense night attack on the compound. However, we were not to enter or try to push home a full assault on the location.

Prior to the attack, we would need to place pre-timed explosives. We'd maintain the attack for an agreed number of minutes then rapidly withdraw when the first charge blew, with five more charges blowing at one minute intervals and a further five at two minute intervals. This would hopefully provide the HAF with enough time to blend back into the mountains and patrol out to a helicopter pick up under the cover of darkness.

Sadaqat was convinced that the attack would so shock the opposition it would be forced to move the high value target from wherever he was in the vicinity. When he did, our role would have been deemed successful and it would be up to someone else to capitalise on the opportunity as they saw fit.

I called Sadaqat and told him we really couldn't go it alone on this one so I'd have to upbrief a trusted individual in the Embassy who could help us with top-cover. I met Kevin and told him I would keep the operation low-tech and Sadaqat could provide additional RPGs and explosives but I needed parkway timers, which we could adapt to detonate our escape explosives; he said he could "Sort it if Sadaqat couldn't".

I could feel the excitement building inside of me. This was the big one and my chance to perhaps bring a big boy to rights, even though, in truth and deliberately, no specific name was ever mentioned.

I was acutely aware that we were now into mid-May and I would have to push hard to get the unit to be where it needed to be before the proposed operation and the completion of my contract. Sadaqat too was aware that his men had most chance of contributing to the demise of a 'big fish' while I was with them.

From this point on, until it came time for me to leave Pakistan there would be no let up. Additionally, the heat in the deserts of Balochistan was starting to turn from "oven-warm" to fucking unbearable.

The introduction of the additional helicopters from the Peru programme would ensure the reach and capacity we needed to cause disruption along Balochistan's border with Iran or up into Waziristan.

During the flight to Quetta, I reflected that the operational tempo of the air assets was now at full throttle. We'd just deployed a Caravan to conduct over flight operations in Waziristan to check on the reported locations of Al-Qaeda. Hopefully, they would turn up something linked to our impending operation. I so wanted to poke the 'big fish' if the opportunity presented itself. My mind then drifted to home.

My wife's behaviour had become increasingly erratic and incomprehensible during the past weeks. There had been several times recently when she simply didn't answer the phone. This was totally out of character. I had three months to push. I just hoped her nerves would hold. I had begun to feel an ill-defined sense of impending doom. But I had to put my domestic anxiety aside. I had to survive the minefield that was Pakistan for another ninety days.

The commencement of training for 2 Platoon readily indicated that this group was streets ahead of their earlier counterparts. Clearly, they had gleaned the processes and procedures during conversations in the barrack-room. The consequence was that the skills learned during the early stages training were accelerated. This was additionally helped because the aircrew had already mastered their own learning curve with the first platoon. The pilots now knew exactly what had to be done and nailed the various profiles of flight which were, by now, almost procedural.

Captain Tanveer led number 2 Platoon. He was a mountain of a man and, although I generally can't tell if a particular guy would be judged by the ladies to be good looking, my guess is that Tanveer would have been a bit of a stud.

His chiselled jaw actually made me think of him as the Pakistani equivalent of Jack Hawkins, the British actor from the Fifties and Sixties. This young Pakistani Captain was far more outgoing and inquisitive than his compatriot Pervaiz.

He was determined to soak up as much knowledge as he could. Additionally, he was energetic and wanted to prove himself in command. This man, I reflected, should have a bright future in the Pakistani military.

Over the next few days, we practised basic helicopter drills and patrolling in scorching weather. By the time my Balochistan summer was over, I would be consuming about six litres of water a day and feeling that I was sweating out seven.

Each night or early morning, I would return to the compound absolutely soaked in sweat and covered with sand and dust. At the end of the first week of drills and patrolling Tanveer made the comment that made it all worthwhile, he commented he had learned more in eight days than he had in his previous eleven years in the Pakistan Army. This was progress.

The DynCorp team were also fighting the heat to keep the Hueys serviceable. They were clearly pushing their own stamina envelopes but were relentless in their support and effectiveness so I'd need to rely on Frank (Quality Assurance) to keep a close eye on them and to be wary of exhaustion setting in. Just one bolt left out or a wrench left in a compartment and we would lose an aircraft and everyone in it.

Meanwhile in Wana, the enemy continued to stick it to the conventional forces. On Sunday May 16, three of our Hueys were dispatched to night evacuate military casualties where twenty-two soldiers had been wounded and one killed.

It was becoming obvious that the Pakistani Army was now wholly reliant on our night operating capability and would use it whenever possible. This trend, whilst life-saving, would be a constant drain on our team as we tried to conduct pro-active operations on the border. I'd need to ask Dorothy to look at what could be done to equip other Pak helicopters with NVG compatible lighting and instruments.

I returned to Islamabad after two weeks of training the 2nd Platoon and asked Dorothy about possibly funding a five hundred thousand dollar NVG compatibility for other units' helicopters. She liked the idea and we figured that the path of least resistance would be to offer the equipment to the two ANF's MI-17 Helicopters.

I drafted and submitted a memorandum and, when dropping it off, asked if I could take a long weekend in London to meet Shellie and the girls. Such had been Shellie's tone of late that I had concluded I needed to see her and the girls to try to get things back on track. With that approval, I booked the tickets for my family from the States and my own from Islamabad.

In hindsight, the visit to the UK was a disaster. Shellie was completely cold and disinterested, blaming jet jag, the weather, menstruation and me for dragging her across the Atlantic. We managed to break away from the girls for a dinner during which she reiterated her reluctance to have anything to do with a move to my new job in Connecticut. I could not understand her hesitation.

After a long weekend, I boarded the BA Islamabad "red eye" flight completely pissed off and had to say a painful good-bye to my girls at their flight gate in Heathrow. It just didn't feel right seeing them get on a plane without being there with them.

I was now determined to get Phase Two of the second Platoon's training completed, integrate the HAF in total, and then get back to my family before it disintegrated.

There was no respite in Islamabad and on my arrival Curtis met me with the news that a USAF C-17 Globemaster transport aircraft bearing our three "Peru" Hueys would arrive that very evening. In preparation he had brought Gerry, Jay, Jason and Matt up to Islamabad for the offload. I met with Brigadier Shafiq for afternoon tea to discuss the arrival and also learned that the Minister of the Interior had praised the Aviation Programme to President Musharraf during his vale-dictory speech. We had indeed come a long way in a short time.

At 4:30pm, I headed off to Chaklala airbase, which is the Pakistan Air Force's northern logistic centre in Rawalpindi. At 6:50pm, having flown over 12,500 Kilometres from Florida to Islamabad, the C-17 Globemaster arrived, just five minutes late with its valuable cargo.

No sooner had the aircraft come to a halt on the ramp and its massive rear door opened, than the DynCorp mechanics were "all hands to the pump" with the USAF loadmasters, hauling the Huey's one-by-one out of the aircraft's giant fuse-lage. The USAF crew was clearly keen to be on the ground in Islamabad for as short a time as possible and informed us that, once they had shed their cargo, they would overnight in Doha, Qatar, which was a convenient U.S. Air Force base just an hour and half's flight away.

What was most striking about the Hueys was that they had obviously been dispatched in haste. They were still in the grey and red stripe livery of the Peruvian forces. I didn't care, and we all saw the humour of flying Peruvian livery over the badlands of Pakistan.

It took just one hour and fifteen minutes to unload all three aircraft without incident and, within twenty minutes of the last Huey being hauled out of its belly, the C-17 pilot was powering up his mighty turbo fans to propel his aircraft on the short flight to Qatar and doubtless a five star hotel for some well earned sleep.

I was happy that the extra Huey's had arrived but elated that a case of six M-16 rifles and Six Beretta pistols marked "Diplomatic. Exclusive for Howard" was in one of the helicopters. We were now self sufficient in terms of self-protection.

As I drove back to my house, I felt a glow of satisfaction. We'd gotten the Hueys', we'd gotten the militia, we'd gotten the guns, and we'd gotten the enthusiasm of the military and the politicians in the U.S. and Pakistan. Now if only I could make my wife happy.

Karachi's jihadists welcomed the month of June 2004 with a massive bomb and riots in the city. The situation within the country remained ridiculously fragile, to say the least, and I often wondered if I wasn't a lot safer on patrol in the Balochistan mountains as opposed to being stuck in Pakistan's centres of population.

Additionally, there was strong concern over a chemical weapons threat in Islamabad. This threat was taken so seriously that gas masks and antidote were issued to all embassy staff. Once again, this real WMD event was not broadcast in the U.S.. That silver bullet had been already blown in Iraq.

Back in Islamabad, I was in constant contact with Curtis regarding the new Hueys and I was now beginning to become concerned. Curtis was a good man, I mean a really good man, and he had done more than any man could be expected to do under incredibly difficult circumstances.

From our frequent work alongside each other, I could sense he was nearing exhaustion, not from lack of sleep, but, rather, from three years of sustained bombardment and pressure of events in Pakistan. In short, Curtis had begun to experience 'threat zone weariness' and I was concerned that if continued for much longer he could burnout. I knew that, despite of his best efforts, nothing was going to stop the onset of "zone fatigue". The only cure was to give him a break from the rigors of Pakistan.

I put a call into Paul and raised my concerns regarding the well being of Curtis. To my elation, Paul said that Curtis was already allocated for promotion to Deputy Maintenance Director in Colombia. Although the 'Deputy" title might not sound like a promotion, because of the size and maturity of Colombia programme, it definitely was. I expressed to Paul that I thought, not only was it deserved, but also fair and timely. If a change is as good as a rest, then Curtis, more than anyone, deserved it along with the promotion. There was no doubt in my mind that if Curtis had still been in the military he, just as with the rest of the DynCorp team, would have been highly decorated for what he had achieved in Pakistan.

Having been inspected by the DynCorp team and test flown by Caz, the very next day, the Peru Hueys' left Islamabad for Quetta just in time for a high threat warning in that city regarding a major suicide attack being planned against Brits or Americans.

June 6th marked the sixtieth anniversary of D-Day and I managed to watch the Remembrance Service on the BBC. As I did so, we received news of another land-mine attack by Bugti against the FC, south of Quetta. There were two casualties, another one of whom had lost a leg. Whether on the beaches of Normandy or the hellhole that is Sui, Balochistan, man's ability to be inhumane to his fellow man seemed to remain infinite. The following day, the threat levels continued to rise when it was discovered that five Iranian trained Egyptians had infiltrated Islamabad "looking for a western target." I kept the company of Messrs. Sig, Benelli and Makarov whether in the car or at home.

On my arrival back in Quetta, the Peru Hueys looked resplendent on the flight line. I was like a kid at Christmas wanting to get them into action. Certainly with the threats and carnage that were going on around us, it seemed like I wouldn't need to wait long.

That very day there had been a major attack on an Army Corps commander in Karachi and we received news of another offensive in Waziristan. The Pakistani Army and Al-Qaeda were now increasing the attack tempo against each other and it now became a certainty that our assets would be pushed to full stretch. On cue that evening, I received an anxious call from Dorothy explaining that President Musharraf's office had called the Ambassador looking for more helicopters. I checked with Brigadier Shafiq and Curtis to see what we could do. Everything that we could put in the air with qualified aircrew they already had!

I was called to Sadaqat's office, he was clearly displeased with the frequency of attacks by Bugti's subversives, showed me the target and told me to commence planning an operation.

I briefed Pete and we decided to get some photography of the target area, I called back into the General's office to let him know we would use the Cessna Caravan to "take a look".

We took off and headed out to Bugti's area but only got about twenty minutes out when we were recalled to base without reason.

On landing I was asked to call the General who explained he had ordered the recall. "We've been compromised Howard, there must be a leak at this end. Bugti knew you were coming and they planned to make a concerted effort to shoot you down." Fortunately the General's sources were well placed and he had made sure Pete and I would live to see another sunrise.

The following day, I commenced Phase 2 training for Number 2 Platoon. I threw them straight into Hard Stop VCP drills. This used a number of techniques, including explosive to ensure we forced an unwilling vehicle to stop. It was inconsequential whether the vehicle was drivable after the event. Jay accompanied us up to Pishin to video the training and collected some excellent footage of the low-level flight and the drills themselves.

By the time I got back to the compound that evening, I was totally exhausted but dug deep to plan the following day's training. Our time was short and we had to maintain momentum.

The following days saw us move through covert search, active soft stop VCPs, Observation Post (OP) drills, and a hostage snatch exercise.

Colonel Cheryl from the U.S. Army intelligence had specifically asked to see one of the advanced training manoeuvres and arrived in Quetta specifically to observe the snatch. This was the first time that a woman had actually stayed in the Compound overnight. So, although she was a full Colonel, the use of the showers by the DynCorp team increased significantly in the few hours before she arrived. A cynic might even say that the aroma of the odd splash of after-shave was abounding in the compound. There was no doubt she had certainly and unwittingly raised morale and the levels of testosterone in the compound.

Following the mission orders for a "snatch," we went through the normal procedures in regard to final kit preparation. The trucks were at the ready with engines running. They moved out with their troops to the line of helicopters waiting in the darkness with rotors running.

What we now viewed as normal activity must have been mind-blowing for Cheryl. And as each section lined up in the one-o'clock position of their respective helicopters, I could see Cheryl soaking up the atmospherics of the event unfolding before her.

I had given Cheryl a set of NVG's for the flight to the drop-off point. She would accompany me in the lead helicopter, which was flown by Caz. Thereafter, Caz would fly her back and drop her off by a truck manned by some members of the 1st Platoon and Jim who would assume responsibility for her protection. They would be her bodyguards and guides so that she could watch the takedown of the target from a pre-selected viewing point.

The light levels that evening were atrociously low and the view through the NVGs extremely grainy. The flight to the drop off point was about forty minutes and we carefully navigated our way through the mountain ranges. By any measure, this was some of toughest flying the pilots had been asked to do and the low visibility due to haze was only impeding our travel. At one point, the view from the cockpit was so limited that I wondered whether we would make it to our drop-off or have to climb out of the mountains to abort.

I looked on as Caz reduced his speed to sixty knots to give himself more time to react if the terrain reached out to grab us. The situation then became more complicated.

When we were about ten minutes from the drop-off zone, the Caravan came up with a call we simply didn't want to hear in these marginal conditions. "The LZ is hot! I say again the LZ is hot!" Shit! This was real and all we needed. It meant there was human activity near the landing zone.

The significance was that, at best, we'd be seen landing and, at worst, we would be shot down if we approached the zone. The Caravan went on to report, "No less than four human heat sources within 400 metres of the LZ." My mind raced back to the Bugti compromise; had we suffered another leak? This was a no-brainer. I told Caz, "Switch to the

273

Alternate." He gave me the thumbs up and instructed all the aircraft that we would now go to the Alternate Landing Zone, which was some four kilometres removed from the original LZ.

By this time, I had my map out to refresh my bearings. The Alternate was at least one ridgeline away from the heat sources, so it would be impossible for them to see, hear or reach us. Caz quickly assessed the new route and worked his way through the ridges to get us into the right valley.

It was bloody tight flying by any measure and the mountains looked too close for comfort as he tried to hug the ridge lines, popping over into the next valley at the last possible moment. Behind us, I could see the Hueys in trail tucked in very close tactical formation. The pilots knew that, in such low visibility, to lose sight of the lead aircraft could prove fatal. I glanced into our cabin at Cheryl.

By now she had taken her NVGs off and was sitting on the floor of the helicopter looking down at her feet. What we considered a challenging condition was clearly beyond anything she had expected, she was overwhelmed by the danger.

When the "Two Minute" call came, I signed off with Caz, tapped him on the shoulder and told him, "Good job mate." He responded, "I'm glad we got you in. Just be careful out there." I replied, "Don't worry I will - See you at the pick up." Even though we were on our own Exercise, neither the mountains, the weather, the Taliban or Al-Qaeda knew this. All or a combination thereof would readily kill us if we gave them half a chance.

I removed my headset, checked the safety catch on my M-16, and pulled the cocking lever to the rear before releasing it to push a 5.56mm round into the breach. I pulled the telescopic butt to its extended position and checked my equipment vest pockets to make sure they were all secure. The rest of the Troopers had carried out similar drills with their AK-47s and were already positioned in the doorways of the Huey, eager to get out as quickly as they could. We were now on our final approach.

Just before we landed, I shouted in Cheryl's ear above the commotion, "I'll see you later!" She nodded and, as soon as the helicopter skids hit the ground, I was gone. She must have wondered what the hell she'd gotten herself into. Now she only had the pilots and crewchief for company and the Huey was quickly airborne again.

The patrol into target was long but uneventful. When we arrived in the Final Rendezvous, however, there was still a lot of activity at the site. The two platoon snipers had learned fast but neither had the stalking skills of 'Smiler' in the 1st Platoon. It took them what seemed an age to get eyes on the sentries.

The full sequence of the assault went down. The Frontier Corp that supplied opposing force was totally suppressed in seconds and, although there was some confusion getting the hostage away from the target, the Hueys were super efficient coming in for the extraction, not least of all because such timing had become second nature for them.

On return to the Compound, we debriefed and, after praising them for their performance, I watched, with some considerable pride, as the men of 2 Platoon mounted their truck to head for their barracks and some well-earned sleep. Cheryl and I walked leisurely to the cookhouse for tea. She was blown away by what she had witnessed and admitted that she never thought she would see such capability in Pakistan. She said, "These guys are incredible." I agreed. She went on, "The Pakistani pilots are so skilled and these troops are as sharp as razors. And nobody even knows about them?"

I smiled and nodded. "All we had to do was channel the talent and stay below the radar." We finished our tea and Cheryl went to Caz's vacant room to grab a few hours sleep before Pete flew her back up to Slammy later that morning.

On her return to Islamabad, she apparently attended the next Ambassador's morning brief and described what she had witnessed. I was told that, when summing up, she said, "If we'd have put this guy in charge of finding the 'Big Boys', we'd have gotten them by now." I'm not sure whether she was right, or if the powers that be even wanted any particular man caught; I sensed not, but it was indeed a great compliment and one that she thought would never reach my ears.

Ironically, two days later I received a call from Kevin in Islamabad. It was explained that Sadaqat's plan had been run up the line as a request to use the HAF in offensive action against a specified compound but to stop short of a full assault. Apparently, the proposal was operationally approved but was referred to governmental lawyers, presumably in the U.S., who had decided such action would not be within their legal "comfort zone". Therefore, permission had been denied. Perhaps the powers that be were afraid that a major capture in Pakistan could bring the Iraq operation into question and it is interesting in reflection that the eventual eradication of Osama bin Laden directly coincided with the withdrawal of the last U.S. combat troops from Iraq.

I was careful what I said on the phone and I could hear the disappointment in Kevin's voice. I think we both saw Sadaqat's willingness to commit his troops for such work as an isolated opportunity to enhance intelligence by attempting to pre-empt the enemy response.

Having hung up the phone, I cursed the fucking lawyers. Was it any wonder that both Jesus and Shakespeare believed the world to be a better place without them? However, ultimately I blamed myself. I had made the uncharacteristic mistake of asking for permission; I shouldn't have been surprised by the response.

My abject disappointment over the denial of Sadaqat's joint operation was further exacerbated by the news of American hostage, Paul Johnson, being beheaded - this time in Saudi Arabia. It seemed to me that if we were playing cricket with the enemy and using a bat to hit the ball, then the opposition was using a hand-grenade instead of a ball.

Meanwhile, my calls to home weren't being answered by Shellie, and if all that wasn't enough to lower morale, the chunks of goat meat that Cha Cha, our alleged cook, served for dinner in the compound that evening was easily the most disgusting meal he'd ever prepared while in Quetta. I reflected both the goat and Mr. Johnson had died an unappreciated death.

However, if as one-door closes another opens, then such an event for me happened a few days later. We had decided to push out a snap VCP on the Quetta – Chaman mountain pass road.

We headed out by truck, having ascertained that using the helicopters would be self-defeating if we patrolled in by foot in the heat of the day. The HAF wore their Frontier Corps berets so they would simply look like ordinary troops in transit.

We located a desolate spot where we could pull the trucks off the road and hide them from view. Tanveer sited his cut-offs and main group effectively and I remained out of sight with the camera at the ready.

The Caravan was many thousands of feet above us attempting to pick out an attractive target and, while we waited, Tanveer and I quietly talked. He asked me why I wore British desert camouflage clothing instead of the American issued pattern they had been given. I explained that I didn't want to be recognized as an American because I thought it helped relations and lowered resentment levels. He listened carefully and then shrugged his shoulders and said, "It doesn't matter Mr. Howard. If they catch you, they will cut your head off anyway." I laughed but I knew he was right; there was no safety net here.

The Caravan announced he had a target and the Soft VCP procedure went into action. The vehicle was a covered pickup truck. By the time the driver saw the four Frontier Corps soldiers on the road indicating for him to stop, he could see more soldiers on the road in his rear view mirror and another group some forty metres beyond the main stop group. There was no way out without a shoot-out and the driver wisely did not choose that option.

In the rear of the truck, there were six young men with tribal headdress and beards in various stages of growth. They had all the appearances of being quite radical. Two of them were even wearing U.S. pattern green camouflage jackets. I worked my way undetected along the gulley and snapped away with the camera. I sent instructions on the radio to Tanveer who, by this time, was talking to them. He ascertained their identities and asked them to empty their pockets.

Each man was separated from the others in turn and, as Tanveer took down their details in his notebook, I clicked away on the Nikon D-100. The entire stop must have taken about twenty minutes and 2 Platoon handled the entire event brilliantly. The leadership of Tanveer was exceptional and the team responded quickly to anything he asked. The atmosphere in the VCP itself was kept friendly and cordial by the stop party, lulling the captives in the truck into a false sense of security.

As soon as the men had bid their good-byes, an excited Tanveer came sliding back down into the Gulley. "I think these are Taliban, look!" He'd scrawled down notes in Pashtu with a sketch and directions and explained this was on a piece of paper with a telephone number carried by the guy he thought was their ringleader. "We need to find this place."

I had no way of knowing whether Tanveer was right or wrong, but all we could do was get back to HQ as quickly as we could and see whether Colonel Wahid could tell us if these men were known insurgents.

It took about two hours for Wahid to come back to us. "Howard, two of the men you stopped are known to us. Is there any way we can take a look at where you think the sketch map indicates?"

I told him we could try and told Tanveer it was time for us to put a set of orders together for a patrol. Pete took me up in the Caravan to overfly the areas that we thought the map indicated. We could see two isolated buildings and human activity but it was impossible to ascertain whether it was suspicious or otherwise. We would have to go out to the area between Quetta and the border to take a closer look.

Tanveer gave the orders and, by 11pm, the Huey's had dropped us off and we were patrolling (or should I say slogging) up a mountain pass in order to get eyes on the remote buildings that had been identified on the map. By this time, the Caravan was reporting that the target was quiet except for a single heat source outside one of the two buildings. If this was a sentry, then we were on to something.

By 2:30am, we had dropped down the far side of the mountain pass and had "eyes-on" the two target buildings, as well as the rest of the area. However, the terrain was doing us no favours. There was one isolated piece of high ground, a lone mountain. It would be ideal from which to observe the target in daylight but, unfortunately, it provided us with no escape route, if we got bumped, we'd be fucked.

We'd just have to use a more distant spur feature to site the observation post and stay in that position during the day to observe movement on the target. It wasn't perfect but at least this location would permit us to blend back into the mountains without crossing open ground if anything went wrong. It was a golden rule, "No escape route equals no operation."

We sited the observation post by 4am and posted sentries to the rear around the small whadi where we would be hiding. The desert was characteristically freezing cold and most of the troopers who were trying to get some rest curled up into the foetal position just trying to stay warm. I was just praying for sunrise and, when it came with its warmth at first light, I was pleased to discover that we could rotate the two men to and from the observation post without being observed by the target.

The OP reported that there was movement on target as the occupants greeted the day with morning prayers. As the Sun climbed up the deep blue sky on that June morning, the thermometer started to rapidly climb. I noted the Pathans instinctive movement within the confines of the whadi to seek out shade. The OP had, thus far, seen no women, which was odd, but it was too early to tell if anything was suspicious. We didn't have to wait very long, however, to know that all was not well on the target.

At about 9am two men armed with AK-47's were reported coming from one of the buildings. They had started to walk along the track towards our position. The entire Platoon was woken up and "stood-to." If these guys discovered our position, we'd shoot the bastards. I used my Thuraya satellite phone to raise Caz back at base to inform him we might have a problem. He brought the aircrew to Alert-5 (meaning they would move out to the aircraft in order to be at five minutes notice to deploy).

Fortunately for everyone, the men on the track decided they had walked far enough and turned round to proceed back from whence they came. My main concern was whether we'd been detected, either we'd got away with it or these guys were excellent at not letting on they'd spotted us. We would just have to wait and watch; there was nothing to make us move out; not just yet.

Once the men on the track were back at the buildings, more men came from behind one of the structures and the group moved onto open ground on the far side of our position. They then proceeded to take turns handling the AK-47s and fired some rounds towards the isolated high ground in some ad hoc target practice. I had crawled up to the OP to watch the events and thanked God we didn't choose the isolated high ground for our own position.

I called Caz again and told him we'd got eyes on a possible enemy and would extract one hour after last light to head for the designated Pick-Up-Point (PUP). I then called Wahid and gave him a situation report. He asked if we could move in to make an arrest. I told him we couldn't because there was too much open ground to cover and without surprise we'd be shot to pieces. We would have to return to base, re-arm for an assault, and combine 1 and 2 Platoons to put fifty troopers on target. The risk was that the bad guys could leave the target in the interim, but there was little else we could do in order to mitigate the risk to the HAF.

By 4pm all was quiet on the target, not least because the temperature was above forty-five degrees Centigrade. I made my own shade using my shemagh and bungee cords and just tried to stay cool. I reflected that, at 4am, I'd been so cold that all I prayed for was the sun to come up and now; here I was, just twelve hours later, sweating my arse off just willing it to go down.

Meanwhile, no one moved in our whadi unless it was necessary to relieve the men in the observation position. Tanveer and I chatted quietly about what had occurred and what we would have to do next. We'd extract that evening and plan for an offensive operation on the following night alongside 1 Platoon. They would doubtless be chomping on the bit, hoping for yet another bounty!

Tanveer's conversation during the late afternoon hours drifted to various subjects and he surprised me when he said, "You should be a Muslim, Mr. Howard."

I smiled and said, "How do you know I'm not?"

Ignoring the comment, he went on, "You go through all of this heat and cold and risk with us. You really care for the men and they know it."

I told him, "I don't plan for any of us to die, Tanveer. That's why we train so fucking hard. I just simply never ask any man to do anything I wouldn't do myself."

I paused. "Hopefully, the men believe I will never leave any man behind if he is wounded. So, if they have this faith in me, that is all I ask."

He nodded. "They know this and they see you are always first on the ground and last off the ground. They talk about this."

"When I'm gone, Tanveer, this is what you must do."

"I will Mr. Howard, I give you my word, but I still think you should be a Muslim."

He was being persistent, so I explained, "Look Tanveer, we are all accidents of birth. If my parents had been Muslim, then I would be Muslim. Likewise for you, if your parents had been Christian.

He countered, "But the Holy Koran is one hundred percent the truth."

I replied, "And I am glad you believe that and would never seek to change your mind. It is not religion that is the issue, Tanveer, it is what men try to do with it for their own gain that is the root of the problem." It was then time for us to take a doze. In this blistering heat, my bet was that the men on the target were doing the same.

There was no more activity on the target that was of any particular interest. Before sunset, the troopers packed what little equipment they carried and the patrol was stood-to, just in case we had been compromised and were ambushed. One hour later, we moved out quietly undetected and headed for the pick-up-point from where the Hueys would take us to the relative safety of Quetta.

The following day was a hive of activity with the Caravan checking the target three times during the morning and afternoon. All the flights confirmed continued activity around the target but it was impossible to know whether the armed men were still there. Pervaiz and Tanveer came to the compound early in the afternoon and we compiled the mission orders.

This would be a fifty-man lift to an area about six kilometres from the target, then a strenuous climb onto the ridge and plateau area. We would use a large, moat-like gulley around the isolated high ground for our concealed approach to the target. We'd then have to move over the open ground in order to get to an assault distance from the target. Our mission was to detain those individuals at the target and bring them back to the authorities in Quetta.

Crossing the expanse of open ground undetected would be a significant challenge but, it would be dark and on the left side of the approach there was a low wall that one platoon could use as cover, the other platoon would have to move over open ground using what undulations they could to get within about thirty metres of the target.

We would deploy two snipers and they would have to take out the sentry if we were compromised. However, we needed to take the occupants of the camp alive so two flanking sections would overpower the sentry during the take down if our approach was undetected. Before the assault, I'd move forward in the centre with the demolitions trooper and plant two sizeable sets of explosive charges.

Once the two platoons were ready for the take down following the "Go" command, Tanveer and Pervaiz would lead the assault teams at break neck speed over the ground that remained between them and the target. I would wait two marching paces and blow the charges with the intent causing sensory deprivation and confusing the enemy during our initial vital seconds of the assault. One section from each platoon would cover the flanks; we'd have no rear guard.

Hopefully, by the time the occupants were awake, they would be staring down the muzzle of many HAF AK-47s. We'd bag and cuff the occupants, retrieve any evidence, and move it all out of the zone on the first two Hueys. Once we'd formulated the plan, I briefed Pete and Caz.

That evening the briefing room was packed with fifty troopers, seven Huey crews, and the entire Caravan crew. Just as we were about to commence the orders, General Sadaqat arrived unannounced. The entire room sprung to attention including myself. I think everyone was taken aback by his presence but I was elated.

For Sadaqat, these fifty HAF troopers going out on a fighting patrol represented the culmination of his vision in creating the Rapid Interdiction Force. The only real surprise of the evening was when Colonel Shaheed (CO of 50

Squadron) announced he would be flying lead. This had not been planned and it was clearly his way of trying to impress the General, but "What the heck," I thought. "It was, after all, his Squadron and it couldn't hurt anyone, right?" Had I known then that I would almost pay for his decision with my life, perhaps I would have thought differently.

The sight of seven Hueys with rotors running on the flight line was impressive by any measure. The DynCorp team had done a fantastic job getting them serviceable. As we moved to board, I looked down the line to see the six sections of the most specialist militia in Pakistan, the HAF, stream forward in an orderly walk to the Hueys, indicating they were ready to go.

After the drop off, which we'd chosen to be well away from the zones of the previous two nights, we patrolled from the low ground up on the plateau for an approach completely shielded by the isolated high ground. Number 1 Platoon took the left hand file; Number 2 Platoon took the right side.

This would put us in the required formation once we had to move out of the final rendezvous toward the target. As we patrolled up a steep incline about four kilometres from the target, my leg muscles were reminding me of my age and I recall thinking with mixed emotion, "This will probably be the last time in my life I will ever do this." My job with the HAF was almost done and I was getting too fucking old for armed slogs up mountains.

The "fifty" were, in any case, now a highly capable fighting patrol in every way. On this occasion, with the exception of water and essential equipment, each man was carrying additional ammunition. If we bumped into any bad guys tonight, they would be against fifty heavily armed Pathans; proven killers, who were probably the best night fighting troops in the whole of Pakistan.

As we entered the gulley towards the final rendezvous the tension was beginning to build in my body. However, no one could have ever imagined there were fifty men moving across that stony ground. There was no human sound and, in the shadows, even through NVGs, it was difficult to see more than five well-spaced troops down each line behind me.

The Caravan was calling activity on target and reported two men in the open, presumably sentries. We had decided "no-move" to assault the target before 3am, so we would remain in the gulley until at least 2:45am. I checked my watch; we running a little late but were still good for time.

I hadn't expected the sides of the gulley to be as steep as they were. We had to search along it to find a way onto the open ground without having to scramble up the shingle. This would have caused too much noise. We found a small re-entrant directly to the south of the objective. The two snipers moved up the gulley, taking their spotters with them. Five minutes later, the fighting patrol moved out on the open ground moving directly toward the target. If the patrol made any inadvertent noise at this stage, it could prove fatal for us. Thus, movement was extremely slow. We were, by now, in single file moving directly towards the target.

On reaching a low undulation, we stopped and 1 Platoon moved out to the left, 2 Platoon to the right. The Caravan called out the sentry movements; there was no sound. I crawled forward in the centre with the demolitions trooper to place the substantial distraction charges.

The snipers out on the flanks were the first to call in their Code, "Alpha 1" then "Alpha 2." Meanwhile, my task was to get the explosives as close as I could to the target without attracting any attention. The unseen platoons on either side of me were concurrently closing in on the objective. They would also have to use judgment (and nerve) to get themselves as close as they could without being compromised.

The demolitions trooper and I had prepared the charges and rehearsed the process in the compound. We anchored the electric cable in the place where we would initiate the explosion and crawled forward to a piece of low ground, short of the left hand building, and then to a similar distance from the right hand building. We then crawled back and I bonded the wires together, connecting one of the terminals to the battery.

I pressed my transmit button. "Bravo, Bravo." Pervaiz, Tanveer and the Caravan whispered an acknowledgement across the radio. Now we waited; it was tense. Tanveer was very exposed on the right but I knew he would push it as close as he could. He had been taught the technique of flicking up his NVG's to give him an idea of what someone could see without goggles and I was sure he doing this to ascertain how close he could get to our objective without the sentry noticing him.

Pervaiz, by chance, had an easier time and had used the wall as cover to get his twenty-four men to within striking distance of the right hand building. Over the radio, he whispered "Charlie 1, Charlie 1" indicating he and his men were ready to go. Now we waited for Tanveer.

Minutes passed and I hoped his radio was working. After ten minutes, I gave way to my concern and called a radio check. He whispered back "Okay." He was still closing in on the target and doubtless cursed me for the call. I vowed I wouldn't bother him again and, instead, would concentrate on holding the loose terminal of the circuit well clear from the battery.

It must have been another anxious seven or eight minutes before Tanveer finally made the call. "Charlie 2, Charlie 2." The acknowledgment by me whispering "Bravo" and Pervaiz whispering "Charlie 1" told Tanveer we were still ready in all respects. It was now all down to him to make the call. For the next few nerve tingling seconds Tanveer essentially owned the radio frequency.

No one would transmit except to call an "abort." There was a pause of about twenty seconds of total, tense silence. Then Tanveer whispered, "Standby...Standby... Go!" Both platoons burst out of their hiding positions.

I counted "One hundred, two hundred" and pressed the loose wire to the battery terminal. The two substantial explosive charges instantly detonated and sent a flash and a colossal boom into the silence of the desert night. Shingle showered the entire area but was thrust upwards because I had placed the charges in dips in the ground.

Meanwhile, Tanveer and Pervaiz, with their Pathans, must have covered the first fifteen metres as they led their men fearlessly at full speed toward the buildings. There had been no shots fired by sniper, Sana Ullah, which meant the two flanking sections must have completely overpowered the confused sentries. As the men in the buildings abruptly awoke to the considerable explosion, their first thought must have been, "What the fuck was that?" (Or a similar expression in Urdu.)

But by this time Pervaiz and Tanveer's men were already rushing into the buildings and screaming at them not to move.

Once the dust had settled from the explosion, I sprinted forward and stopped short of the targets, not wanting to be mistaken for enemy. I could hear the Hueys in the distance. They were now closing on our position at a 100 mph. Within a minute, Pervaiz called in, "Charlie 1 secure and clear." About thirty seconds later, Tanveer's voice could be heard. "Charlie 2 secure and clear."

The Caravan acknowledged and informed the Hueys that the target was secure and they were clear into the zone. I worked with the demolitions trooper to lay an NVG strobe and a "Y- shaped" marker to give Colonel Shaheed a wind indicator for his landing. On the target, there were eight men lying on the ground with bags over their heads and their hands plasticuffed behind them. There were at least half a dozen AK-47s in a pile outside one of the buildings. I saw Pervaiz and asked, "Everybody Okay?" He responded *"Atcha"* (yes in Urdu). I turned around see Tanveer directing his soldiers on the target. Everything looked good and we hadn't lost any of our men.

As the Hueys approached, we moved the prisoners to the landing zone. We would have to cram these subversives into the first two aircraft along with as many troopers as the crew-chief would permit. The rest of us would have to get into the remaining Hueys.

I told Tanveer to bring in his flanking section and make sure the last man was just that. Pervaiz, now a veteran of assault raids, was already calling in his men. The two prisoner handling teams moved with the prisoners down to the landing zone Pervaiz and Tanveer moved their men into linear in depth in order be prepared to defend their positions and to efficiently mount the stream of incoming Hueys.

As the lead helicopter landed, the dust enveloped all of us and, to my surprise, a figure in combat clothing came walking out of the dust. It was General Sadaqat; he just had to come out onto the ground! I could hardly believe my eyes. At first, I didn't recognize him in his camouflage uniform. I think he thought we would be in less of a hurry to get the hell out of there. I quickly pointed to key locations in the area and asked him to move to the third aircraft, not wanting to mix him with the prisoners or seem too hurried to ruin his own adventure.

However, the Hueys had been on the ground long enough. I put the General on his new ride and ran to the lead aircraft.

The crew chief was standing by and waiting for me. Just as I reached the helicopter, I turned to sit on the floor and, with only half my arse in the Huey, Colonel Shaheed lifted off. The crew chief wasn't even in the aircraft but was on a retainer strap. He grabbed one of the straps; I grabbed him. Unlike the chief, I was not connected to the Huey and was now in very real danger of falling out of this helicopter as it climbed away.

Two of the troopers on board immediately realised what was going on and grabbed me by the shoulder straps of my equipment vest as I twisted, squirmed and kicked trying to get myself into the aircraft. As the aircraft opened its distance from the ground, Shaheed was totally unaware that his crew-chief and I were literally fighting for our lives.

We were desperately trying to get each other into the aircraft with the help of the troopers who now were grabbing any part of us just to get us into the Huey. If either of us had fallen, we'd have certainly been killed. Oh to have survived all of this and now fall out of a fucking helicopter, that would be ripe.

We both managed to use whatever method we could to get inside. When we landed, I asked Shaheed if he realised he'd almost killed us. He was completely unaware of the crisis and thought he'd heard the words "Go-Go-Go" from the crew-chief. I reflected that perhaps it had come from an inadvertent transmission from the aircraft behind him.

Our return to Quetta saw Sadaqat address his troops in congratulation - and all before 7am in the morning! As the General spoke, I knew the bulk of my job was finished in Pakistan. I had done all I could and now it was time for someone else to consolidate the programme. Following the General's address, we drank chai with Pervaiz and Tanveer and we chatted about the operation and the way ahead. Sadaqat let slip that there was an operation coming up close to the Iranian border and that we should "stay sharp."

The men departed for some well-earned sleep and I packed my bags for Slammy wondering, even hoping, that I had been on the ground for the last time. Nearly falling out of the Huey had been too close a call. My luck was almost certain to run out soon.

CHAPTER 13

The Last Supper

My feelings leaving Quetta were mixed. On one hand I was glad to see the back of the godforsaken place, on the other I knew I might have to return for one more patrol. Time was now running very short, however, and even if I didn't get my boots dirty again I could feel somewhat satisfied that I'd actually achieved what I had set out to do in Pakistan.

My main objective now was to affect a smooth transition for my replacement, while coping with the continuing political and departmental bullshit that had transpired in the Embassy during my absence. The immediate problem, however, was the DoD.

Such had been our success that General Stone's office had issued a letter to the Pakistan Army offering them our Hueys.

Unfortunately (or perhaps fortunately in this case), the State Department's assets were simply not the DoD's to offer and it would be a disaster for border security-specific operations if the Huey's were swallowed up by the Pakistan military. Not least because they'd be unlikely to ever be returned.

I remained calm, giving them the benefit of the doubt that those various issues had not been recognised. In the event it would be another five years before the DoD replicated the programme with very limited success, but by this time they would spend about $1billion a year of U.S. taxpayers' hard earned cash.

While all the posturing was occurring in the Embassy, one Huey was tasked to Gwadar close to the Iranian border and the HAF, along with a Caravan and the new Bell Hueys, were deployed to Sibi in an attempt to flush out more militants. This event was good news. It soundly demonstrated that 50 Squadron and the HAF were working as an integrated unit without any supervision. They remained deployed for four days but found nothing and so withdrew. It had been a good proving operation for Number 2 Platoon.

At a mid-week meeting I had a chance to engage with USAID. I had long been concerned that the locals in Balochistan saw our helicopters as carriers of bad news. An example was when we flew across villages the children would still run out to throw stones at us in a futile signal that we were not welcome; I wanted to change that.

I explained to the very refined and rather seductive lady who headed up USAID in the Embassy that I needed to procure rice and blankets for my Hueys. My concept was that we would carry the supplies in the aircraft on an opportune basis and simply drop them off over the villages as we flew by.

She listened attentively and then abruptly informed me that she was sorry but no such mechanism existed for them to make "random" provision without it being part of an approved USAID programme. I asked her whether they had any active programmes in Balochistan. She told me, "No, it's too dangerous."

I asked, "So it's better to do nothing than something?"

To which she told me that she didn't make the rules.

I was clearly wasting my breath and it was to be another four years before USAID launched a significant programme in Balochistan. To this day, I still think USAID missed an opportunity of gargantuan proportions to assist an allied hearts and minds campaign in Balochistan.

They had the opportunity to use State Department air assets to get aid onto the ground in some of the most desolate regions of the border area. It was a vital element of the strategic jigsaw puzzle that was so sadly missing from the allied counter insurgency matrix in Pakistan.

July was welcomed much like June. The threat level in Islamabad was sky high due to a proposed rocket attack by jihadist against the British and U.S. Embassies. The intelligence was taken so seriously that the U.S. Embassy was evacuated and, unusually, remained closed for more than two days.

It gave me the opportunity to work on the detailed HAF training document for the reference of future advisors. Following three days of uninterrupted work, it encompassed every aspect of the training and was intended to provide any future Advisor with a template from which to work. Interestingly the men keenest to get their hands on it were the DoD and Amir.

Ironically, it was they and not the State Department who capitalised on what had been achieved either for the purpose of attaining promotion or increased sales.

As I worked through the entire training programme and tactical descriptions, my mind drifted back to treasured events that had occurred during the process of implementing the entire procedure twice.

I recalled the moment when we patrolled close to a Bedouin encampment and three filthy and dishevelled children came out to see what was going on. I stopped to offer them food and only the little girl amongst them had the courage to come forward and snatch it out of my hand before they all ran away. It had been like feeding a timid wild animal.

I wondered if they had ever had contact with a white man before.

I remembered the discovery that one of the troopers had a chronically septic finger that he would have doubtless lost if it had gone unattended. The base's military doctor refused to get out of bed to treat him. I called the doctor directly and threatened to call General Sadaqat on the spot if he didn't get his arrogant medical arse out of bed to treat my man immediately. The sleepy doctor, who held the rank of Major, got the less than subtle message and appeared. I told him to sort the finger out or I'd have him in front of the General in the morning. He knew I could. The finger was lanced and bled and treated with anti-biotics and, inevitably, this treatment saved the trooper's finger.

Then there was the discovery that some of the troopers didn't have decent or, for that matter, *any* socks. They were patrolling with blisters. I remember the look on their faces when I demonstrated on one of them how to treat their blisters and foot injuries. They were equally astounded when I distributed amongst them 100 pairs of loop-stitch socks that I'd bought whilst in America.

Then there was the surreal experience of taking Jerry the cop on a patrol in Pishin and, with stunning mountainous scenery behind us, having him explain to Jim and me, in the most eloquent and intellectual style, that the Pathans were a high-content, low-context race. Having let him complete his five-minute diatribe, I recalled the laughter when I replied, "All that might be fine, but out here (in Balochistan) an AK-47 overcame such convoluted and fucked up explanations because it was high-context, low-content in extremis."

I recalled being invited to the trooper's barracks for chai and them being thrilled that I would even think to accept and their pride in showing me their "elite troop" accommodation that was separate from all other FC soldiers. The laughter when they discovered I didn't take sugar in my chai and my realisation, during conversation over that chai, that they were totally relaxed in my company.

My long chats with Pervaiz and Tanveer and watching them develop into the two of the finest military junior officers in the Pakistan Army. These memories would stay with me forever.

My fond recollections and daydreams were broken when I received a call from Colonel Wahid. He told me that I must return to Quetta at the weekend at the express instructions of General Sadaqat. He removed my option of any excuse by saying, "Howard, it's a direct order from General Sadaqat." He added in a gentler tone, "We want to bid you farewell."

I hadn't been sure whether anything would be done to say goodbye. However, after the Colonel's call, I knew I should leave some mementos with those who had done so much to help me; namely Brigadier Shafiq, General Sadaqat, the 50 Squadron pilots and aircrew, the men of the HAF, the NAS Annex staff, and the DynCorp team.

I decided to visit a decorative metal-ware shop in the Blue Area of Islamabad behind the Mobilink office. There, I explained that I needed six inscribed silver platters (for the Pakistanis) and ten hip-flasks (for the DynCorp team). I knew that these brass flasks might serve as a decoration but they'd also be useful if a tipple was ever needed during life after Quetta. Having picked out the silver-plated platters, I explained to the craftsman exactly what I wanted.

He was to carve the insignia of the U.S. Department of State in the centre of each plate. On the outer rim, he would carve the words "Department of State" on the upper aspect, and "Air Wing" on the lower. I had come to know that the Pakistani's ability to copy or fix something was second to none. When these people were skilled, they were really skilled and their ability to innovate should have gotten them much further in the world than it actually had. It was a case of so much practical skill, but Pakistan sadly lacked the direction or structure to harness the talent of its people and create synergy from it.

I decided to personalise the hip flasks with the first name of the recipient with the Department of State Air Wing's insignia on one side. On the rear, I had the craftsman carve an adaptation of the last verse from Rudyard Kipling's poem "The Young British Soldier."

The following morning it seemed quite strange to be going to Qasim airfield to rendezvous with Pete and the Caravan. It was the first time since my initial journey to Quetta that I hadn't been laden with kit and equipment. It was also the first time that we hadn't left Islamabad before sunrise in order to "Carpe Diem" at the other end.

It was a delightful novelty to wake up in my villa and have breakfast at a leisurely pace. I had no concerns about which sets of equipment would be coming from where. I genuinely enjoyed the absence of anxiety over wondering if the drivers were following their instructions in order to get everything to the plane at the allotted time.

That morning my stress-free tea and Alpen slipped down as I looked longingly at the voluptuous Jenny Harrison on CNN. I didn't care that she was needlessly explaining what the weather was going to be like elsewhere. It was strange how such little communication with real women makes a man truly appreciate the female form.

When Hussein Shah arrived at my house at 10am, I was ready in all respects with one small backpack, my rifle bag, and a suit carrier. It was a real novelty to travel so light!

It was about 4pm when Pete commenced the now familiar approach to the little airstrip outside Quetta. As he did, I enjoyed looking out over the Cantonment and viewing the Army's Command and Staff College under the aircraft's final approach.

I had wanted to visit the college, which I was sure, must be like a screwed up time capsule of the British equivalent at Camberley. Unfortunately, however, I never seemed to find the time.

However, on today's approach I noticed considerable troop activity beyond the Cantonment. A massive canvas tent and temporary compound had been erected. This thing was huge. I guessed that there must be a very prestigious wedding about to happen.

When we landed, I asked Pete if he'd seen the marquee and surrounding partitions. He said he hadn't really been looking. Upon arrival in the compound, Major Javed was there flapping around and greeted me like a long lost brother telling me he was relieved I'd finally arrived. He immediately called Colonel Wahid to let him know that I was in Quetta.

My itinerary for this valedictory visit was then explained to me. Moussa would be ready with a car at 7:30pm to take me to say good-bye to the HAF and RIF. I would have dinner at that function. The following day I would go to the General's Headquarters Officers Mess for dinner that evening with all the high-ranking officers so I'd brought a suit with me. Before flying back to Islamabad on my third and final day in Quetta, I would breakfast with 50 Squadron.

When it got to about 6pm, I asked Caz if he could gather the DynCorp team in the cookhouse. I wanted to catch them for a few words before I was whisked away or they were scattered between the compound and the flight line.

When they were all gathered, I explained how immensely grateful I was for what they had done in Quetta. I knew that these men were viewed by some of the civil servants in the Embassy as being second-class citizens simply because they were contractors. What those "Sheep" didn't realise, or chose not to acknowledge, was that each and every one of them had served his country in uniform and now continued to serve it in the most arduous of conditions out of uniform.

The only difference was that nowadays there would be no medals for time served in an intensely operational environment and they would get little or no recognition for their vital role in this hazardous jigsaw puzzle.

I kept my speech short but said that, in my mind, they were the unsung heroes of what we had achieved. The difficulty of the conditions in which they lived and worked only made their contribution that much more remarkable.

I reflected that I had wanted to provide them with a memento that could be potentially useful as well as denote the period we had served together. I pulled one of the hipflasks from the bag, which happened to be for Jay. I handed each flask to the individual named on each. They did seem genuinely moved by what they had received; the combination of their name and the Air Wing insignia on one side and the poem on the other:

When you're wounded and left on Balochistan's plains,
And the women come out to cut up your remains,
Jest roll to your rifle and blow out your brains,
An' go to your Gawd like a soldier.

I had substituted *"Balochistan"* for the Kipling's original *"Afghanistan"* but the sad fact was that his advice was as valid in 2004 as it was when it was he wrote it in the 1890s. I simply hoped these men, who were the pillars of the aviation programme in Pakistan, never had to use this advice and that they truly realised how much I appreciated what they had done.

At 7:30pm, as instructed by Javed, I was ready to go.

The first real hint of an unusual event was when I saw Ed all spruced up. This was when I deduced the DynCorp team was coming to dinner too. Moussa was like a cat on a hot tin roof. He was so excited he had been assigned to drive me that he could hardly contain himself. He was even making *me* nervous.

I'd stuck a pistol down my belt just in case anything untoward went down. I didn't want to get zapped on this last trip. Moussa drove out of the compound and jovially asked if I knew where I was going. For only the second time since being in Pakistan, I had to admit I didn't have clue. The previous time being the secret meeting with the senior Generals in Islamabad.

As soon as we accelerated gently up the road toward the area of the Staff College, it became patently obvious that something was different about this from any other evening. There were armed soldiers everywhere. Each junction had sentries and there were ad-hoc checkpoints scattered along the road that led out to the desert.

Moussa asked me how it felt to be going home and reflecting that I should miss Pakistan. I knew in a weird way that I actually would miss this place. However, my drifting thoughts were broken when Moussa's phone rang again and he drove towards a glow of lights in the desert.

By now, I really didn't have a clue what was going on but, whatever it was, looked like it was going to be adjacent to the wedding tents I'd seen on the Caravan's approach that afternoon. The density of soldiers intensified as we got closer to the lights. By the time we approached the brightly lit area, there were soldiers lining the route at ten-metre intervals.

I finally cracked and asked Moussa, "What's happening here? Is there a wedding or something?"

He laughed in a raised voice and exclaimed, "Mr. Howard, this is for you!"

I was momentarily stunned.

As we pulled up at the entrance to the marquee, I could see the Deputy Commander and Colonels Wahid, Shaheed and Shaheed waiting by the entrance on the ornate carpets that had been laid in the entrance area. As Moussa pulled alongside the welcoming group, his grin was so wide his teeth must have been dry. A soldier with white gloves moved to open my door, which I quickly unlocked from the inside.

I felt a wave of emotion come over me as I heard the uniformed soldiers all around me being called to attention and I felt the raw emotion of pride welling up inside of me. "These guys had done this for me? Surely not." I fought to contain myself as the Brigadier came forward and shook my hand. "Welcome to your tribute, Howard." I could hardly speak as the uniformed soldiers saluted, but squeezed out a "Thank you Brigadier. I didn't expect this."

I shook hands with all the officers in the greeting line that included the field rank officers of 50 Squadron, Majors Wajid and Javed, and Captain Bahtti. The last two officers on line were Pervaiz and Tanveer. It was the first time I had seen them in civilian clothing and we laughed about them having some real clothes. I think it must have been obvious to all looking on just how dear these two brave officers were to me.

The Brigadier guided me into an area where there were several rows of chairs where the DynCorp guys were already seated. They were all giving me a "gotcha" smile and I looked at them and mouthed, "Bastards". They had successfully concealed everything that was going on. We all laughed as I was seated with the Brigadier front and centre. I asked the Brigadier if General Sadaqat was coming and he told me that it was against tradition for the General to attend because all the attention at such functions must be on the guest of honour. He quipped, "The General will have his turn to say good-bye tomorrow."

He then nodded toward a group of men with traditional musical instruments. The drums and the pulsating music of the border region filled the Marquee. Three male dance troops entertained us in turn with their tribal dances. First, the spinning Balochis with their swords; next, the Punjabis and last, but by no means least, the Pathans each with their own distinctive style of dance and music. It was a magnificent display of dancing mixed with athleticism and strength. I must have had a fixed smile on my face and just kept pinching myself that they had done this for me.

Following the dancing I was ushered to the rear of the tent which had been made into a large canvas compound. Decorative flags and carpets hung from the perimeter partition and large carpets covered the desert floor. In the centre of the arena was a troop of chefs surrounded by serving tables that were adorned with food. Around the outside were at least twenty round tables with white table clothes each seating about ten men.

I presumed I had met all of the individuals that were sat round the tables at some point during my time in Quetta. I was invited to the Brigadier's table with the Colonels, Major Wajid, and Captains Tanveer and Pervaiz. I could see the forty-eight men of the HAF sitting around one group of tables and some of their compatriots from the RIF adjacent to them. I made sure the HAF knew that I'd seen them and, were I able, would have sat with them. However, I was acutely aware this would break all bounds of etiquette. Once we were seated, the feast began with the "VIP" table being waitered while the troopers delved in for an opportune, all you can eat feast of the best food produced in anywhere in Balochistan.

Following the extensive curried and spiced dinner, the Brigadier stood up and made a very kind speech, which Wajid translated into Pashtu for the troopers. He described me as a man who had come into all their lives and, whether I intended to or not, had made change for each of them for the better.

He went on to say that, by leading from the front, I had taught all of the people at the dinner some important lessons. After a few minutes more of platitudes that made me feel quite embarrassed, he turned to me and asked me to stand up. He then looked at me and said, "There are many people today who think that HAF stands for Helicopter Assault Force; however, given what you have done for us and who you have been to us, everybody here, we all know that HAF really stands for *"Howard And Friends."*

The Brigadier and Colonels presented me with several inscribed unit plaques and regimental mementos. After the officers had given their gifts, Iqbal from the HAF, my Punjabi amongst Pathans who spoke the best English, was called forward. He was clearly nervous in front of the senior officers and his comrades but, in his best English, told me the men had wanted to buy me something themselves. He presented me with a traditional Sawal Kameez. I reflected that this gift was something that they had clearly thought about and, more than of any other gift I had received on that evening of gifts, it was the one I treasured most.

In response, I presented the inscribed plates to Colonel Shaheed of 50 Squadron and to Major Wajid for the Rapid Interdiction Force and the Helicopter Assault Force. Each plate bore a personal message to the individual units.

Following the presentation, it was now time for me to say a few words. I thanked the Brigadier for his kind comments and for arranging and hosting the dinner. I then turned my attention to the pilots and the RIF.

I explained to them that what they had achieved in such a short time was nothing short of miraculous. In the past year, I had asked them to undertake incredibly difficult, arduous and hazardous manoeuvres in the extremes of climate and terrain. All of this they achieved under the noses of a determined enemy and had not only done so unquestionably, but with stamina, courage and sheer tenacity.

They were, in short, simply magnificent but - and it was a big "but" - I explained that in the UK's SF we had a saying, "You are only as good as your next operation." They needed to know that the interpretation of this saying was that the better you perform, the better operations you will be allocated. This is because the powers that be always need to use their best units for the most challenging operations. It was now up to them to aspire to be as good as their next mission.

This would be their test without me. I thanked them for their trust and for their friendship. I told them that the time I had spent with them would be a treasured period of my life and would provide me with fond memories until I died.

I closed by looking at the HAF and taking a few steps towards them. "Remember your drills. On your way to the target, stealth is everything; speed is nothing. When you hit a target, speed is everything, stealth is nothing." I could see some of them mouthing the words back to me as I spoke. "Know compassion for those who are harmless, know severity to those who are harmful."

They had heard it before but appreciated this final reinforcement; the officers, on the other hand, were hearing these words for the first time. "He who hesitates is dead. Always be better than your enemy, he only has to be better than you *once*. Look after each other. God's speed and may the blessings of Allah be upon you. It has been my honour to serve with you. Aqabar and Allah Hafiz."

I walked back to my chair amongst the standing applause. Some of the pilots came forward to shake my hand; others quickly followed their initiative. As I sat down, the Brigadier shook my hand and told me the speech was just right. After a few minutes, he said I should start to say my goodbyes. I then walked to the HAF. It was an emotional goodbye. I knew I would never see many of these men again and I knew that some of them would not live through their service. Such was the danger of their task. It was an inevitable fact there would be losses. I didn't know at the time that one of them only had two weeks to live. Several of them who had cameras asked if they could take some group photos. They would be a lasting memorial for all of us. I bade them a sad but bravado farewell and left.

On the drive back, I was still amazed by the number of soldiers standing guard and commented on their numbers to Moussa who explained that there were over 1,500 soldiers guarding the event and needlessly reiterated that security was very high. I assumed the reason was the many unarmed soldiers at the event itself and that all the key figures of the headquarters were in attendance.

When I arrived back in the compound, I received a call from Robert. He asked where I was and what I was doing. He then went on to tell me not to travel by road in Quetta. "Something is definitely going on," he explained, "Are you going to any functions down-town?"

I told him about the officers' mess dinner the following evening. He advised in typical Englishman's understatement, "You might want to give it a miss because there is a credible threat against a westerner visiting Quetta." What he *really* meant was that I could get my brains blown out if I did go! Robert then elaborated, "I think it's you, mate. They missed you before and now I think they want one last poke at you." My mind was racing; perhaps this was the reason for such heavy security.

How the hell would I get out of the officers mess dinner the following evening? I couldn't exactly tell the General that there might be a threat against me. I imagined his reply would simply be, "So what's new?"

Thank goodness, I needn't have worried. About half an hour after Robert had called, while I was pondering how to handle the situation, I received a call from the General's ADC. Following the niceties of telling him how the evening's event had gone, he told me, "There has been a change of plan for tomorrow, Howard. The dinner is cancelled."

"Thank fuck for that." I thought.

"But the General wants you to come to his house for lunch instead."

"At least the timing had changed," I thought, "but would this be enough for a successful run of the gauntlet?"

"Howard," the ADC continued, "You must tell no-one, absolutely no-one of this change of plans."

They clearly knew about the threat. He went on, "Only talk to me about this if you have any questions. Do not use any of your usual vehicles. I will send a driver and car; it will pick you up at 1230. Please do not tell anyone."

He hadn't told me that the threat was specifically against me but, in truth, he didn't have to. The 1,500 guards; the Brigadier hurrying me away after dinner; Robert's call; and now the secrecy over the change of venue and time. It didn't take the brains of an archbishop to figure out what was going down.

As always, I would sleep that night in Quetta with my two guns close by. If they came for me in the night, the first few men through the door would pay a heavy price.

The next day I told no one what was going on and, shortly before 1230, changed into my suit trousers and put a scruffy top over my shirt. I would put my jacket and tie on when I reached the General's house. The car showed up right on time with two armed plain-clothes soldiers, including the driver.

I sat alone in the middle of the back seat leaning forward. From this slightly uncomfortable position, I had a clear forward view but onlookers wouldn't get a good look at me thanks to the shielding the front seats provided. I had my machine gun alongside my right leg and my pistol in my covert belt holster under my scruffy jacket. I assumed the soldiers in the car were Sadaqat's bodyguards but didn't ask. I was in the back seat so had total control over them anyway.

They whisked me through town by a route I hadn't travelled before. It brought us to the back entrance of a large house, which I assumed was the General's. We pulled up by a side door where a uniformed sergeant was waiting. I moved into the lobby and told him I needed a bathroom so that I could change clothes. I didn't think it appropriate to tell him I needed to unload the machine gun I carried in my canvas bag along with the silver plate I had brought the General.

I was subsequently ushered through to the drawing room where Sadaqat awaited me, cigarette in hand. He apologised for all the secrecy but explained, "You can't be too careful and we don't want any harm coming to you at this stage." He'd said all he needed to say on that subject.

We then sat down for a two-hour lunch covering a compendium of subject matters. Of course, we inevitably kept reverting to the two main subjects favoured by military officers, namely work and women. The General again mentioned the intelligence report concerning a foreigners' training camp toward the Iranian border. He wished I would stay long enough to go on the operation. I told him that, if I did, there would always be another operation to keep me there, and another after that. He nodded pragmatically, "Yes, you need to get back to your family."

It was a delightful and precious two hours and quite remarkable that it was all happening in the middle of Quetta. When it came time to leave, the General presented me with a beautiful Frontier Corps rug and I presented him with his commemorative plate.

The inscription on the plate read:

To Major General Syed Sadaqat Ali Shah.
It is only he who can see the invisible
Who can achieve the impossible.
It has been an honour to join you in your vision.
Howard Leedham, July 2004

We said goodbye but were to remain in contact and good friends until his untimely death from a heart attack in late 2009.

Once out of his house, it was back to business and the last run of the Quetta gauntlet. If I survived the next fifteen minutes, the chances were I would get out of Quetta unscathed. Before we left the ground of the General's house, I discarded my jacket and tie and reloaded the M-16 SWAT. The close protection team could sense that I meant business.

I could feel the level of aggression rising within me and, if anyone decided to take us on, then I was ready to take the fight to them. For if this represented the enemy's last chance to kill me in Quetta, it would also represent my last chance to kill them, so bring it on.

Within fifteen minutes, we had travelled an entirely irrational network of Quetta's back streets and I was deposited safely back in the compound. Immediately, I bumped into Caz who was eager to know where I'd been and we then had a chat over a cup of tea.

Besides being an exceptional pilot, Caz was a budding philosopher and I always enjoyed listening to his pontifications regarding a diverse range of issues. He was one of the guys who, like me, had come to Pakistan for the adventure and to tick his own, been-there, done-that box. The unit and the programme was a sojourn in his life but it *wasn't* his life. In due course, he would return to the world of the airlines to fly for Delta and we spoke about that at length. He clearly envied the fact that my days in Pakistan were getting few and I could almost taste his eagerness to get back to civilisation.

That evening, I popped to Robert's house to say goodbye and enjoy a final, contraband, Murree beer in Quetta. It was as good as ever to chat with Robert and the British lads. I enjoyed the "same wavelength" discussions of what was and what might have been during the past twelve months. We reflected on the unparalleled levels of operational cooperation between the Brit and the U.S. programmes and the laughs we'd had along the way.

Robert presented me with an 1885 Henry Martini rifle, wonderfully straight out of the days and poems of Rudyard Kipling. It was a little spooky that this particular model of rifle had mention in the very same poem that I had chosen for the flasks. The rifle had an inextricable connection with the region and it was a marvellous gift. As I left the house, I wondered if, in the murky shadows of Quetta that night, the potential assassins were waiting for me to journey to the Officers Mess. Thankfully, the bastards would be deprived of their target on this evening.

The following morning, I went to a farewell breakfast with the pilots of 50 Squadron. On my final return to the compound, Tanveer, Pervaiz and Wajid came around for a final cup of tea. It was touching that they had come round unannounced. I really hated to have to say goodbye to these guys. I hoped they would live through the seemingly endless turmoil of their country's existence.

Saying farewell to the DynCorp team was as matter of fact as a bunch of former military guys can make it. Caz drove me out to the ramp. It was a beautiful day and, as I stood on that ramp, I soaked up the presence of the Hueys and Caravans. I once again felt pride in what we had accomplished.

Ed, the Caravan mechanic, was the last guy I shook hands with. He was a genuinely fine man and I kind of wished he would pack it all in and go home to his grandchildren. However, that was none of my business. He had decided his extensive service to his country, in whatever form, was not over just yet. My feet left Balochistan's soil and I boarded the plane for the last time to Islamabad.

It was finally time to bid farewell to the Sleeping Lady of Quetta and, as I looked towards the mountains where she lay against the deep blue sky, I must admit she became one of the few women in my life that I had no desire to see again. As the aircraft climbed out to the northeast, I looked down on Quetta. For all its problems, it had given me a heck of a send off.

My relief, Dan, was at Qasim to meet me and we both agreed it would have to be a sprint finish to get everything else done before I departed. As ever, in such end of tour days, the administration was a complete pain in the ass. In between handing my villa back in an immaculate condition and signing out with all the departments in the Embassy, Dan and I went over all aspects with a fine toothcomb. Fortunately,

Dan had spent years in Air Wing and was a very experienced operator. He was also incredibly intelligent.

With just two days to go, I received news that the Hueys had deployed with the entire HAF and FLIR Caravan to the Turbat area of Balochistan. Their mission was to take out a foreign camp. That said it all. The HAF no longer need me to show them how. They had their own operational capability and Brigadier Shafiq had his Operational Control. They were as good as their next operation and this capability represented probably the very best gift I received from the entire deployment.

That afternoon, I met briefly with Dorothy. I informed her of the Turbat operation and that, so far as I could make out, everything was taken care of in regard to the handover. During the conversation, I asked if the Ambassador needed to see me for a "don't let the door hit you in the arse on your way out" interview, but Dorothy informed me that, if I wanted to see the Ambassador for a farewell interview, I would have to request it! The only word that sprung to mind was one I had learned in Quetta. "Un-fuckin-believable!"

It was actually a sad comparison to the thanks and appreciation I'd experienced from the Pakistanis and, unfortunately, spoke volumes about the mindset of some within the embassy.

Dorothy accompanied me to a lunch with the NAS annex staff. It provided me an opportunity to present them with one of the engraved silver plates. Following the lunch, Dorothy said a few kind words and presented me with a plaque from the Narcotics Affairs Section. The inscription read:

Presented by NAS Islamabad staff to
Howard Leedham
Your professional guidance and leadership in
organizing

and making M.O.I. Air Wing fully operational,
shall always be appreciated
July 2004

That evening the Sheepherders gathered at Ed the Cop's house, the affable former cop who had taken over from Jerry, and I was elated that the Brits and Pakistanis turned up, too.

Robert gave me a very rare edition of the Foreign and Commonwealth Office plaque and Ed presented me with a fabulous Pathan short sword in a presentation case. The DEA gave me a beautifully engraved and mounted Bowie knife. I must admit, I was overwhelmed by it all.

The following day, deeply hung-over, I bade farewell to the Embassy and spent two hours with Brigadier Shafiq over lunch before a meeting to hand in all my personal weapons to the appropriate departments and personnel. Just as I arrived in Pakistan unarmed, I would leave unarmed.

That evening, I ensured that Dan was content with everything and told him to keep his head down during his tour of duty. At 4:00am Hussein Shah drove me to the airport where the Brigadier had come especially to see me off. I joked that he just wanted to make absolutely sure I was gone but, in the reality, I was deeply honoured.

As I sat on the British Airways Boeing 777, I experienced extremes of mixed emotions. I was elated to be on the plane and silently willed the flight attendant to hurry up and close the door. I could at least then fasten my seat belt and know that I was out of the country.

On the other hand, I felt abject sadness to be leaving it all behind, but I knew that I needed to get back to my family. The aircraft door closed along with a year's chapter of my life that, with the exception of my diving training twenty-five years earlier, had made demands on every skill I had ever accumulated during my military career.

The political and diplomatic situation had required operational entrepreneurism in the extreme in order to get the mission completed. My year in Pakistan, in short, had been a culmination of all the stepping-stones from the earliest time in my life and, by luck and coincidence, I had managed to arrive at the right time for the programme and the wrong time for the enemy. It couldn't have been any better than that.

With the aircraft now climbing above the beautifully rugged landscape of the unforgiving Hindu Kush, I pulled my journal from the seat pocket and wrote: *"I did this and I think I did it well. I'm very proud to have managed to do what we've done. I'm even more pleased that I lived through it; there were times when I didn't think I would."*

The brown surface of the earth below the aircraft turned to green, and then from green to blue, and back to green again before my plane touched down at Washington DC Dulles. I'd made it home and no one on that plane could imagine how elated I was to be back after a year away from my family.

CHAPTER 14

The Fat Lady Sings an Encore

I was on 'cloud-nine' as the U.S. immigration controls officer took a good look at my diplomatic passport. He swiped it, studied his screen for a while and simply said, "Welcome home." Permitting me to walk excitedly into baggage claim to pick up my luggage.

The last time I'd walked through the doors that permitted passage into the Dulles Arrivals greeting area it had been the best welcome I had ever received in my entire life.

This time, however, I could not see my family anywhere so moved out of the way of other passengers arriving behind me. With other greetings going on around me, my excitement at arriving home was by now plummeting.

My hand fumbled for my mobile phone and I switched it on hoping the damn thing worked after all this time away. It took what seemed like an age to get a signal and, when it did, I dialled Shellie's number. She picked up. I tried to conceal my irritation and disappointment, "Hi. I'm here, where are you?"

"Yeah," came the casual tone, "We're running a bit behind, we left late and then traffic hasn't been good."

I had daydreamed about this homecoming for weeks; it was not at all what I had imagined. I felt gutted - but in relative terms, I would find out I wasn't anywhere even close.

I stood outside the Dulles terminal for about ten minutes when the horn sounded from a white Land-Rover Discovery; she'd bought a new car.

I went straight to open the rear passenger doors where the girls were strapped in and gave each of them as big a hug as I could without crushing their precious little bodies. Shellie stayed in the car as I loaded my bags in the back.

The drive back occurred in a stilted atmosphere. When we arrived home, I put the girls to bed. Shellie said she had a headache and was going to upstairs. I sat in the kitchen and thought "Welcome home Howard."

The following morning I woke up late and felt exhausted. I was alone in the bed; so thoroughly jetlagged I dragged myself out and went downstairs where the girls were already eating their breakfast in front of weekend TV. I asked Shellie how she was feeling and she abruptly told me she was fine and that they were going to her father's house that afternoon for a cook out. I didn't know what was wrong, but she was as cold as ice.

There were to be no yellow ribbons for this homecoming and two hours later she announced that she wanted a divorce on account that she was fed up with me. I questioned, "How can that be? I haven't been here for a year," and instinctively blurted back that I'd never agree to a divorce.

I had been home only sixteen hours, I was exhausted both physically and emotionally, and now this. Unfortunately, I was soon to find out that I had a lot further to fall. The only solace I subsequently retrieved from the entire event was that some forty percent of men returning from combat zones go through similar domestic trauma within six months of their return. Unfortunately, mine was closer to six hours.

Living in a small town has the disadvantage that people talk. It also has the *advantage* that people talk and it quickly transpired that three months before my return Shellie had fallen for a builder who was brought into our house for repairs prior to sale and that the relationship was ongoing.

Perhaps it was because she didn't want me to be put under additional pressure in Pakistan that she hadn't told me and I reasoned that it was probably the right thing to do. However, I kept asking myself, "How could it have come to this over a few months? We had been so happy at Christmas".

As the days rolled painfully by I said nothing to Shellie about my discovery but noticed that she was keeping her mobile turned off in my presence.

Then some really tragic news arrived from Caz.

The operation in Turbat had gone down but some idiot of a local commander had insisted that the HAF make the attack in daylight, using the Hueys in a direct assault. This might work in the movies or as a last resort, but it was the wrong thing to do against Al-Qaeda, not least of all because there would always be another day to catch them. I had implored Tanveer and Pervaiz at the end of their training to be strong with senior officers and to impart that, given a mission, it was *they* who would use their training to figure out how to complete it.

Unfortunately, the Pakistani Army is so rigid in its style, whereby rank means everything, that I could imagine them agreeing to a hair-brained direct assault even knowing it was absolute folly. (And how many junior officers have been in that position in history?) The result was that two of the Hueys were tasked in the daylight pursuit of a pickup truck carrying armed men. Without the element of surprise and in broad daylight, the lead Huey was a sitting duck.

Taliban techniques for shooting down helicopters came straight from the Mujahedeen tactics developed against the Soviets. They were pros. The truck let the Huey close without engaging, then poured bullets into it. Shooting down a Huey is no easy task and, fortunately, Al-Qaeda would fail in their attempt. However, as the rounds from the AK-47s found their mark, they either embedded themselves in the Kevlar protection or passed right through the flimsy metal and empty component spaces. Inevitably some found their way into the cabin. Two members of the HAF were hit and one of the pilots was wounded. The experienced Crewchief, Muhammad Iqbal Butt (Iqbal), took a high velocity bullet directly in his right eye and died instantly. Only his flight helmet prevented his brains being splattered all over the helicopter and its occupants.

As always, with events like this, it is probable that most of the HAF in the rear of the Huey were single men with no children. Iqbal, however, was not only one of the finest crewchiefs on 50 Squadron; he was the father of four children.

My feelings of guilt were overwhelming. The General had been right. I should have gone on that operation. If I had done so, I would have negotiated with the idiot of a local commander in order to get my way. I knew that if I'd been in Turbat, Iqbal would still be alive. At that moment, I felt I would have to live with the guilt of his death forever.

My journal entry that day read, *"More pain, more hurt, I'm nearly at the end of my tether; am thinking about ending it all."*

In the cold light of day contemplation of suicide is extreme to say the least. However, only five days prior, I had just left a "kill or be killed" environment where I had vowed to never be taken alive and, if ever I got down to my last pistol magazine, or if capture seemed imminent, I would turn my pistol on myself and go to my God like a soldier. I would never give the men who do evil in the name of God the privilege of slitting my throat for their own entertainment.

So the mindset and the resolute decision to get the hell out of life if the situation dictated was one that I had accepted and lived with for a year. I suppose I was still in that mindset during this first week at home, but the entire contemplation was in response to the prospect of losing my family and my questioning the point of life itself. Given what I'd gone through the decision seemed so very matter of fact.

It is though, in reflection, a period of intense vulnerability and is a crucial "preventative medicine" phase that is often tragically omitted by the families who end up mourning combatants who decide to take their own lives when they return to shattered homes or relationships.

All I knew at that moment was that I was staring at the abyss of losing my daughters anyway so at that moment I just wanted it all to go away.

The emotional desolation that was all in such stark contrast to the previous week and the send off and tokens of appreciation I had received from my team in Pakistan. I went upstairs and, in the top cupboard of my wardrobe, pulled out a small black, plastic carrying case that contained my Glock 9mm pistol.

I checked the pistol and then scratched around to find some bullets. If I were going to do this, I'd go to the tranquillity of the woods where I'd find solace in my final moments and disturb no one and I just wanted to get it over and done with, but I couldn't find the damn rounds for my pistol!

I put the Glock back in the wardrobe, went downstairs and told my eldest daughter, Olivia that I was popping into Hagerstown for "some stuff." She immediately jumped up from her desk where she was working diligently on her colouring book and said, "I'll come, Daddy."

We drove down Interstate-81 with Olivia chatting about anything and everything that a ten-year-old girl can think of. Arriving at Keystone Sporting Goods I asked Olivia, "Do you want to come in or stay in the car?" She could see a Springer Spaniel sitting inside the shop. Olivia eyed the dog and decided it needed to be stroked. She said, "I'll come in."

While Olivia poured her affection over the deeply appreciative Spaniel I meandered up to the counter and asked for two boxes of 9mm parabellum. To this day I have no idea why I asked for two boxes. For my plans that day, I only needed one bullet from one box.

Olivia said goodbye to the dog and we headed north up Pennsylvania Avenue to cross the 50th northern parallel of latitude, the Mason-Dixon Line, into the State we called home. As we did, Olivia was now recounting the merits of the dog and was comparing her to Hardy, our own Springer.

As she chatted away, I looked in the rear-view mirror at this beautiful and innocent blonde ten-year old and the realisation hit me that this little human-being trusted me implicitly and was chatting to me as if I had never been away. Whatever was I thinking? How could I leave her forever? The permanent deprivation was unconscionable and, in that moment, I mentally left Pakistan and came to my senses. I would have to tough it out for my girls no matter what and try to fight to preserve the integrity of my family. She had unwittingly brought me back to the world that was my real life and, in doing so, *had* brought me back from the abyss.

The following week my family was invited to the U.S. Department of State in Washington. I was introduced to Richard Armitage who, as the Deputy Secretary of State, was Number Two to Colin Powell.

Mr. Armitage was a veritable mountain of a man with remarkable record of service in Vietnam. Despite being in his mid-fifties, he allegedly "pumped iron" every morning to sustain his considerable physique. As I shook his hand, which was about the size of a JCB excavator bucket, I reflected on three things: The first was that this guy would never get mugged. The second was that he had visited Islamabad during my tenure but, thanks to the 'layers' in the Embassy, I'd had more chance of walking on Mars than being allowed to share some truth serum with him. The third was that this was the man who, according to President Musharraf, shortly after 9/11, presented Pakistan with demands for assistance in the campaign against Al-Qaeda and the Taliban. The demands were non-negotiable and, should Pakistan accept, it would be considered a United States ally. Should it decline, Pakistan would be considered an enemy.

According to Musharraf, Armitage added that, should Pakistan decline, the United States would bomb it "back to the Stone Age".

As Mr. Armitage and I exchanged brief niceties, it was neither the time nor the place to raise anything contentious. I was simply glad to have met this man. Sharon escorted my family and me to the offices of Assistant Secretary of State and Head of the Bureau of International Narcotics and Law Enforcement Affairs, Bobby Charles.

That Sharon had travelled to DC just to manage my family's visit, spoke volumes of the way she demonstrated a caring for her team and an understanding that good leadership is achieved by a constant effort to maintain an equilibrium between "Task, Team, and Individual". Today, she was ensuring that the needs of the individual were tended to.

We were ushered into a conference room and I was introduced to several people from the Bureau. These were the people who, from behind the scenes, had either backed or implemented what had been requested from Air Wing on my behalf, so I owed them thanks.

Bobby swept into the room and came over as being a genuinely nice guy. He made a big fuss of my girls and, while coffee was served, he made sure they each got a Coke. After some chat about the programme, he asked everyone in the room to sit down but for me to remain standing. He then made a short address.

He talked about what had been achieved over the past year by the programme in Pakistan and how it had been brought from something that many thought would fail to what it was today.

He recounted. "In my job, for whatever reason, I get a lot of bad news and, before Howard went to Pakistan, the only news I would get from there seemed to be bad news. But then, within a week or two of him arriving, there was a little good news; and as the months rolled by, the news just got better and better. Eventually, I came to the conclusion that there was bad news and then there was news about Howard." He paused, "I would literally drive to work thinking, I wonder what Howard was doing last night? Then, a few weeks ago, came the worst news of all. Howard was leaving us. And although today I can see the beautiful reasons why," he indicated towards Shellie and the girls, "I know I speak for everyone in the Bureau when I say we are very truly sorry to see you go."

Bobby was then handed a certificate, which was tastefully mounted on a dark wood mount. He asked me to accept the certificate as a token of the Agency's esteem and that of Air Wing, which he then read to all in attendance in the room:

United States
Department of State
Certificate of Appreciation
Howard Leedham

Mr. Howard Leedham distinguished himself through the outstanding meritorious service to the Department of State, Bureau for International Narcotics and Law Enforcement Affairs, Office of Aviation during the Period August 2003 to July 2004 while serving as the Senior Aviation Advisor, Narcotics Affairs Section, Islamabad Pakistan. He orchestrated the organization, training and operational employment of an effective aviation unit engaged in countering cross border trafficking in illicit drugs, arms and terrorist activities. He has made the single most important contribution to the Air Wing's counter-narcotics/counter terrorism mission in Pakistan and garnered for himself the admiration and respect of those involved in this important national programme. Mr. Leedham's dedication, tenacity and superior professional skill in this assignment are in keeping with the finest traditions of public service and reflect great credit upon him and the Department of State.

It was signed, Robert B. Charles.

As I accepted the certificate, I fought hard to suppress the wave of emotion that was rushing over me. I shook his hand and thanked him and everyone in the room.

I smiled and looked at Sharon and kept it short "I owe a debt of gratitude for the help that has been received. I am very sad to leave. I have made some good friends, but real life beckons and I'm not getting any younger. Thank you again, you have no idea how much I appreciate this event and this award." I left it at that.

On the drive home, I tried convey to the girls what they had both experienced but I think it was a bit too much for them. I also reflected that in Quetta, Islamabad, and now Washington, I had been afforded touching and heartfelt send offs. Now came the task of trying to save my marriage, coping with a baptism of fire into the hedge fund industry and, unbeknown to me at that time, narrowly surviving one more terrorist attack.

The Epilogue – The Bomb

Ultimately, as is the common template for returning combatants, my wife and I failed to keep my marriage together in the wake of Pakistan. Much as I tried to understand that the adultery was a symptom of other things that were magnified by my absence I couldn't reconcile myself to the physical and emotional deceit or lack of remorse on the part of my wife. Like many families, my children paid the heaviest price for the combination of their father serving their country and their parents' collective failure to keep their marriage together.

Like so many veterans I had thought it couldn't happen to me and I was mentally prepared for injury or death when deployed but I was ill equipped to deal with the emotional turmoil of infidelity on my return. Despite moving on in life, like many men on whom such situations are thrust, that inability and its shattering effect on my family still haunts me almost every day.

Three weeks after leaving Pakistan, I transitioned into the world of hedge funds and convertible bonds. The world where a million dollars is seen as pocket change and there was many a moment when I thought, "What the hell am I doing here?"

My task was to take the business global and resulted in establishing the first Hedge Fund in the Dubai International Financial Centre.

Meanwhile, I was approached on several fronts regarding a return to Pakistan. Paul and I continued dialogue and, on one occasion, he jovially mentioned that I had received the highest accolade from Dorothy that any man could ever receive. She apparently commented, "Howard was the right man at the right time. He did a great job but was 100% unresponsive to me." I recall laughingly saying to Paul, "Well there you go. It doesn't get any better than that!"

Regrettably, at that time, Paul was not aware of my ongoing domestic crisis. Also, my request for the government to match my salary at the hedge fund company was deemed impossible. The U.S. Government was spending in the region of sixty five million dollars over two years on its Aviation programme in Pakistan and yet it could not invest less than one percent of the programme's cost in proven operational leadership.

This lack of flexibility within the manpower procurement system of USG is one for which they have paid heavily. Not just in Pakistan, but also in Iraq and Afghanistan where the pendulum swung at immense financial and political expense towards expensive private security firms.

Their PSC contracting policy financially precluded me from being able to return to Pakistan. The inevitable consequence was that the programme began to crumble to the distinct benefit of the terrorists and at significant cost to the U.S. taxpayer.

Additionally, there were further operational complications when a State Department commentary on the events for their own magazine was acquired and plagiarised by Khalid Hasan of The Daily Times, one of the Pakistan's most distributed daily newspapers. It was published to the world on September 22, 2004 and went viral in the Middle East media thereafter. It read:

US training Pakistanis for terror hunt

By Khalid Hasan, WASHINGTON: Special Pakistani forces are being trained at an air force base in Florida and in Quetta by the Americans to conduct air assaults on terrorist cells, free hostages, and search for Osama bin Laden.

"We are training pilots, mechanics and ground forces into a rapid interdiction force. The unit (under training) is cutting edge. There is nothing like it in Pakistan," according to Paul O'Sullivan, director of Air Wing operations at the Florida base. The 50th squadron of the Frontier Corps is one of the crack units being prepared for these special operations. Frontier Corps operates under Pakistan's Ministry of the Interior.

A part of the corps is being trained in Quetta that Paul calls a "hotbed of drug lords and terrorists." Working from a desolate 3,200-foot dirt runway, the unit has grown from five Huey helicopters and three Cessna Caravan turboprops in July 2002 to ten helicopters. U.S. Congress appropriated sixty one million dollars for the corps. The training programme is being managed by Howard Leedham, the State Department's senior aviation adviser, and several contractors. According to an official publication, the corps is a highly manoeuvrable unit that thrives on stealth and "shock actions" with an emphasis on night operations.

According to Leedham, a former British Special Forces commander and Royal Navy pilot, "We bring in the troops and get them out quickly." He personally has trained the Pakistani helicopter assault force and integrated both the ground and air components into an "elite day and night strike team." State Magazine, published by the Department of State, reports in its July-August issue, "To demonstrate the Corps' deadly coordination and speed, Mr. Leedham played a video recorded by a Department aircraft that captured an intense night hostage rescue.

The dramatic footage, shot through the surreal green tint of night optics, shows a squad rushing to a structure where hostages are being held. Within seconds, rescuers overcome the sentries and burst into the building". Another tactic called "Spot Stops" along roads and highways keeps terrorists and other outlaws off balance by creating "instability." "When rumours get out about our patrols just popping up, it provides the impression we're everywhere," said Leedham. Known mainly for spearheading the department's drug eradication programme in Colombia, the Air Wing's mission has expanded to Pakistan. "While still committed to drug addiction, the Wing now provides surveillance and a strike force committed to Pakistan's Western border. Brig S, Pakistan's Air Wing director at the Interior Ministry, has called the programme "a great success." He claims that his helicopter pilots are the "best trained." He said on an earlier occasion that Pakistan's Western border is politically a "region of extremism" and difficult to manage. "It's not a border with checkpoints that can be sealed. It's mountainous and the climate can be very hot or very cold."

The article wasn't entirely accurate but it was there for the whole world to see and had linked my name to the hunt for bin Laden.

The publishing of the article raised my profile in Pakistan and I needed to let things cool off. However, little did I realise that my Pakistan clock was still ticking.

On October 26, 2004, I returned to Islamabad and checked into the Marriot Hotel. The aim of my visit was several fold. I'd explore business opportunities that we could lever from Dubai and meet with several DoD personnel.

They had commenced the procurement of twenty-seven Bell 412 helicopters for the Pakistani Army. It was a painfully slow attempt to mimic what had been achieved with 50 Squadron and the HAF. In doctrinal terms, this seemed more like an attempt to replicate air cavalry than to achieve manoeuvre for a small, operationally secure, raiding force. As with so many aspects of life, it was difficult to convince the audience that size wasn't everything.

The meeting ended and I sensed a very conventional approach to the implementation of a programme that was way too large and didn't have a visionary like Sadaqat to help them. Hence, with two strikes down, an effective operational equivalent of the HAF, or air cavalry for that matter, has yet to be achieved but the media reported in 2011 that the DoD had committed 120 trainers and was purportedly spending $1Billion per year on the effort.

On the Thursday, the 28th of October, I agreed to meet Amir for dinner in the Marriott's Thai Restaurant, which was directly adjacent to the glass-fronted entrance area, close to the security scanner and a waiting area.

The restaurant's glass doors were open, a feature that was soon to become very significant. The delightful waitresses, wearing traditional Thai dresses, greeted us and one of them guided us down three steps to reach the main dining area. A waist high wall separated the entrance area and the main restaurant. The dining room was almost full. A beautiful young Thai lady was sitting cross-legged playing soothing traditional music on a Thai xylophone for the entertainment of the patrons.

We sat down at a table just two metres from the small dividing wall and were handed our menus then - boom! An explosion rocked the hotel and the pressure wave swept through the restaurant.

There was the sound of shattering glass and human screams from the direction of the lobby. A black cloud of smoke poured through the open restaurant doors. The doors hadn't shattered because they were open. Two men staggered in through the opening, their clothes were flash burned but they seemed relatively unscathed.

I looked at Amir and, as if to convince myself, I said the first stupid statement of the evening (I was to make two). "That was a bomb." If Amir hadn't been in momentary shock, I think he would have said something like, "Well, aren't you the fucking genius!" But he actually said nothing. Had he known this was the fourth time I'd been hit by an explosion he would have doubtless wondered why he even dined with me in the first place.

I looked around and noted that everyone in the restaurant was still sitting in his or her seats, clearly stunned in momentary confusion and not knowing what to do or even realising what had happened. I jumped up and moved towards the entrance to look into the lobby. I was concerned about a follow up attack by gunmen.

Who was it that said the most likely time you'll need a gun is when you don't have one? Shit, I didn't have one.

I knelt on one knee using an entrance pillar as cover and cautiously glanced around it into the lobby. It was in darkness. The entire front of the hotel had been blown out and much of the ceiling had collapsed. There were wires and pipes hanging down from the ceiling, and water was spraying from a broken water pipe. Thankfully, there were no gunmen just yet.

I turned around and, to my amazement, many of the would-be diners were still sitting stoically in their chairs. It seemed like no one had moved. They had unilaterally made the cardinal error in their choice of reaction to the danger. Their choices were, and always will be, "fight, flight or freeze" - in other words, go towards the danger, get away from the danger, or do nothing.

Unless you are being hunted and are in cover, the "freeze" choice is seldom the one to take and such a decision has cost many people their lives.

I spoke loudly in an authoritive tone, "Okay, I want everyone to stand up and exit the restaurant in an orderly fashion through the kitchen." I pointed to the kitchen door. To my surprise, everyone did exactly as I had instructed. I looked at one of the waiters. "You lead the way," and then looked at the diners again. "Okay, let's go. Everyone go through that door and, when you get out of the hotel, please get as far away from the building as possible." I reinforced, "Keep walking, let's go!" The diners, as if on automatic response mode, filed out of the restaurant in an orderly fashion into the kitchen and presumably out of the tradesman's entrance.

As soon as the last diner was gone, I turned my attention to the lobby and gingerly entered the bombed out area which was ringing with the various alarm systems that the bomb had activated. There was glass everywhere but the lights were still on at the back of the large lobby. Most people had gone, but I could see a few bewildered staff in the lit area.

I walked towards the security area and, as I came past one of the pillars, there was a Pakistani lying amongst the glass. His left leg had been severed just below the knee and, what remained of his lower leg and left foot, dangled by a piece of skin. He was attempting to lift his leg in a vain attempt to make it work as blood was pumping furiously out of the stump. My initial thought was, "Oh Jesus Christ," and then, having given myself that fraction of a second to get over what was happening in front of me, I knew I had to stop his bleeding.

I knelt down beside him. He was conscious and breathing. He looked at me with absolute desperation in his eyes. I asked, "Do you speak English?" He answered a simple, "Yes." I then said, "You're going to be alright," followed by the second stupid statement I made that evening. I kept his bewildered gaze and said, "Don't move, I'll be right back."

My only hope, in retrospect, is that this man was in deep shock because, otherwise, he would have been thinking, "Don't move? I've just had my fucking leg blown off, for Christ's sake! Where am I going to go?" Of course, what I meant to emphasise was that I wasn't leaving him and I would be back. God only knows why I said what I did.

I ran to the back of the hotel to the staff and I asked, "First aid kit? First aid kit? Do you have one?" The woman behind the reception desk was in tears. She said, "No we don't." I was very irritated and told her "Okay, I've got a man who is dying over there. Call an ambulance." She reached for the phone but I hoped that the responding services would already be on their way.

I dashed back to the severely wounded man and, as I did, I grabbed a couple of small cushions from one of the couches. Quite predictably, he hadn't moved.

I started talking to him, "You're going to be okay, stay with me, stay with me." I pulled off my belt and pulled it as tight I could about halfway up his thigh and then tied it off. I lifted his leg to elevate it, wrapping my right arm round it and holding it close to my chest and, with my left hand, pressed one of the cushions against his stump. Hopefully, the combination of the belt tourniquet, the elevation of the limb, and the direct pressure of the cushion would control the haemorrhage. I was squeezing his limb with my arm to also make it as difficult as I could for the blood to leave his body via his severed extremity.

Then, in a surreal moment, I looked up and there was a businessman standing about six feet away. I don't know why but I assumed he was English but all I can recollect is that he was wearing a grey suit and bright yellow tie. He had a dazed expression on his face as he stared at the gruesome scene of the injured man's blood all over my shirt and splattered on my face, and me hugging and pushing on the severed leg with all my strength.

I looked at him and ordered, "Give me your tie." He did nothing; I paused and barked again, "Give me your fucking tie!" It was as if he'd been suddenly awakened and hurriedly loosened his tie, took it off over his head, and handed to me. I don't recall saying thank you. I never saw the man again. I was simply grateful he had left the tie knotted.

I released my grip on the cushion and managed to get the tie over his bleeding stump. The useless part of his calf and foot that was hanging on by the skin was really getting in the way, but I didn't have a knife to cut it off so had to work around it. I slid the tie all the way up to the groin and pulled it as tight as I could. I grabbed the cushion again and, as before, rammed it on the stump.

The flow of blood had diminished to a steady ooze. Either his bleeding was contained or he'd lost all his blood. That he was still conscious, led me to hope it was the former. Then, out of nowhere a camera flashed. I looked up and there was an individual with a camera. The last thing I wanted was my face in the newspapers the following day. I barked at the photographer, "Fuck off, you sick bastard." And to my surprise he did.

I'd now have to wait for the ambulance in the unlikely event that the woman at reception had managed to get one. I could hear sirens and the first few policemen had arrived. What was strange is that, up to this point, they seemed to be keeping a wide berth of this repugnant scene. I then heard an American accent, "Do you need a hand buddy?" I couldn't look up since the man's leg was still elevated against my body and I was continuing to applied pressure.

I said, "Yeah, I've got him in tourniquet and I've stemmed the flow, but I need to get something on the end instead of this cushion." The American voice then shocked me, "Howard? What the fuck are you doing here?"

I looked up and saw that it was one of the junior men from the U.S. Embassy's security detail (bodyguard). He had arrived just before I'd left. "How are you?" He continued. By this time the casualty must have been thinking, "Oh my God, I'm dying and they're having a fucking reunion."

"I'm about as good as I can be under the circumstances?" I replied.

The bodyguard looked at my shirt and asked, "Is any of that blood yours?"

I said, "No I'm fine." And he left to reappear about a minute later with a pile of napkins.

He then suggested, "You keep it elevated and I'll get the dressing on the end." As I removed the cushion, he pushed about four folded napkins onto the end of the leg and then secured them with other napkins. I looked at the patient. He appeared very weak and I now noticed he had burns on his face and two fingers on his left hand were obviously badly broken. I reached out for his right hand and told him, "Squeeze my hand as hard as you can." I wanted to see if he had any blood pressure, he didn't have much. I then asked, "Do you have any children?"

"Two Boys," he answered

I said, "That's good. You think about your boys and keep thinking of them." I wanted him to stay conscious.

The bodyguard had mastered the napkin bandage. We had done all we could. Someone said, "The ambulance is here." I looked outside and two medics with a stretcher were coming towards us. The four of us lifted the patient onto the stretcher. The lobby was now filling with police and soldiers and I kept hold of the patient's hand as he was carried to the rudimentary ambulance. They slid him in and I never saw him again; I had forgotten to ask his name.

He had apparently been one of the security personnel who had responded to a hotel guest, saying that someone had left a laptop computer in the waiting area. He had picked it up and was placing it by the security scanner for safe keeping when it went off. It had blown off his leg. As the ambulance disappeared down the road, the bodyguard looked at me, "Do you think he'll make it?"

"I don't know," I replied, "He lost a tremendous amount of blood."

He went one stage further, "I'll be surprised if he lives."

With that, we shook hands, not caring about the stickiness of the blood, and I made my way to the back of the hotel to find the stairs. I was determined to get my bag and get the hell out of there. I went to reception and paid for the days I'd stayed prior to the bomb going off. Their credit card machine still worked.

I found Amir at the front of the hotel and we went to his house to clean up.

At the airport, I called Ken at the Embassy to let him know what had happened. I asked about the guy who was injured and whether he'd made it, to which Ken said, "He lived Howard; good job!" I boarded the plane to Dubai.

One week later, I received a call on the matter of the bomb from an FBI investigative team. I told them what I knew, not knowing whether it would be useful or not. They had already spoken to the bodyguard and were aware of most of the events. At the end of the call, they asked me if I'd heard that there was a second device planted that night. I told them I didn't. They explained that a second, larger device had been laid with the intention of killing the responders but, for whatever reason, it had failed to detonate.

I asked them, "How close was it?' One of them simply replied, "Close enough." Clearly, death didn't have an appointment with me on that particular day and, whenever an incident like this happens to me I am mindful of an Arab fable that was told to me several years prior by Bahraini Major Abdul Al-Khalifa.

He had described a man in Damascus who walked round a corner to come face to face with the figure of Death. On seeing the man, Death jumped back and raised his arms above his head. Fearing that Death would grab him, the man ducked back around the corner and sprinted to his horse. He then rode the horse at break-neck speed across the Bekka Valley to Beirut. On arrival, the man and horse were exhausted, so he tied up his horse and crossed the road. Unfortunately, the man was so tired that he failed to see a runaway Ox cart that hit him and killed him instantly. Death then appeared over him and picked him up. He looked at Death and said, "I don't understand. Why did you not just grab me when you had the chance this morning in Damascus?" To which Death calmly replied, "I wasn't trying to grab you. I was leaping back in surprise because I knew I had an appointment with you in Beirut this afternoon."

Hence, in my view, we all have an appointment and will keep it when it's due.

Shellie and I finally divorced in 2006 and, for the sake of our daughters, I knew it was my duty to overcome my animus and hurt and simply revert to the hope that Shellie one day finds some inner peace and emotional stability.

I eventually found myself living in Dubai with the lucrative hedge fund company leveraging my regional relationships but where truth was stranger than fiction.

Concurrently, private companies seeking to establish their own initiatives in Pakistan were pitching me. But, to be candid, it was difficult to see how this would work unless it had the full blessing of the Pakistan military and the ISI.

On reflection, I look back on my adventure in Pakistan as one where the stars aligned to bring me together with fifty noble Pathans the individually courageous Sheepherders in the U.S. Embassy in Islamabad; the Brit team under Robert; Curtis, Caz, Pete and the DynCorp few who enabled us to fly; Steve Schrage and John Mackey who were the modern day Charlie Wilsons; Sharon and Paul who were stalwarts of support in Air Wing and in particular with Brigadier Shafiq-Ur-Rehman Awan, who is now retired and working in civil aviation, and with General Syed Sadaqat Ali Shah, who remained in the Army until 2007.

Both the Brigadier and the General hardly knew each other. One was an aviator, the other an infantryman. But they were special men and truly a breed apart from their fellow officers. They were also an exception to a Clausewitz observation that *boldness becomes of rarer occurrence the higher an officer ascends the scale of rank.* Their vision and courage to implement our programme and their quick decision to place and keep their belief in me was unwavering. I shall be ever grateful for their friendship and steadfast trust.

We all knew that we had to push the operational envelope in order to drive the programme forward and combine fixed wing with rotary wing with an effective ground force. We had to build momentum and enthusiasm and nurture respect between each element in order to enable the willing men involved to face extreme danger as a team. And at the end of the day, each man, be they aircrew, militia or aircraft mechanic, achieved what needed to be done not for any political agenda but with a soldier's knowledge that no one really fights for their country. They fight for their family and those they love and, when the shit goes down, they fight for the man on their left and the man on their right. It wasn't that our grouping in Pakistan derived pleasure or wilfully set out to do things that we knew the bureaucrats would tell us we couldn't do.

We simply knew that, if we didn't make it work, then the beneficiaries would be the subversives and Narco-terrorists. We unilaterally pushed forward without any conscious discussion amongst us. Our small and isolated team instinctively and collectively concluded that, in order to alleviate our superiors of any responsibility if anything went wrong, we would shoulder the burden ourselves.

It was another high stakes game in the land of the "Great Game" and, while hundreds of thousands of coalition troops were deployed to Iraq, (where there had been no Al-Qaeda,) less than 100 men from three different cultures formed and enabled a raiding force that annoyed, hampered, and ultimately deterred one of the greatest threats to the honest and decent people of that region.

Perhaps our superiors sensed that they should let us run in order to achieve the mission and, if they asked no questions, we could tell them no lies. Or perhaps they might have been shocked by our actions. I suspect that none of us will truly know until this book is read. All we do know is that we made it work to the detriment of the enemy and to the benefit of the US Department of State, the American and British taxpayers, and honest, hard working Pakistanis who simply wanted their country back. We did it for those we love and seek to protect and, when it counted, for the man on our left and the man on our right. By what we achieved, I think we proved that in such circumstance, and in order to reach your own Aqabar, it is better to ask forgiveness than permission.